How Africa Developed Europe
Deconstructing the His-story of Africa, Excavating Untold Truth and What Ought to Be Done and Known

Nkwazi Nkuzi Mhango

Langaa Research & Publishing CIG
Mankon, Bamenda

Publisher:

Langaa RPCIG

Langaa Research & Publishing Common Initiative Group

P.O. Box 902 Mankon

Bamenda

North West Region

Cameroon

Langaagrp@gmail.com

www.langaa-rpcig.net

Distributed in and outside N. America by African Books Collective

orders@africanbookscollective.com

www.africanbookscollective.com

ISBN-10: 9956-764-94-9

ISBN-13: 978-9956-764-94-5

© Nkwazi Nkuzi Mhango 2018

Table of Contents

Acknowledgements

This book was enabled to come into being by the humungous contribution from my wife Nesaa that I cherish and relish who, as always, has never complained about my academic adventures. Her cooperation and support are second to none. I remember how I used to change many family topics into academic discourse in order to get her responses on various issues I raised in this compendium. Boring, as they always are, academic topics and its general narrative need a person who seriously care, especially when such a person is specialised in a different discipline.

So, too, I am indebted to:

My young professors our children Ng'ani, Nkuzi and Nkwazi Jr. who oft like to help even where they do not know what they are doing. They have always been around my computer giving me a hard time of explaining almost everything since they believe that their dad knows everything. One important thing I appreciate about these little creatures is the fact that they know that their dad makes book.

My brother colleague and friends professor, Eliakim Sibanda (University of Winnipeg) spent much of his precious time digging hole on my manuscript so as to improve it. Brother professor Munyaradzi Mawere (Great Zimbabwe University) spent his precious time to assess the title not to mention my mentor professor Sean Byrne who reminded the importance of touching on her-story along with his-story as Europe concocted, doctored, desecrated and fabricated it. Brother Artwell Nhemachena (University of Namibia), as well, liked the idea and told me to tweak it.

My friends and readers Salih Hassan Ibrahim aka Darfur (Winnipeg, Canada) and Sirili Akko (Arusha, Tanzania and friends who always want to be the first to grab the copy of whatever comes out; and Langaa my publishers that have always been instrumental to my writing adventure, to all I am, indeed, beh.

Preface

Although Africa has sadly always been seen as a doomed continent, it played a very pivotal role in the development of others, particularly Europe. This is because its actual history has never been known. What is known is a besmirched, distasteful, miswritten and misrepresented story of the white man on Africa or his-story that is taken as the history of Africa. Factually, without Africa's contribution through blood and resources, Europe the world knows of today would not be or look like it is. It is only through Africa's profound and humongous contribution that produced the Europe the world knows of today. Through slavery, colonialism and neocolonialism, Europe garnered the capital that propelled to the development and success it boasts of today. However sadly, despite such leg up, Europe has never appreciated Africa so as to do justice to it. Instead, Europe has taken Africa for granted as its backyard for bullying and plundering.

Now time has come for Europe to do justice to Africa and itself based on the rationalisation and the deconstruction of the centrality of true history of Africa by redressing Africa for the all evils it has caused resulting from slavery, colonialism, and neocolonialism. Under deconstruction theory, every aspect of the so-called African history that Europe fabricated and launched to the world by killing its true history needs to be doubted, interrogated in order to be deconstructed, detoxified. In addressing Africa's role to Europe's development and Europe's role in Africa's underdevelopment, this discourse seeks to deconstruct everything revolving around this oxymoronic interdependence so that truth can come out. In so doing, history but not monolithic his-story built on blatant lies is used as a tool that can help both parties to come up with a viable and just way of addressing the problem. The author shows how, when and who did and what; and who is responsible for what. The book seeks to show how Africa developed Europe at the expenses of its underdevelopment. This is why the international community is not left out. For, it has always been predisposed so as to let Europe off hooks *vis-à-vis* taking responsibility for destroying robbing and violating Africa for its benefits among which is the development of the former as opposed to the latter's underdevelopment.

In a nutshell, this cutting-age volume in that it has used current information and references aims at presenting the case for Africa to the world so that the world can reciprocate by presenting Africa's worth to Africans and the world but not Europe alone. Nothing this book seeks to demystify, detoxify and deconstructing the "his-story" that the reader needs to investigate and interrogate as Europe and its allies and cohorts fabricated and subscribed to it. This is the history and story that portrays and shows Africa in a bad light. This is how Africa developed Europe.

Abbreviations

AD–Anno Domino
ATO–Alternative Trading Organisation
B.C–Before Christ
BAKWATA–Baraza la Waislam Tanzania
BBC–British Broadcasting Corporation
BBD – Big Black Dog
CAR–Central African Republic
CDC–Center for Disease Control
CIA–Central Intelligence Agency
CNN–Cable News Network
DRC–Democratic Republic of Congo
EAC–East African Community
ECOWAS–Economic Community of West African States
EEC–European Economic Community
EU–European Union
FAO–Food and Agricultural Organisation
FDA–Food and Drug Administration
GDP–Gross Domestic Product
GER–Gross Enrolment Ratio
GMF–Genetically Manipulated Foods
GNP–Gross National Product
Heavily Indebted Poor Countries
HIPC–Heavily Indebted Poor Countries
HIV–Human Immunodeficiency Syndrome
IFI–international Financial Institution
IMF–International Monetary Fund
IRT–Institute of Responsible Technology
ITEC–Indian Technical and Economic Cooperation
KFC–Kentucky Fried Chicken
MCC–Millennium Challenge Corporate
MDG–Millennium Development Goals
MIT–Massachusetts Institute of Technology
MPLA–Movimento Popular de Libertação de Angola
NAB–New American Bible
NCD–Non-Communicable Diseases
NLT–New Living Translation
ODM–Orange Democratic Movement

OECD–Organization for Economic Cooperation and
Development
PEV–Post-Election Violence
PM–Prime Minister
PNU–Party of National Unity
R2P–Responsibility to Protect
RF–Rockefeller Foundation
SADC–South African Development Community
SAPs–Structural Adjustment Programmes
SDT–Self-determination Theory
SSA–Sub-Saharan Africa
TMK–Traditional Medicinal Knowledge
Tsh.–Tanzania Schilling
UK–United Kingdom
UNITA–União Nacional para a Independência Total de Angola
UN–United Nation
US$–United States Dollar
USD–United States Dollar
USSR–Union of Soviet Socialist Republics
US–United States
WB–World Bank
WTO–World Trade Organisation
WW–World War

Chapter One

How Africa Developed Europe

Introduction

> "*The last four or five hundred years of European contact with Africa produced a body of literature that presented Africa in a very bad light and Africans in very lurid terms. The reason for this had to do with the need to justify the slave trade and slavery. [...] This continued until the Africans themselves, in the middle of the twentieth century, took into their own hands the telling of their story*" Achebe (2000) cited in Kasapovic (2015: 7).

As Achebe, above, succinctly lucubrates, the true history of Africa has neither been told nor written due to its oxymoronic nature and lack of truth about both parts. Arguably, the current so-called history of Africa was miswritten and misrepresented, as fake and fickle as it has always been, and "left in the shadow" (Womack 2013: 154) if not in the oblivion or warp of white history. It is, therefore, shrouded with fabrications, lies and, above all, distortions that European bigots created in order to discredit Africa. For, this very history was miswritten without the consent or the participation of Africa which denies it legality in any field of social science. The way it was doctored, miswritten and mispresented definitively defies academic, ethics and logic. For those who studied research ethics and methods, especially on indigenous people, understand how the history Europe wrote about Africa is against academic tenets due to the fact that researching on somebody living; and publish the findings without his or her consent is totally unethical (Brown and Strega 2005). This is what happened *vis-à-vis* the history of Africa which this volume calls his-story of Africa European bigots wrote that needs to be decolonised (Shultz 2012) in order to address the concerns of the victims as the part of decolonising social justice and general education. This is because both colonisers and colonised people need to be decolonised; and above all, vacuum cleaned from colonial toxicity that has made it difficult to see the injustice Europe committed against Africa. It should be noted from the outset that his-story or call it *histoire colonial,* as (Blanchard and Snoep 2011) puts it, represents Africa in general to mean even her story. It is only an animal about which one can write without necessarily seeking its views simply because animals do not communicate in human language and sense. So, as you will see hereinafter later, Africa's history was miswritten by white bigots without necessarily seeking any inputs from the subjects which is totally bigoted, unscholarly, untruth and unethical. To make matters worse, these bigots fabricated such toxic versions that sadly though have been taken as truth while they actually are mere lies that sought to justify Europe's criminality against Africa. So, too, much of what is known as the history of Africa is much opined instead of presenting the facts as they are. History is about facts, and possibly, figures but not fabrications and opinions. There is no way a Eurocentric history can define Africa or the world (Marks 2006) as it actually was when such toxic history was mendaciously written. This, therefore, undergirds the importance of deconstructing and detoxifying it to see to it that justice is done for both sides.

Fundamentally, what is known as the history of Africa is nothing but historical fiction (Msiska and Hyland 2017) in which writing history has no border between it and fiction. There is a famous understanding that always "history is written by the winners" (Remember the Titans (2000) cited in Marcus (2005: 65). This is colonial mentality under which any history written based on it must be decolonised and detoxified in order to as to do justice and avoid legalising propagandistic and colonial history on any people as it is the case for Africa among others. This is very important due to the fact that whenever winners write history of their victims, they commit many injustices to the losers as it is in the case of Africa which needs to write the history of the loser. The thug will never write an accurate history even a story of his victim[s]. When colonisers wrote the history of Africa, like any colonisers, they enacted many lies, big misrepresentation; and above all, injustices. In such history, all colonised people suffer from what Memmi cited in Shohat and Stam (2014) refers to as "the mark of the plural" whereby they are projected as "all the same." In such a chicanery, one member's ills are generalised as representative of the entire community. If one member of a certain society is a thief, the entire society becomes the society of thieves including babies and unborn ones. This, by and large, is where the journey of historical tragedy commences. The butcher will never bother about the justice of the cow. For him, all cows are fair game. The Bible, Quran and other religious and misogynistic books provide an ideal example. When men authored these books, they doomed all females in order to exploit, own and rule them. For example, when the Bible and the Quran condemned one woman Eve (Bible) or Hawa (Quran) all women were wholesomely condemned. It has taken many generations for feminists to battle this injustice; which up until now, has never been rectified. Essentially, with this "one-size-fits-all mentality", European bigots were able to dupe the world by fabricating all mendacities about Africa; and got away with murder for a long time simply because Africans did not rebut their "his-story."

I have picked his-story but not her-story due to the cadence his-story makes in connection to history. So, his-story is her-story that makes the miswritten history of Africa as Europe concocted it. His-story epitomises Europe's arrogance, animality, veristic idiocy, criminality and shamelessness if we underscore the crime against humanity Europe committed in Africa for many years without being brought to book. Achebe's quote above speaks volume as far as Africa's history and predicaments are concerned. As Achebe crisply puts it, Africa was painted in a bad light for the purpose of justifying animalities and brutalities Europe committed against it. The question we need to ask is: When will the evils Europe committed against Africa be corrected? In answering such a pivotal question, the author comes up with some suggestions that revolve around the theme of the title of this book namely *HOW AFRICA DEVELOPED EUROPE: DECONSTRUCTING THE HIS-STORY OF AFRICA, EXCAVATING UNTOLD TRUTH AND WHAT OUGHT TO BE DONE AND KNOWN.* Arguably, Europe has the duty to pull Africa out of the devastation it caused. And this devastation equally needs and involves Europe and Africa that need to cooperate in addressing all evils as discussed in this volume. In deconstructing his-story through excavating distorted and hidden Truth about Africa, this volume seeks to make the case for Africa *vis-à-vis* colonial evils as Europe committed them; and thereby create a system that enabled it to get away with murder for some times. Lincoln cited in Boeschoten (2013) notes that "you can fool some of the people all of the time, and all of the people some of the time, but you cannot fool all of the people all of the time" (p. 18). All the same, Europe will never fool all people all of the time. This is why deconstructing his-story or narrative it fabricated is *conditio sine qua non*.

No doubt; Europe is a materially-developed continent compared to Africa and some other continents of the world it once colonised or exploited. However, Europe's development came at the cost of the development of others, particularly Africa which is the continent of plenty but whose population lives in abject poverty and dearth materially though not morally. Due to this, Africa has a profoundly huge contribution to the development of Europe which however occasioned its underdevelopment. If we peel back the layers of time, no doubt; without Africa, Europe we know today would not have existed in terms of economic prowess it has always boasted about undeservedly so to speak. Despite this fact, Europe has never either admitted or appreciated the role Africa played in bringing about its development. Therefore, this compendium aims at showing how Africa practically, and for a long time, contributed overly to the development of Europe that resulted to the underdevelopment of Africa (Amukowa and Ayuya 2013). To do so, the author of this book decided to revisit the history or his-story of Africa as it was dubiously authored by European bigots ever since they came into contact with Africa. In doing so, they created what is known as the history of Africa. However, it is nothing but *his-story* of Africa whereby his stands for a European coloniser who also represents an archaic, colonial and patriarchal Europe. This is why her-story is represented by his-story. Likewise, the book examines the current situation in which Africa contributes hugely to the development of Europe premised on the plunderage of resources, mainly by the way of either unfair international trade or by the way of fueling and sponsoring violent conflicts that revolve around the quest of controlling and extraction of resources that end up in the Western markets under neoliberal policies and free market (Hahn 2007; LeBron and Ayers 2013). On the one hand, the hunch of this corpus, henceforth, gyrates around slavery, colonialism and neocolonialism as the phenomena Europe used to rob Africa. On the other hand, nonetheless, the hunch of the book gyrates around ever-changing *realpolitik* of the world as it currently is under the Western dominated so-called international community. To be precise, Europe is used as the representative of the West.

Achebe's quote reflects on the big and true picture of what can be said to be behind the development of Europe, as opposed to the underdevelopment of Africa therefrom. No dispute. Despite having no resources and land mass compared to Africa, Europe is one of a leading continents in many aspects such as economics, politics, science, technology and many more; which gave it; (and still does) an advantage over others based on how Europe achieved such an edge in development. Notwithstanding, the causes, the secrets and the truths behind Europe's advancement are typically dubious, felonious, fictitious, grim and rapacious due to the fact that Europe has failed to appreciate the role Africa played in achieving such development. Therefore, the naked Truth about Europe's development has never truly come out for every eye to see how it came into being; because many bigoted European and partly Asian thinkers and writers told a one-sided story that, on the one hand, glorified Europe while it belittled and demonised Africa on the other hand. Mhango (2017a) names such jaundiced thinkers to include, *inter alia*, G. W. F. Hegel, Darwin, Ibn Khaldun, François-Marie Arouet (Voltaire), Ibn Sina or Avicenna, David Hume, Emanuel Kant, Ibn Qutaybah and others who maliciously viewed Africa as the continent inhabited by a bunch of mere androids whose brainpower was nothing but *tabula rasa* that will never do anything meaningful for itself; while at the same time, it has, for many years, contributed immensely for the prosperity of the world, Europe in particular. Such bigots condemned Africa to nihilism and neophytism while eulogising and uplifting its Europe to fictional *supermanship*. Essentially, colonial his-story produced two antithetic people namely Africans as subhuman and European as superhuman. All such distortions and misrepresentations were based on the pigment of the colour of the skin. What makes the sin of the above bigots even graver than anyone could imagine is the fact that Africa bought into it so as to allow their lies to eat into Africa's future. For Africa to self-reinvent, it needs to distance itself from long time fabrications such sick thinkers fanned for many years without any deserving confutation.

Demonstrably, Europe has practically been a trailblazer in many areas of development for many decades thanks to the roles it played in international affairs legally and illegally. For, example, Europe invented many things among which are not so good such as slavery, colonialism, and above all, reinventing a distorted Africa. The evils Europe invented gave it a lead in advancement and development by providing it with a capital as the means of excelling over others, especially its victims (Easterly and Levine 2016). Therefore, when I talk of Europe's development, I mean the one attained criminally and fickly. The first aspect of Europe's leading role in development can be traced on the economics of exploitation which Europe has been enjoying since inventing and using them against others while the so-called international community, in its conspiratorial stance, ever since kept on condoning; and watching not to mention benefiting from such a setup as well. By enjoying this advantageous position premised on exploiting Africa and others, Europe and Africa became what they antithetically are presently despite one contributing incredibly to another's development for its underdevelopment. Noticeably, such unfettered position freely gave Europe a comparative and competitive advantage that shaped its currently leading role in the world economy (Barbier 2010). Europe's leading advantage, as indicated above, emanates from slavery and colonial times to present due to the fact that even in modern times, after colonialism and slavery came to an end, Europe still has the advantage over Africa. This is because the former has an upper hand in international affairs while the latter does not have the same advantage and privilege. For example, currently, Africa does not have any meaningful say the international organisations such as the International Monetary Fund (IFM) the World Bank (WB), the United Nations (UN) and World Trade Organisation (WTO) among other which have always been serving Europe in stark contrast to disserving Africa. For example, when it comes to world business, under exploitative policies towards

Africa, Europe has grown economically exponentially in doing business with Africa that, to the contrary, has sadly grown poor exponentially. One of the advantages the current WTO's stance has is that Europe is allowed to bankroll its farmers and exporting their products to Africa (Bond 2006; and Harrison 2013) without any policy based on meaningful reciprocity due to the fact that Africa either has no wherewithal financially to subsidise its farmer or it is not allowed under Western neoliberal policies. In such a situation, there is no way subsidised European farmers can compete with unsubsidised subsistence African farmers. This is one of the major neoliberal drives that allow European subsidised farmers to exacerbate the conditions of African subsistence farmers that are invariably *in extremis* due to depending on nature (Hydén 1980 cited in Herbst 2014). By being subsidised, European farmers, like Europe, have an advantage over African farmers. Their produces seek cheap price compared to same African produces. Thus, this advantageous position is multifaceted in that it enabled Europe in the past, the present and the future to lead others in development shall the current anomalies not been decisively dealt with to see to it that justice is done for the two.

Essentially, in this book, I will delve into the history of how Africa developed Europe to end up in underdevelopment itself. Therefore, this tome is like a long lecture given in the form of a book. The major aim of this book is to demystify and deconstruct Europe's development based on re-writing the true story of Africa as a maker and victim of Europe's development. Notably, the aim of this book is not to accuse Europe or punish it. Neither is it to romanticise Africa while demonising Europe as Europe did. Instead, I must say from the outset; the aim of this book is to put records straight as one way of doing a right thing; doing justice to the duo namely Africa and Europe as far as their roles in the development and underdevelopment of one another are concerned. Doing so aims at chastising the two parties to come together and address all historical wrongs in order to practically and truly enter in a true partnership of equals in its true meaning and applicability between them.

Whoever believes in Europe's unexplained legerdemain can easily believe that its development was achieved because of its solo initiatives and ingeniousness. However, the Truth shows that there is no static society of humans. This is why currently; unexpected countries such as Brazil and India, among many, are evolving as competing powers in world economics. Many would ask: Why is it that Africa is not evolving as well? The answer is quite clearer; what would have helped Africa to reach desired development went into developing Europe and now it is going to the evolving powers due to unfair international systems of business and finances under neocolonialism and neoliberalism. For, without a push from Africa, nothing like Europe we know of today would exist. Therefore, all braggadocios and pomp Europe has always displayed to celebrate its achievement are more of abracadabra than truth shall we revisit the true history of its development. Due to this duplicity based on fake history, we need to revisit history of Europe's development (Nunn 2009) in order to see a true, big and real picture of how Africa developed Europe economically. This is the Truth Europe has invariably kept a secret for many reasons among which is to maintain its comparative advantage in development not to mention portraying itself as the teacher of development to Africa despite hoodwinking Africa under dubious and pseudo-Afro-European treaties such as a 'partnership of equals (Bach 2011) that ironically, have never and will never be equal shall the *status in quo* remain *de-deconstructed*. The history and story of how African developed Europe start in the 15th century when, for the first time, the duo came into contact. This is when a Portuguese criminal Bartolomeo Diaz purportedly declared that he *discovered* the "Cape of Storms" (*Cabo das Tormentas*) (McAllister 2012; Mafe 2013; Liscák 2014) which Joao II, king of Spain (1481–1495), renamed Cape of Good Hope (Estreicher 2014; and Major 2017) or *Cabo da Boa Esperança* as if it was not inhabited. This was on 12 March, 1488 when Dias sailed on the current Cape of Good Hope he renamed however, in reality it came the Cape of Miseries not only for South Africa but also for Africa in general due to the fact that this act led to the colonisation of Africa therefrom. For this breakthrough for Europe, like Christopher, Vasco da Gama; and Amerigo Vespucci and other criminals of the time, Diaz became a hero-cum-icon so as to be knighted while he actually was a criminal who was supposed to be charged even killed had his hosts knew his evil mission and the

8

consequences it would cause for many generations. Essentially, this is where the history of Africa turns murky and spooky. Diaz's mission opened up Africa; and thereby provided an opportunity that would turn Europe into the most powerful and richer continent than all at the time. It gave Europe *carte blanche* to rob Africa and develop itself as Africa became underdeveloped thereof. Severino and Ray (2011) note that Europe got a boost from gold and slave trade in the 17th and 18th centuries that made it rich whereby Timbuktu was believed to be paved with gold. Essentially, Africa became Europe's goldmine to dig wealth from for its development. Consequentially, Africa became the Dark Continent. This was an introductory phase of the story of Africa and its *his-story* due to the fact that what is now known as the history of Africa is the product of his (European's) story with all of its bigotries and fabrications. For such reasons therefore, the True history of Africa is still untold. This is because; the current history was written by colonial agents with the aim of portraying and mispresenting Africa in bad light so as to justify their quest for occupying and colonising it. In so doing, one can say; either the Europeans such as Leo Africanus, Lopez, Pigafetta and Dapper dubiously deconstructed and reconstructed the African (Curran 2011) in order to look the way they wanted him or her to but not the way he or she naturally was. The *his-tory* in question refers to Africans as barbaric, savages, uncilivised that ironically, needed killers and thieves from Europe to civilise them by colonising and enslaving them! The same still goes on today when Europe still takes Africa as a continent of savages thanks to the way it has unvaryingly exploited and maltreated it. I will touch on this when I address trade imbalance under the so-called international community chaperoned by the WTO. Sometimes, I wonder. How killers, rapists and terrorists like Diaz are today celebrated as heroes.

Recently, many cities in the US woke up from their slumber by celebrating Aboriginal Day instead of Columbus Day that has always been celebrated in North America while actually the hero they celebrate is nothing but a criminal who is supposed to provoke anger, crossness and indignity whenever his name is mentioned. The Holley (2015) reports:

For the past 81 years, Americans have celebrated Columbus Day on the second Monday of October. That won't change this year, but a growing number of cities are seeking to abolish the traditional holiday and replace it with a day that acknowledges and celebrates the millions of people who were already living here when Christopher Columbus arrived.

Ironically, such criminals are now aware of their past criminality but are still taught in African schools as discoverers, explorers, missionaries, merchants and heroes while they actually were criminals who led to the sufferings of Africans and others at their time and thereafter by being the harbingers of colonialism. Unluckily, some of suchlike are the ones who with malice doctored, miswrote and misrepresented the True history of Africa after destroying whatever they could to see to it that it should not be known. All sacrilegious crimes Europe committed against Africa such as murder, rape, extortion and enslavement, *inter alia*, were pushed under the carpet. Again, how did Africa allow itself to be fooled this way? I shall offer the answer when I touch on our European educated elites colonisers put in power to keep on vending their people. Now, it is the right time to accurately rewrite African history by at least, deconstruct the one Europe wrote for Africa. English adage has it: Fool me once, shame on you; fool me twice shame on me.

There is more evidence about Columbus' criminality. Bigelow (2015) argues that Columbus deserves to be remembered as the first terrorist in the Americas whose accomplices spread terror among the First Nations to show them how strong and powerful the Christians were.

Demonstrably, the *African* and *Africa* the Western-written history presents are completely different from what they actually are. The African Europe presented to the world is in a bad shape almost in everything. He or she is demonised, pilloried and reduced to the status of sub human because of the pigments of his or her skin (Smith 2011). To show how colour was the major factor of sub-humanising an African, he or she was less human than another human who was reduced to becoming an item any man could own in Europe, namely at the time the fake history of Africa was written. Since the invention of a fake African, he or she has always suffered under the weight of misrepresentation (McKoy 2012) derogation, exploitation, exaggerations, fabrications, stereotypification, and above all, racial discrimination internationally. For example, India recently faced the wave of brutal acts of discrimination against Africans (*Telegram*, I October, 2014 cited in Mhango 2017b). Arabs too are not spared of this sin of discriminating against Africans simply because Europe constructed them so (Poggo 2009 cited in Mhango *forthcoming*). Chinese, too, discriminate against Africans. For example, Jaffe (2012) discloses that "experts say, just because there is a historic prejudice against dark skin in China, it was never a given that this prejudice would automatically translate into prejudice against races with darker skins." All those discriminating against Africans, ironically, live more comfortable lives in Africa than Africans in diaspora. Discrimination against Africans does not end up with non-Africans but also with some Africans themselves. Generally speaking, Europe broke and divided Africa right in the middle based on ethnicity, regionalism, religion, language, and whatever weakness. In Cameroon, Europe divided African linguistically based on Anglo-French divide that has threatened national cohesion (Biloa and Echu 2008; DeLancey, Mbuh and DeLancey 2010; Echu 2013). The same toxic strategy extended to neighbouring Nigeria that was divided between Christian South and Muslim North (Berger 2009). In Sudan for example, colour and partly religion became tools of division whereby northern Sudanese, with a little bit blighter blackness, refer to themselves as Arabs. Provided that northerners are the ones that have been in power since Sudan's independence, they turned Sudan into an Arab country while it actually is an African country. After they learned how to dream and dress, drink and eat like Arabs, think and sing like Arabs, talk and walk like Arabs, pray and play like Arabs, they deemed themselves Arabs. The artificiality of Sudan's transgenic identity is one of the reasons that led to the breakout of Sudan. For there were some fears that if Sudan remained one under the leader from the South, it would be turned into an African country and, therefore, revise discrimination by targeting Sudanese Arabs (Deng 2007). They also discriminate against other Africans simply because they are blacker than they are; and some are Christians but not Muslims

(Deng 2011). This signifies the danger the reconstruction of an African poses not only for African from the non-Africans but from him or herself. Despite this chicanery O'Fahey (2006) notes that:

> The ethnicization of the conflict has grown ever more rapidly since the coming to power by military coup in 1989 of the Islamist regime of President Umar al-Bashir. The present regime is not only Islamist but also Arabo-centric, a fact often underestimated by outside observers. Arabism ('arabiyya or 'uruba) has deep roots in Northern Sudanese nationalism, going back to the 1920s. The paradox here is that many Northern Sudanese have experienced racist incidents while travelling in the Middle East (p. 27); also see Sharkey (2008); Flint (2009); Luqman; and Zambakari (2012).

As if the division of Sudan along religious lines was not enough. Even the South Sudan that ceded from the North is now facing the same sin whereby violent conflict revolving around ethnicity is between two major tribes namely Dinka and Nuer. In Burundi and Rwanda the situation has been the same for many years whereby the Hutus (majority) and Tutsi (minority) are always at loggerheads labouring under the divisions colonisers enacted. Furthermore, Somalia, despite having people of the same tribe and religion, the scrimmage is gyrating colonial master between Somalis who were under Italian (Italian Somaliland) and those who were under Britain (British Somaliland) rules while in Kenya is between two dominant tribes, Kikuyu and Luo not to mention the CAR between Christians and Muslims. The same pattern of division was extended so as to be embraced based on under whose colonial regime a country was. This phenomenon has been repeating itself whenever African countries meet to elect the heads of the African Union. There is visible linguistic division that hinges on Africa's colonial past. Francophone countries vote together against Anglophone countries (Mhango 2017b). If there is anything that colonialism fully achieved in Africa is nothing but killing its language; and installing its language on their place. This is why Francophone countries are more at home with France than their African sister states. Anglophone, too, are at home with Britain than their African neighbours who happen to have adopted other colonial languages. Some feel more at home in Europe than in Africa. For such peoples, helping in robbing Africa, is not the matter of being manipulated. It is the matter of patriotism to their fake mother Europe as opposed to their true mother Africa. To see how Europe divided and poisoned Africa along many lines, the 1994 Rwandan genocide can sum everything up in showing the destructive nature of Europe's division of Africa. Rwandan genocide unearthed the danger toxic ethnicisation of the country or Africa poses to the future and wellbeing of Africa. If there is any destructive thing Europe did to Rwanda and the likes is nothing but confining them in toxic tribal cocoons whose climax was the genocide of 1994. Nobody can be accused of this carnage and madness more precisely than colonialism that created a Hutu-Tutsi toxic divide (Samuelson and Freedman 2010; Carney 2014; and Mamdani 2014). As argued above, all was done to see to it that Africa becomes a danger and a threat to itself something that gave Europe the opportunity of exploiting Africa perpetually and safely.

How Europe Laid the Foundations for the Exploitation of Africa

By tone and tenor, for Europe to bully and exploit Africa, it had to dubiously and surreptitiously lay foundations for doing so in Europe before executing its macabre mission using various deceptive methods such as religion as a signature of colonialism. As I have indicated hereinabove, Europe dispatched its agents to spy and map up Africa ready for invading, occupying and colonising. Essentially, this is where the foundation of how Africa developed Africa or antithetically, how Europe underdeveloped Africa was laid. Rodney (*Ibid.*) maintains that there is no way one can know how Africa became underdeveloped without knowing how it started, augmented; and how it has been going, up until now, when manpower and resources are still going to Europe and other non-African countries without any evocative interplay or appreciation. Currently, the same phenomenon of syphoning unquantifiable wealth from Africa to Europe can be seen in the ongoing unequal trade between the duos. It is from the oddities of rooting Africa Europe was able to fill its vaults with diamonds and gold it is now boosting of having while Africa was left poor (Iliffe 2017). Although Europe has never admitted such a boost, there is evidence to prove that it made economic headways during the gold economy in which gold was king after slaves. For example, in Tanzania, gold was discovered in 1900 (Jønsson and Bryceson 2009). With the discovery of gold, Europe was able to amass tons and tons of gold that are now used as the standard in international economy. After owning African gold, European countries in the mid-1920s (Eichengreen and Temin 2010) decided to introduce gold standard that was later internationalised to the advantage of Europe as opposed to the disadvantage of Africa that ended producing tons and tons of gold without having anything in its reserves. This said, Tanzania's attempt, above, to decolonise its economy is but the way forward shall all African countries take a leaf from it. Economists know how European countries forced other countries to peg their currencies with gold knowingly they had a lot of it while other countries, especially African countries had none. This has been ongoing for the advantage of Europe. As said above regarding a leading advantage, by introducing gold standard, Europe was able to secure its economic and financial future easily. Eichengreen and Flandreau (2009) note that the gold-exchange standard piggybacked on the so-called international financial centers despite being Western ones with the aim of safely holding external reserves that could be easy to access whenever needed to all depending on the liquidity or the means to pay foreign countries easily (Machlup 2014). This helps to avoid converting local currencies between two countries. Gold is the same; and its value is equal internationally while currencies fluctuate depending on country's economic performance at a certain time.

Also, it can be seen on how Africans, among others, from poor parts of the world are immigrating to Europe looking for jobs but not colonising or destroying its culture and development. Mhango (2015) calls such a move by immigrants the *exodus of the mass* that Europe is supposed to accept and welcome as a *quid pro quo* if not a payback due to the fact that Europe sent its illegal immigrants namely predatory *explorer*s, missionaries, and traders all aimed at paving the way for full-fledged colonialism. When such invaders arrived in

Africa, they were not expelled up until they started their criminality in colonising and robbing Africa. In so doing, Europe indebted Africa which is now paying back however in a very progressive way provided that this exodus of the people from Africa does not seek to colonise Europe. Instead, they are going there to work but not to rob or destroy Europe's civilisation as misguided hardliners tend to wrongly assert. In other words, the so-called illegal immigrants are nothing but modern-day missionaries whose missions is not illegal as Europe's was then when it invaded, occupied and colonised Africa for many years. Going on referring to economic immigrants, that colonialism sired, as illegals is nothing but displaying international racism against Africa. Mhango goes ahead proposing some solutions to this dilemma arguing that Europe–shall it want to avoid the burden it is facing currently–must stop exploiting Africa. And above all, Europe must redress Africa for the ills and miseries it authored for it. For, it is a *sine qua non* for both to "extracting Africa from the quagmires of its 'lost decades' and to meeting the aspirations of an increasing vocal citizenry clamouring for a decent livelihood (von Holdt 2010) just like their counterparts in Europe and other so-called developed countries. Redressing Africa, apart from doing justice for both Africa and Europe, helps to avert violent conflicts that normally revolve around struggles for controlling resources in order to sell to the same beneficiaries of the colonial past robbery on Africa.

Principally, the underdevelopment of Africa, on the one hand, and the development of Europe, on the other hand, touch on the very systemic and international exploitation of Africa which was officiated in Berlin in 1884; and has been ongoing ever since up until now. Therefore, without addressing this very system, there is no way Africa can develop so as to be at par with Europe. For, for many decades, Africa has been filling a black hole that is Europe. Things are likely to become worse if we underscore the fact that other powers and emerging powers have unitedly, under neoliberalism, joined the race of fleecing Africa (LeBaron and Ayers 2013). If the trend goes on, we will be contemplating about writing another volume, *How Africa Developed the World*. Currently, China and India are doing the same thing Europe did to achieve its edge in development. Resources are massively moved from Africa to these countries in the same manner Europe did. However, the difference is that the type of colonialism used to actualise and perpetrate this plunderage is different in that Africa is deemed to be free though partially in which African homemade agents are abetting with their foreign masters.

In 1884-85 European colonisers divided Africa into the modern weak states Africa has. If anything, this was the first blow on Africa. Ironically, while they divided and partitioned Africa among themselves, they were united in occupying it. The ever-waring European colonisers decided to cooperate in occupying and pillaging Africa in order to avoid creating schisms that would force them to face each other militarily. So, for Europe to enjoy peace, it had to suffocate its victims. Essentially, this cooperation acted as shock absorbers for Europe of the time. Instead of fighting over scarce resources in Europe, colonisers had a continent of extremes to exploit and occupy; thus saw no need of fighting among themselves while Africa was able to provide whatever they needed and wanted. This is how Africa ushered peace to Europe which acted as ideal environment for production that led to producing massive surpluses.

In the first episode of this colonial project, the colonial masters owned African countries after dividing them carelessly so as to perpetually destroy its organic God formation. This ownership was not like any other one known. It was brutal, exploitative and destructive altogether. African economies were destroyed so as to benefit and suit European ones. African cultures, mores, religions, political institutions and a single country that existed were brutally destroyed. For example, they destroyed African crucial institution of marriage by introducing theirs as if Africans did not how to marry or get married. They realigned Africa's ways of doing things. For, example, Africans did not believe in superiority and inferiority among themselves. They were an egalitarian society despite having some insignificant differences such as kings and his people. Nowadays, some Africans believe in the superiority and fake brotherhood resulting from religions. Famina cited in Peek (2005) says that:

> The whole issue of identity, in Islam, you don't support nationalism in the first place. That's what brings community. Right now you see so many different colors here among the [Muslim] sisters. If your brother

16

or sister is not Muslim, but a stranger is, you're closer to that stranger than your own brother or sister (p. 230).

This is sad for African identity, future and wellbeing. It shows how mentally and morally some Africans, especially proselytes have been brainwashed so as to disown their blood. How many Famina does Africa have currently that can kill their brothers and sisters simply because they do not share the same religion? Such ideologies have suffocated African brotherhood and sisterhood so as to set Africans against others for the benefit of foreign countries and ideologies. As well, thanks to the divisive nature of foreign religions, even Christianity has the same mentality and philosophy of destroying an organic African bond under what is known as *concorporatio cum Christo* or the oneness of Christians in the body of the Lord (Ratzinger 2013) not of their originality and natural relationship. Where is *concorporation cum Africana*? Unfortunately, when Africans were sold as slaves such brotherhood and oneness evaporated so as to surface after Africa gained its independence! Those who believe in foreign ideologies and their brotherhood are likely to subvert whatever efforts those who do not belong to them do to emancipate Africa. They are likely to side with their fake and foreign *brothers and sisters* even if doing so means nothing worthy to Africa as it has been under the church and the mosque. It is sad that such Africans, labouring under foreign influences, have never learned that those they ape are their nationals before anything. Arabs are Arabs first then Muslims so are Europeans. You can see this in the wave of immigrants that Europe is now facing. No European is saying that provided that some of those going to Europe are Christians, should be left to join their brothers and sisters in Christ. As well, Arab countries have been watching while Sudanese from Darfur have been suffering for many years without giving them refuge status. Where is this brotherhood? Come to African brotherhood and sisterhood, you can see them on African countries whenever there is a violent conflict in a neighbouring country. They automatically offer refuge despite being poor and unable to support such people in need.

However, Mhango (2015a) deconstructs such an anomaly maintaining that:

You cannot teach a goat or a chicken who its brother or sister is. They know their siblings. So, too, they know their relations for granted. Even trees know their phylum sakes however they do not speak. Even bees and other pollen-carrying insects know the differences among trees they pollinate (p. 49).

Africa needs to redefine fake relationships based on faiths but not reality as it is in the two cases above. If needs be, Africa must deregister such religions. They cannot be allowed the freedom of scuttling Africans. For, such freedom can create betrayers who will see nothing wrong to destroy or sell their brothers and sisters that they ceased to recognise due to labouring under the toxicity of foreign and racist dogmas. After destroying the institution of marriage, thus, family, they did the same to African notion of the nation. The new concept of nationalism was introduced to replace African natural confederacy in which all small kingdoms lived side by side sometimes peacefully and sometimes disharmoniously all depending on the needs of the time. Again, no war of large scale has ever been recorded involving these confederacies of Africa. This is contrary to Europe which at the time was immersed in individualism. Evidence can be drawn from the US confederacy that was aped from the Americas' Iroquois (Mhango 2015). They used to trade together, fight now and then, raid, and helped each other for many years without necessarily resorting into any megalomaniac self-destruction such as the one the world experienced in the WWI and WWII among others. So, it is obvious that the destruction of Africa is a new thing that Europe exported to Africa so as to turn it into the collective war zone for its benefits as it currently is. This is why Europe has been selling arms to African countries so that they can be used to fight each other in some violent civil conflicts such as the one in the DRC. This is an irony that Africans fought to help Europe in its WWs to end up being betrayed. Through selling, and partly supplying factional groups in Africa, Europe has for many years been able to get the supply of resources bought for cheap prices fixed by colonisers which have gone on to add to its economic and financial muscles.

As luck would have it, in the early 16th century when the first colonial agents, mainly missionaries (Gallego and Woodberry 2010), traders, explores (Dalton 2016) and others arrived in Africa, they found an already advanced society with its well established institutions of administration that covered all sphere of life according to the needs of the society so as to make Africa operate and live independently and self-reliantly of any power. Such institutions did not come out of the blue. They were established and supervised by the governments or the powers of the time such as early African empires (Rodney 1972 cited in Matunhu 2011) among which are Ashanti, Buganda, Luba-Lunda, Ghana, Mali, Songhai, Mwenemutapa, the East African Coastal Swahili City States, Maravi and many more that had already established trade links with the Middle and the Far East (Reid 2012) before the arrival of Europeans. These empires and kingdoms were developed and well established before the arrival of colonial Europe (Michalopoulos and Papaioannou 2013). This is why the term development is not new in precolonial Africa. However, the difference is how the concept is defined today based on tyrannical European lenses. Regarding as to how Africa became developed, Blaut (2012) disclosed that "Africa was densely populated before the slave trade, and utterly slave trade devastated the continent, destroying state and civilizations, depopulating vast regions, and leading, overall, to disastrous underdevelopment" (p. 79). Some of these kingdoms and empires had already advanced so as to become stable confederacies (Antwi-Boasiako and Okyere 2009). Here I am not talking about the most ancient civilisations such as Axum, Egypt, Kush, Meroe and Sudanese Nubian empires that were ahead of the first European civilisations such as Roman, Greece and others. Here I am not talking about Sino-Africa trade that started in 10th century BC (Aning and Lecouture 2008) going way far back than Europe's internationality and universality as colonialism envisaged them. Despite the existence of such strong states and their institutions, colonial Europe maintained that they were *uncivilised* so as to need it to *civilise* them. However, they are colonial minds that still maintain that colonialism civilised the world. Margret Thatcher, former UK premier, cited in Sautman and Yan (2006) maintains that "the story of how Europe explored and colonized–and yes, without apology–civilized the world, is an extraordinary tale of talent, skill and courage" (p. 8). What a shame such nonsense to be aired by such a criminal in the 21st century without being brought to book not only for colonialism but also new colonialism! Some bigots go further alleging that colonialism brought development such as the construction of infrastructure like roads, schools and railways. What were they for if not for robbing Africa? Was infrastructure a new thing to Africa? Reid (2002) cited in Heldring and Robinson (2012) provides the answer testifying that "infrastructure, the Bugandan state had constructed an extensive system of roads prior to being colonized" (p. 7). Further, there were even more expanse once such as the Trans Saharan trade networks (Lydon 2009; Nixon 2009; and Wilson 2012) in the West and the route from the Swahili City States to Zimbabwe and the DRC that were established many centuries before the first calamitous contact. This does not include the sea route to India and China (Kim and Kusimba; Vernet 2009; and Fleisher, Lane, LaViolette, Horton, Pollard, Quintana Morales, Vernet, Christie and Wynne-Jones 2015). Africa established the above routes for its development but not for underdevelopment as those Europe established intended to achieve.

So, those asserting that Europe civilised Africa simply because it constructed infrastructure for full exploitation of Africa, need to know that Africa had its own institutions and means of communicating; and doing business with others. In reality and deconstructionist logic, there is a catch; Europe did not bring any civilisation to Africa. To the contrary, Europe destabilised, desecrated and exploited Africa. Essentially, colonial Europe did not find Africa in a vacuum or backwardness or the lack of administrational systems and civilisation as it has always alleged. For example, when the first Europeans arrived in the East and West Africa, they found that gold business had already been established in these areas (Guerra 2008) on which they built, seized and later ruined. Further, (Habashi 2009) notes that when the Arabs swept through North Africa in the late seventh century, they found that there was gold beyond the desert which rich Sahelian kingdoms traded, and they hoped to find its source so that they could control it not to mention Ethiopian gold (Jackson 2015) which has been established in Africa for many centuries before. This is more than ten centuries before the advent of Europeans who pretend to have civilised Africa while in actuality they just learned and scooped from it without crediting it.

Furthermore, Swan (1994); and Sinclair and Håkansson (2000) cited in Beaujard (2007) estimate that gold from the Limpopo and Zimbabwe was probably exported from the 7th century and seems to have made an impact on the coastal economy from that period as well on the Mozambican coast, 'from ca. 650 AD onwards' (p. 19). At this time, Europe was still in dark as far as where to obtain gold was concerned. It makes more sense even to assert that gold technology was scooped from Africa provided that Europe did not have gold mines. This is why when Europeans evidenced how some African kings were sitting on golden stools while their courts were pregnant with golden ornaments when they first arrived in Africa. Despite such contribution to the development of Europe's technologically and materially, Europe has never admitted and appreciated it.

Demonstrably, when European colonialists arrived, this beautiful history was purposely felled in order to portray Europe as a civilising agent for Africa while, actually, it was but a barbaric and destabilising argent as history proves. Of all criminals that destroyed Africa's history and its ways of life missionaries are second to none. These missionaries, wrapped in the holiness of their God, were able to penetrate the continent easily as they spied under the guise of preaching the *gospel of God* that turned out to be the gospel of colonialism (Tignor 2015). Equipped with the Bible with its contradictions and fabrications, missionaries paved the way to colonialism without underscoring the fact that there will come some Africans and other thinkers to hold them accountable for the destruction of Africa so as to develop Europe. Instead of being the word of God, the Bible became a satanic tool that enhanced the plunderage and defecation of Africa. Through Christianity and later Islam, all African ways of life were condemned to purgatory. They were completely destroyed so as to end up producing the current seed of Africans who abuse and deny their own ways of life. African cultures and ways of life were demonised and deemed uncouth while European ones were glorified, spread and superimposed on unsuspecting Africans. Due to this toxic indoctrination, "it is more surprising still that the educated Africans have never stopped to think whether it is not possible to make some good out of what we generally term "devilish" (Igboin 2011). In other words, the venom Christianity and Islam (Mhango 2017) injected into many Africans is still working so as to make them believe that abandoning, demonising and negating their ways of life is civilisation; while it actually is to the contrary. I may argue that this is why Africa has always lost its wealth simply because it is managed by such poisoned minds from which Rodney openly seems to distance himself. If anything, this is the journey this volume has embarked on. It seeks to deconstruct all such baloneys and toxicity that colonialism, Christianity, Islam and other colonial agents inculcated in the heads of Africans. The time at which Africa was called names must be history. So, too, as we will see later, this is why Europe is currently making a lot of money by selling its fashions to Africa without any reciprocity. Africans were confined to looking after Europe for almost everything meaningful.

Further, the volume seems to debunk insults such as new world in which Aiyejina (2010) notes that African cultures were treated as devilish, inferior, rowdy, vulgar, chaotic, scandalous, disreputable, and bacchanalia. All this aimed at demonising and cheating Africans so that they feel their ways of life were wanting; and thus needed a boost while all such mudslinging meant to pack more punches on African ways of life so that they could give room to European ones. It worked. For, many Africans still believe that everything African is evil as opposed to everything Western that is still presumed to be advanced, holy and modern. Ironically, they forgot that they and their foods and resources were African too. This is nothing but colonising food. Emielu (2006) argues that everything African was either excluded or demonized. He cites an example of how "African songs and African musical instruments" (p. 36) were excluded and considered unfit for worships of God. To show how malice this was, nowadays, all churches use African music and instruments. It is only Islam that still latches on the same tradition of demonising and excluding African music.

As well, Islam still make Muslims believe that dates are a special food just like Christianity that prays for bread but eats everything. More so, you can see how discrimination against Africa still exists in these institutions. No place in Africa has ever referred to as holy (Mhango 2015). Africans need to interrogate the holiness of *holy lands*; who conceived the idea; and who decides which is holy and unholy land based on what criteria. For, if one looks at how Africa is blessed materially and morally, wonders how the lands of amoral people can be holy but not Africa that contributed to the development of many without complaining despite all maltreatments. Apart from the farfetched concept of the *holy lands*, no African saints have been taught by hegemonic foreign religions. *Holy lands* in what while they can neither even support vegetation nor have enough water for its inhabitants to drink not to mention crucifying dusts and heat among many hardships such lands face? No prophet Mohammad's friends or sahibs are black apart from the crier or *muezzin*, Bilal bin Rabah (Prophet's black companion from the modern time Ethiopia, who is believed to have died in Tafilalt in southeastern Morocco (Oussedik 2012) for his powerful voice (Spadola 2013) or *mu'addin* (Crier for prayers) (Arafat 2013 cited in Stadler (n.d year) whose status was negligible compare to other due to playing the role of the cockerel at the times of Mohammad. Looking at the position Rabah held, practically, it was very important. He was like a timekeeper for Muhamad's project in its embryonic stage. Again, provided that Rabah was black, he did not become a powerful member of Muhammad's inner circle just like the Arabs of his rank became so as to secure places in the history of the enterprise. Although many apologetic thinkers tend to take the choice of Bilal as a respect that promoted him from being a slave to a crier who was married to the daughter of one noble Arab Abdurrahman bin Auf from the Banī Zuhra family of the tribe of Quraish (Demirel and Kılıç 2014), in Arabic culture, this did not make any difference. How Arabs maintain their blood lineage can be observed on those who immigrated to Africa; and on those who remained in the Middle East. Refer to how Middle Eastern countries do not offer citizenship to non-Arabs despite sending their people to gain citizenships in other non-Arab countries (Parolin 2010). Even with respect to who took over after the death of Mohammad, you find that virtually all Caliphs were Arabs. Even if you go further and look at who is who in mosque's administration, the *muezzin* or crier is a no-brainer compared to the Iman or a caliph.

How blackness was viewed at that time can be seen in Spadola (*Ibid.*) who discloses that "black stands for slavery" since it was practiced in Morocco if not *lila* or night. This has always been the take of many cultures in which blackness is insinuated as a bad thing if not inferior. Additionally, Toledano (2007) notes that during the Anglo-Ottoman reins, racial insinuation was exploited for the aim of getting free labour under which blacks or Africans were fair game. Due to this mentality, even Arabs who migrated to Africa still maintain the same culture of taking advantage of Africans. They are allowed to marry African women without any meaningful reciprocity. In East Africa where I grew up, I used to see people with Arab pedigree–who were, mainly half caste–marrying African girls but not *vice versa* (Chami 1998; LaViolette 2008). Due to the laxity among Africans, this has become an accepted norm.

Apart from African language, almost in all Eastern and Western languages, the term black is synonymous with dirtiness, inferiority, (Curran 2011), negativity, being neglected, otherness (De Weever 2013) and wickedness and slavery. This is because neo-religions did not want to embark on self-defeating teachings that would unearth their hidden *holier-than-thou* strategy so as to colonise them culturally. They, therefore, decided to subvert the Truth; and got away with murder. This needs to be debunked. Neo-and colonial religions still demonise and discriminate against African names and their ways of life simply because without doing so, they would not have been accepted as holy and perfect despite the fact that all is but a hoax because there was; and still, there is no international agreed *modus operandi* and criteria of assessing and deciding about this deceptive holiness. Sometimes, what is holy or moral for one person can be unholy or amoral for another. I would agree if we confine such holy land or their holiness to a certain people who believe so but not the whole world as it currently is. This needs, at least, an international decree *nisi* for Europe's development to make sense. The churches and mosques must be made to pay and make formal apologies for the suffering they have always caused Africa and its ways of live. For example, to justify racism and white superiority, if not supremacy, Jesus who is said to either be an African or Arab from Egypt, Ethiopia or Palestine, was deliberately made a Caucasian. To make matters worse and work for them, under Roman Empire, the headquarters of Christianity–that is supposed to be either Bethlehem where Jesus is allegedly to have been born or Jerusalem–was moved to the Vatican in Rome, Italy. As for Islam, Arabic was made a godly language all aimed at portraying others as ungodly that need to be converted; and ruled under Arabic *diktat* aka Islam.

Criminality resulting from colonialism perpetrated by religions cannot be left to go on destroying Africans' minds and souls. Africans need to take on it to see to it that they restore or salvage their lost civilisation. Aiyejina (*Ibid.*) goes further noting except for our foods, minerals, weather, and waters, animals everything black was bad and everything bad was black; and was condemned to being devilish and unfit for humans. And all this was aimed at the far demonisation of an African and his philosophy whose "God-fearing grandparents had nothing to do with those aspects of what we would call our culture" (*Growing in the Dark, 2-3*) (p. 11). Instead of growing in the dark, Africans now need to make their culture glow in the current dark that all sorts of colonialism created in their minds, souls and societies.

Pro tempore, every victim is asking one question. When will this brutal and freeloading system end? There is no simple answer to speak to this unless the victims become aware of the system and untold sufferings they have caused since their inception.

Apparently, after arriving, equipped with lies and mythologies, colonial agents started spying on Africans. They duped Africans who wrongly thought that their guests were as civilised and human as they were so as to get away with murder. It is from this tenet; one may argue that it became easy for European invaders to colonise Africa. Africans had a cyclical belief in the universality of all human beings regardless their creeds or colours. So, the first reason why Africa was colonised can be traced on their trust and belief in human equality. So, too, Africans had good experience with non-Europeans such as

Arabs, Persians and Indians they used to trade with before they turned against them during slavery.

In his august book, *Africa Reunite or Perish*, Mhango (2015) alludes that Africa needs to reunite and become a single country as it was before the introduction of colonialism that saw it divided and fractured into foible and weak states Africa boasts of having today for its peril. Mhango's argument is that Africa knows how, when and why it was divided and partitioned not to mention its ramifications. He argues that Africa needs to follow the same trend by which it was divided in a fast track by reuniting it in the same manner shall African countries aspire to have a formidable force internationally. Experience shows that Europe was able to exploit Africa continually due to its superimposed divisions. The lesson[s] from such a condition is worthy being revisited and deconstructed in order to enable Africa learning from its past and current weak position resulting from its division and partition. With one united Africa, just like Canada, Russia and the US, Africa will have one authority that will enable it to manage its affairs so as to have a clout in international affairs something that is amiss currently. As well, the author argues that African countries should establish inter-trade among themselves in order to do away with the current farrago and sick mentality of preferring to do business with former colonies while shying away from their sister states. African countries need to establish synergetic internal cooperation and coordination of their businesses instead of depending on their former colonial masters that have always bullied and exploited them. For, so doing will bring down the costs of production and supply not to mention boosting Africa's economy. Without African-engineered *quid pro quo* among African countries, it becomes hard for Africa to evolve economically. This is why it is very crucial to take the lesson from over sixty years of post-colonial exploitation as a tool by which African countries can do things differently at these different times from those they used to live in desperations and humiliations due to their unnecessary dependency on Europe. I think; if African countries and Africans in general are educated about how they contributed to the development of Europe that ushered in their underdevelopment are able to start contemplating about developing themselves without necessarily wrongly believing that Europe would reciprocate or contribute to their development.

So, too, Mhango proposes that Africa needs to form cartels for its chief products such as oil, minerals, and agricultural produces; while at the same time import technology in order to add value to its products not to forget investing in its people to run the show as far as Africa's development is concerned. Further, the author suggests that, apart from being reunited to the tune Africa was before 1884 when it was deformedly divided in 50 plus sick states in Berlin under what came to famously knows as the partition of and scramble for Africa (Michalopoulos and Papaioannou (2016) that kept changing names according to the needs of the times, (Frynas and Paulo 2006; Ofodile 2008; Keltie 2012; and Moyo, Yeros and Jha 2012) must decolonise its institutions and systems. No doubt that when colonial Europe divided, partition and, later, invaded and occupied Africa, apart from pauperising it, destroyed its systems first. The empire of Ghana provides a window for us on how rich Africa was. The monarch of Ashanti or Asantehene used to sit on golden stool (Lentz 2010; and Edusah 2011) while other European counterparts were sitting on wooden chairs in their thrones that were not as opulent as Ashanti was. This shows how Africa was relatively rich before the arrival of European colonial power that sucked it dry to end up becoming poor and dependent on them.

Chapter Two

How Europe Decreated and Reinvented Africa Ready for Exploitation

So as to justify and make its project successful, colonial Europe had to decreate and reinvent a fake Africa that would justifiably been brutalised, colonised, exploited and merchandised. If there is anything sinister that Europe did against Africa is nothing catastrophic like redefining, reinventing, decreating, and above all, misrepresenting an African and Africa. One would ask: why did Europe do what it did to Africa but not to other continents? There is no a single answer to this question. In fact, Europe did colonise and exploit many continents. However, regarding Africa, the situation was different due to the fact that Africa is endowed with a lot of resources. So, too, Africa is the only continent that was occupied by only black people. Therefore, Europe decided to pick their colour; and thereby use it as a means of exploiting them by demonising it. Now, why did Europe violate Africa? The answer is clearly logical that Europe did all that it did in order to have an upper hand over Africa's people and resources as its major capital for its development.

By its criminal nature, what Europe constructed as an African and Africa are currently discriminated against and exploited by almost every race that is not African. This cannot be a true history of Africa but European story or his-story. Such his-story cannot serve the interests of Africa. For, it was written at this time European colonial powers sent their agents such as explorers, merchants, and missionaries to spy and survey Africa already for colonisation which resulted into many unfathomable miseries that have continued up to the present day. This criminality partly ended after decades of plunderage, sufferings and misrepresentations of African people, history and everything meaningful. It is at this time, missionaries, like any other colonial agents, sedated Africans and destroyed their civilisation and all ways of life by replacing with theirs under the guise of religion which, essentially, was a major agent of colonialism which will always be accused "of imposing alien ways of thinking" (Zeleza 2010: 22) on African so as to force modern Africans to refuse to accept or negate their ways of life.

Essentially, religion has never been a good thing for Africa. For, it is through religion, Europe was able to occupy; and thereby colonise and fleece Africa. It is through religion; especially the Roman Catholic Europe was able to fleece Africa and built big, many and magnificent churches in Lisbon, Paris, and Rome other European capitals that we see today. It is by the help of the church Europe was able to create many investments that saw it through up until today. Through religion, Europe was able to pauperise Africa under the pretexts of *feeding the soul* while depriving the body which is totally different from African perspective of religion. In African religions, the soul and the body are equally important. None can live without another (Mbiti 2015). It is through condoning bestiality and criminality religion became a very dangerous tool that Europe used to rob Africa in all aspects of life. It created a savior-sinner dichotomy whereby, despite being criminally liable, ironically, Europe became the saviour and Africa a sinner. Now, that Africa has suffered gravely under superimposed religions, it is the right time to deconstruct such religions by linking them with colonialism so as to hold them legally accountable for whatever miseries they created in what is now known as westernisation of Africa (Arowolo 2010). By westernising Africa, certainly, as noted hereinabove, Europe destroyed important African institutions, systems and ways of life. This has a lot or ramifications such as lack of confidence, creating animosity among Africans, exploitation, colonialism, divisions and weakening the fabric of what used to hold Africa together. For example, if Adam and Eve committed the so-called original sin (Granger and Price 2007) so as to lead to the punishment of the whole gamut of humanity, what is wrong with wholesomely holding foreign religions accountable for their past evils and vicarious liability or "the absolute liability of one party-generally the legal 'principal'-for misconduct of another party"? (Kraakman 2009: 669). What is wrong with following God's rationale in dealing with predatory foreign religions whose role in the colonisation of Africa is huge and palpable?

Despite their roles in destroying, holding Africa back through robbing it, colonisers and their agents such as missionaries have never admitted that they are the major mainsprings of profound miseries colonialism unleashed to Africa enhanced by the roles they played in fulfilling the evil aims of the project that enabled Europe to surpass Africa almost in everything. There is no way we can stop blaming foreign religions for corrupting Africans. For example, they taught Africans that the heaven is for the poor but not for the rich. Therefore, Africans should not waste time on chasing wealth. For, it would not take them anywhere except to the hellfire. Sadly, when such toxic teachings were inculcated upon Africans and taken as true, colonial regimes were stealing Africa's resources center, left and right. They used the bible they robbed from Jews to justify their ploy of pauperising Africans. In fact, they injected toxic mindsets that have ever since negatively affected on Africans wrongly thinking that being poor is one of the prerequisites of going to the heaven. The weapon they deployed in duping and fleecing Africans, *inter alia*, is Mark (10: 25) which says "it is easier for a camel to go through the eye of a needle, than for a rich man to enter into the kingdom of God." To hoodwink Africans even more, they were told that they are the sheep and the clergy are shepherds. All this prepared Africans for onslaught and slaughter that have cost Africa dearly under the exergies of faiths.

Other exploitative and misleading verses are, among others, Matthew (3: 5) which says "blessed are the poor in spirit, for theirs is the kingdom of Heaven"; and Luke (4: 18) which says that:

> The Spirit of the Lord [is] upon me, because he hath anointed me to preach the gospel to the poor; he hath sent me to heal the brokenhearted, to preach deliverance to the captives, and recovering of sight to the blind, to set at liberty them that are bruised.

If you clinically look into the verses above, you can understand how Catholicism contributed hugely in duping Africans by making them believe that rich people will not go to heaven. Ironically, when religious quacks were preaching such hokum, they were becoming rich by grabbing land, soliciting money and services from unsuspecting Africans. So, when I say that the church has some

31

explanations to make, I mean such misleading dogma it inculcated into its believers and African children who went through its seminary schools. In my coming volume on how to detoxify colonial education, I propose that Africa deconstruct and decolonise everything neo-religions brought so as to get it rid of the toxins currently tormenting Africans among which is religion and God (Brett 2008); also see Crowell 2009; and Grisham 2010). Africans need to deconstruct virtually all tenets of religions in order to accommodate them practically. For example, the bible says God created man in his image. Ironically, those who taught this to Africans are the ones who referred to them as beasts in the jungle, savages, Niger, the Dark Continent, uncouth, infidels, kaffirs and whatnots simply because they received these religions. The same have since discriminated against Africans even the very institutions such as Christianity and Islam as I shall prove later the coming chapters.

As per Desmond Tutu cited in Mhango (2017), the missionaries told Africans to close their eyes to find that they received the bible in exchange with their land; and cultures. Missionaries did not end up here. They supported slavery and colonialism (Pitkänen 2014) although, later, they pretended to turn against these two evils that benefited Europe a great deal. I think this is because, like in politics, the Church decided to replace white colonisers namely white priests with black ones. Quite so, the church has maintained its presence through its institutions the same way colonialism maintained ties through embassies and multinational organisations. Another hypnotic tactic the church used is to pretend that it transformed itself from a colonial agent to moral agent. I think; the mistake African post-colonial governments made is to allow foreign religions operating in Africa to keep on conning and duping Africans to end up divided even more along religious lines. Being a type of colonialism, foreign religions were supposed to be abolished the very day African countries acquired their independence. This would help Africa to go back to its true religions. Arabs did this after gaining their independence. Almost all Arab countries either are under a secular government that has Islamic elements, theocracy or monarchy all operating under traditional Islamic tenets. This is because Islam is their traditional religion they succeeded to export to other countries keeping their cultural imperialism which "is firmly rooted in the critical political economy tradition" (Kraidy 2017: 22) as way of exploiting other subjugated cultures as it is now in Africa *vis-à-vis* its contribution to the development of Europe. To see how deeper cultural imperialism is, imagine; how many African historical treasures such as arts, symbols of African heroes, insignia regalia and other institutional tools are still detained in European capitals' museums. What are they doing there if not to conceal their centrality and symbolism for new generations from both sides whereas for Africa, it to erase its true history while for Europe shows its prosperity and domination over Africa?

In a nutshell, for Europe to justify its criminality against Africa, it deconstructed Africa by reinventing an African as a subhuman if not a mere animal anybody would buy, sell and use as deems fit. To erase Africa's identity, Europe robbed and detained Africa's symbols and treasure. So, what has been ongoing–whereby an Africa is discriminated and exploited because of his/her colour and resources–is not an accident. Europe created and envisaged everything for its benefits as opposed to that of Africa. In order to develop quickly, Europe decided to use Africans and their resources without necessarily bothering that doing so is illegal and immoral. Ironically, Europe used religion, among other tools, to destroy Africa. Due to the magnitude of the criminality Europe committed on Africa, Hasian and Wood (2010) suggest that the artifacts stolen must be returned back to Africa; and the formal apology must be made. This is a very good approach and the beginning shall such ideas be put into actions so as to come to their fruition. Therefrom, Africa may start addressing all crimes Europe committed; and treat them as thus. Bringing artifacts without redressing Africa will not make any sense provided that those who robbed Africa and detained its cultural wealth benefited many folds from such acts.

How Europe Corrupted African Brains as Means to Colonisation

Despite corrupting and Africans from the first contact, Europe has kept on corrupting; and thereby fishing African academics so as to keep Africa perpetually starved and strangulated academically. Apart from creating conducive milieu for lulling African experts trained in Europe, there is another bad face of this crime. For, most of those fished out of Africa had their education paid for by African poor governments to end up working in Europe while they are badly needed at home. For those who return back to Africa face many hurdles such as not being appreciated or utilised by the authorities in their countries, for they are presided over by Europe-cloned black colonisers. To do away with this, many have joined politics in order to make quick money by robbing those whose taxes financed their studies. This has recently become a norm in many African countries where many professionals are rotting in political positions. Ishengoma and es Salaam (2007) cite an example of Tanzania noting that out of the 20 politicians surveyed, five, representing 25% had attained the academic ranks of full professorship in their respective specializations before they joined politics (p. 44). In this politics of the tummy, Africa is losing big; and if this is not changed, Africa is going to lose even more under the internal brain drain whereby many academics serve in urban areas by neglecting rural ones. Ndulu (2004) cited in Mhango (2017c) argues that Africa loses almost US$ 17.5 billion annually through brain drain compared to only US$ 4 billion Africa receives as technical assistance from all sources from Europe. While this goes on, Africa receives many quacks posing as experts that collude with African corrupt rulers to rob it by being paid bigger salaries than true African experts or those with who they are at par with in knowledge and skills. By refusing to stop brain drain, Africa suffocates itself for the development of Europe. To corner Africa, the West has always presented itself as a generous partner with Africa. It has been offering scholarships to African countries which the recipients see as a good gesture while it actually is not. Cuba is one of the countries in the world with a vibrant patriotic *crème de la crème* that it produced after the West slapped it with sanctions as the means of coercing it to comply with its *diktat* to no avail. Why can't Africa emulate Cuba by creating its own intellectual tarns? What have scholarships African countries receive from Europe helped in creating their own intellectual pools? The question we can pose here is: are such scholarships well intended for the development of Africa really? They may seem as a good thing to do. However, when they are critically looking into, the intentions behind the intended ramifications are nothing but keeping Africa at bay intellectually. If Africa were not colonised, it would not need such disgrace and sabotage. Elhadi, Kalb, Perez-Orribo, Little, Spetzler and Preul (2012) maintain that Egypt was the center of many ancient sciences that gave rise to the current ones. This was during the 2nd century A.D. But, later, such edge was destroyed after Europe invaded it. After destroying such a civilisation thought to have one of the first libraries on earth, Europe robbed everything and plagiarised and claimed to have invented everything.

Regarding brain corruption, currently, China and India are doing the same. They are offering many scholarships to Africa in order to be able to influence their future academics and leaders. McCormick (2008) discloses that China offered 15,600 scholarships to 52 African countries in 2005. So, too, India offers technical training through the Technical and Economic Cooperation (ITEC) after assuming the role of emerging powers. Why now not then? McCormick provides the answer noting that whoever receives Chinese aid must accept and succumb before being tied to the use of Chinese goods and services; and is required to hew to the 'One China' policy. Through cultural troupes and scholarships, China and India have opened Africa up; and their leverage in the continent is growing exponentially for the disadvantage of Africa provided that the duo is after resources (Rotberg 2009); also see Wang (2007); Youde (2010); and Haugen (2013). Looking at the hegemonic nature of the relationship between the duo and Africa, Africa is likely to lose the same it did in its colonial and exploitative relationships with Europe. Aid is not a bad thing shall it aim at helping a person out of the problem he or she is facing. It becomes a problem when it pushes such a person in more poverty than that person was. Africa now is losing a lot of resources to China and India due to imbalanced trade. For example, Broadman (2008) and Mhango (2015) note that Chinese and Indian entrepreneurs bring consumer goods from home into Africa and thereby displace African producers in domestic sales and exports such as in textile and apparel sectors which create more poverty resulting from unemployment and sound investment. Arguably, such anomalies show how African rulers have not learnt anything from their long time exploitative relationship with Europe. Mhango cites examples of Angola, Ghana and Zambia where visible rifts have already surfaced between Africans and Chinese due to the threat the latter poses to the former.

Ironically, due to not reckoning with the trap such countries are pushed into, they just receive such scholarships openheartedly without considering future ramifications. Essentially, China and India copied the trick from Europe knowing that in the near future they will need China and India trained personnel in Africa to safeguard their interests. This is obvious provided that the duo is still backward academically compared to the West. Therefore, had it not been for their self-preservation and self-serving, the scholarships they are offering to Africa are badly needed at home. You can see this on how China and India are exporting their jobless people to Africa to take up jobs from Africans and indulge themselves even in illicit activities due to not benefiting from the job markets at home. When Shinn and Eisenman (2012) were conducting interviews about the relationship between Africa and China, they were shocked to find Chinese ditch diggers in Sudan. Does it mean Africa does not have ditch diggers really? The situation is likely to become worse shall Africa not put a stop to it. Gong (2007) notes that:

> While China's investment in Africa raises eyebrows around the world, the vast number of Chinese migrant workers in the region rarely attracts attention. China has quickly become a prominent presence in many key industries in Africa, including petroleum fields, construction sites, mines, and textile mills. Unlike the western investors in Africa, who only brought managers and engineers and hired, mainly local laborers, the Chinese have brought along their own workforce. Many of them, especially the illegal ones, are determined to stay. This will have profound impacts on the Sino-African relationship.

This means; whenever China invests in Africa, just like Europe, there is no technological exchange. This cannot happen for the situation in which an investor comes with his or her workforce from home. There is no way such an investment can be referred to as the one Africa desires or needs. Again, China and India are likely to succeed thanks to not interfering in Africa's internal affairs. They do not care about democracy, human rights or rule of law. Theirs is business by all means. Sautman (2006) cited in Gill and Reilley (2007) notes that by 2006, approximately 74,000 Chinese workers were involved in Chinese projects in Africa on a temporary basis, ranging from higher-paid "foreign experts" to menial laborers (p. 41); also see Gill, Huang and Morrison (2007); and Park (2009). Does it mean that Africa does not have people, mainly jobless that can do such menial jobs? Provided that the number of Chinese and Indians are swelling in Africa, thanks to their racism, soon Africa will see another wave of greener pasture seekers namely prostitutes who will be brought to serve this new group of contingent workers.

While China and India are exporting their jobless armies to Africa to take up even menial jobs, Europe has been doing things differently by sending only technocrats and diplomats who use Africans to do their works. Instead of sending such unskilled people, Europe has been attracting Africa's experts under the so-called brain drain. As indicated above, drain brain cost and hurts Africa heavily. Arguably, it is important to note; such lossmaking setting does not only end in brain drain but also in other aspects such as trade, technical assistance and the horse-jockey relationship (Mhango *forthcoming*) between Europe and Africa. I shall address this later when I touch on capital flight and aid; and the way Africa does not need aid but to plug the gaps through which its resources and capitals are syphoned to Europe. Despite such vivid evidence, European colonial agents asserted that Africa was uncivilised; and whatever they did was out of their savviness but not out of the help Africans freely and generously extended to them. To crown it all, they claimed that they discovered Africa. Evidence, clearly, shows that they discovered nothing. An ideal example can be drawn from the Americas that they fumbled on after failing to reach the Indian subcontinent. Ironically, despite such generosity, profound beauty and help, the same Europe that brutally robbed and heartlessly violated Africa is the one whose thinkers have always told Africa's story.

As aforementioned, the aim of this tome is to accurately recap the history of Africa from victim's narrative and point of view. This is because whenever anyone allows another person to tell his or her story, chances of distorting everything are high, especially when a person doing so is culpable of committing actions resulting to the crimes committed as it is the case between Africa and Europe. It is only the dead whose story can be told by another person. Africa has suffered a lot. But it has never died. To do away with this, African thinkers need to retell the true story of Africa the same way Rodney told it; and they must avail themselves of this truth not to mention disseminating it to others. They need to prove that Africa was not actually *terra nullius* (Buchan and Heath 2006; Fitzmaurice 2007; Samson 2008; Fitzmaurice 2012; Geisler 2012; and Mhango 2015) as European colonisers maliciously claimed in order to avoid criminal liability later. Accepting that Africa was *terra nullius* or No Man's Land, means saving those who robbed it from facing criminal liability resulting from the plunderage they committed. Doing so was done purposely to make sure that, in future, Africa would not legally reclaim for redress not to mention apology or anything[s] like that. How could a country already occupied by millions of people be referred to as *terra nullius*? Who in his or her frame of mind do that and fail to commit a crime not to mention show his or her racist nature as it is in the case in point? This is like calling someone's spouse nobody's partner while everything is clear.

What surprises is the fact that this the archaic and criminal doctrine of *terra nullius* was propounded by the so-called famous thinkers such as Adam Smith, John Locke, Grotius, Purfendorf and others who reduced humans to animals that do not own the land they own. Some of such pernicious and toxic thinkers went as far as claiming that those whose land was taken had no right over the land simply because they were gatherers and hunters which is a lie. I do not think that when European came to Africa Africans were gatherers or hunters. As noted hereinabove, Africans had already established trade with far Asia not to mention a very advanced agricultural system in which they built on when they introduced colonial crops or cash crops (Austin 2009; and Mhango 2015) which destroyed natural African crops something that resulted into acute food shortage (Shokpeka and Odigwe 2009) in many places due to the fact that much emphasis they received. The danger cash or colonial crops posed to Africa did not only affect Africans at colonial times. Korieh (2010) maintains that development and economics-oriented studies have concluded that economic reforms driven by cash crop production in both the colonial and the post-colonial period led to agricultural decline and threatened rural survival. Again, while cash or colonial crops are threatening the rural survival, things are different for Europe which process them and make more money by supplying the world with the same crops it buys cheaply from poor countries. An ideal example can be drawn from coffee which is one of the major sources of income for many European companies dealing in cash crops. Most of the coffee sold all over the world is processed in Europe that does not have even a single coffee tree. Western companies buy coffee from Africa and other producers at fixed or throwaway prices to end up making super profits after processing and packaging it while producers suffer from poverty.

Interestingly, in regard to how Africa developed Europe, exploitation does not end up in agriproducts. It goes as further as covering other products such as precious minerals, demand and supply, production and processing and the general international trade regime whereby Africa sells raw materials and buys processed goods from most of the same products it sells to Europe. This trend started a long time ago during the trans-Atlantic slave trade in which Africa supplied agricultural goods and slaves who were sailed to the Americas to produce sugar for exporting to Europe and then to Africa. Since then, Europe formed cartels that ever since have controlled the business globally. Notably, Europe did not only create cartels but also created smuggling regime under colonialism. This it to say: during the whole period Europe occupied and colonised Africa, it used to import and export goods without paying and taxes. To whom it would have done so while there were no governments except colonial ones? How much money did Europe make out of such criminality? How many tons of goods did Europe import and export without paying even a dime? Such tons of money, had it been paid, would have contributed enormously to Africa's development. Instead, it contributed significantly to the development of Europe.

Jaffee (2014) discloses that Europe created cartels known as Alternative Trading Organisations (ATOs) that established a network of "world shops" (p. 12) in many cities in the West and other emerging big economies of the world to sell these craft products, as well as some coffee and tea. If we calculate how much such parasitic cartels have already made by fleecing Africa, we can easily know how much Africa developed Europe economically. Ironically, such vivid exploitation is blessed under the so-called the WTO and other International Financial Institutions (IFIs) whose role[s], as noted above, is no different from those of colonial agents. Slaughter (2009) admonishes us to stop viewing the international system as a system of states—unitary entities like billiard balls or black boxes—subject to rules created by international institutions that are, apart from "above" these states due to the colonial and toxic roles such institutions have always played, especially against poor and non-western countries. Slaughter goes on noting that to make it look nice, such a system is called a New World Order. Is there anything new in this *new order* or just an old order of colonialism whose name is changed to suit covert interests of those behind it? If there is a new thing or order or change in this new world order (Drezner 2007) I think is the coming of China and India as new imperial powers all united in exploiting poor countries. Although this is the topic for the other times, the history will one day be written about how Africa developed China and India on top of Europe. Therefore, this new world order is as toxic to Africa as the old one was. Such a view is very important for Africa. Because, under international institutions it was recklessly and ruthlessly divided, partitioned, occupied and ultimately colonised; and still under them, it is still maltreated. Call (2008) notes that primarily European states (and later North American countries) created the system of nation-states drawing from their experience with the aim of extracting resources, fostering colonial institutions with powerful legacies, propping up postcolonial leaders. With such a freeloading system, the West has not only been able to unendingly exploit Africa but also closely control its superimposed systems plus sabotaging whatever alternative system or policy any country would create to oppose these colonial systems. This is why Western countries have always controlled and used the IFIs to keep on exploiting poor countries so as to make them poorer and poorer as days go by. Apart from being colonial tools, the IFIs operate exactly in colonial manners by superimposing their policies on poor countries. They apply conditions and selectivity on their aid (Easterly and Pfutze 2008) so as to build beggar-savior interdependence; and they do not operate democratically despite democracy being one of their conditions for those who need assistance from them. Many dictators Africa has ever had used to enjoy cooperation with these institutions. If anything, this is one of the anomalies this tome seeks to expose and right so that justice can be done for both sides whereby Europe is supposed to redress Africa and make a formal apology for wronging Africa instead of living in the state of denial devoid of reasonable and actionable answers. If Jews were redressed for the wrongs Nazi Germany committed to them, what is wrong for Africa to demand the same?

Given that, as victims and members of the international community, we are duty-bound to make our contributions to the wellbeing of the world; it is time to write *How Africa Developed Europe* in order to right the wrongs Europe committed to Africa without bothering even to admit or taking any initiatives to redress Africa. Doing so will not only put records straight but will also add up to the quest, for Africans as victims, to find solutions to their problems; seek remedy and start afresh. Arguably, one of the solutions to the problems Africa has perpetually faced is knowledge. This is why much of the corpus of knowledge the world has latched on is purely bias and European. What do you expect when you take baboon's case to a monkey? This said, it is only right knowledge as an emancipatory weapon that can help Africa to right all wrongs Europe committed against it. Again, where do we get this so powerful weapon? History and our day-to-day lives have a lot to offer in this search for the solutions. Rodney (1972) observes that:

> In a way, underdevelopment is a paradox. Many parts of the world that are naturally rich are actually poor and parts that are not so well off in wealth of soil and sun-soil are enjoying the highest standards of living. When the capitalists from the developed parts of the world try to explain this paradox, they often make it sound as though there is something "God-given" about the situation. One bourgeois economist, in a book on development, accepted that the comparative statistics of

the world today show a gap that is much larger than it was before. By his admission, the gap between the developed and underdeveloped countries has increased by at least 15 to 20 times over the last 150 years. However, the bourgeois economist in question does not give a historical explanation, nor does he consider that there is a relationship of exploitation which allowed capitalist parasites to grow fat and impoverished the dependencies. Instead he puts forward a biblical explanation! (p. 21).

After scrambling for (Chamberlain 2012), surveying, securing (under the dubious strategy of areas of influence), dividing, partitioning and colonising Africa, European colonisers created a freeloading system that would perpetually exploit Africa economically, politically and socially. It is this malefic system perpetrated under the guise of globalism, internationalism, neoliberalism and other isms–the West has always propounded–that has always held Africa to ransom up until now.

How Religion Made Ungodly Godly as the Colonial Agent

Just like any human society, Africa has a very long history of civilisation which has passed through many epochs good and bad. However, much of the history of Africa was prejudicially miswritten and misrepresented by colonisers who omitted some facts and added some fabrications in order to justify their bestiality and criminality of colonising, occupying and robbing Africa in what this volume calls *his-story*. Tamale (2011: 16) cited in Nhemachena (2016) observes that in the 1960 and 1970, Western researchers inundated Africa to study African sexual orientation in relation to fertility whereby *oversexed, promiscuous, less moral and less brainy Africans were never far from the minds of the demographers and other researchers* interested in the study of fertility control. It is, therefore, clear that Western researchers did so in order to prove that their coloniality civilised Africa while it actually sent it back many decades as far as development is concerned. Nhemachena (*Ibid.*) argues that before the eyes of colonisers, Africans could not imagine or create institutions, history, art, culture or anything except their emptiness and primitiveness. However, when you clinically observe the Truth, you find that the difference is, indeed, the case. I can cite one element that uniquely differentiates humans and beasts. Language is the major element that shaped human acme due to the fact that enables humans to intelligibly communicate and exchange skills based on their needs, choices and interests. Maintaining that Africans were primitive devoid of the powers of creating or imagining is one of the proofs that those making such a statement had some mental problems due to the fact that nobody taught Africans their language. Africans have many more languages and richest culture than any human race on. Demonstrably, who paved the way for such researchers? Through paving the way to colonialism and destroying African cultures, missionaries are liable for this crime that has been ongoing, up until now, when African cultures are demonised and seen as evil and ungodly. Again, were colonialism, cultural imperialism and slavery godly?

For the sake of argument, even if we buy into Western conceptualisation of development based on material success as opposed to underdevelopment that is manipulated to be the natural state of thing, I may argue that the *his-tory* of Africa starts at the time when slavery; and thereafter colonialism were introduced to Africa. Before then, a little is documented (Fage 2010) despite the fact that East and North East Africa are historically believed to be the cradle of mankind. This informs us that we do not know our whole history as a species. This being the case, I state that the current doctored history of Africa started at the time slavery was introduced in the 8th and 9th (Trans-Saharan as it was introduced by Arabs) and the 15th centuries (Trans-Atlantic as it was introduced by Arabs and Europeans) due to the fact that recording, however doctored it is, started at this time. Due the genesis and changing nature of slavery, some scholars either tied it to race or religion (Goldenberg 2009) provided that the duo fully participated in perpetrating this crime against humanity, particularly and latterly African. Evidence can be found books of authority of foreign religions namely the Bible (Leviticus 25:44-46 (NLT); (Exodus 21:2-6 (NLT); (Luke 12:47-48 (NLT)); (1 Timothy 6:1-2 (NLT)); (Ephesians 6:5 (NLT); and (Exodus 21:20-21 (NAB) and the Quran (33:50); (23:5-6); (4:24); (8:69); (24:32); (2:178); and (16:75) legalise and validate this inhuman and ungodly phenomenon in the name of God. Johnson (2010) maintains that at the times and ages when the Bible was written slavery was a universal phenomenon; and it was part and parcel of the culture and people accepted it as a fact of life; also see Meager (2006); and Whitford (2009). However, later, the same Bible was used in abolishing slavery after slavery was no longer productive due to the introduction of industrial revolution that was enhanced by slavery. Ironically, when it is said that slavery was a universal phenomenon, those saying so had never set a foot on Africa's soil. Again, provided that to the West the world is them, Africa did not matter. Goldenberg (*Ibid.*) maintain that Islam did not abolish slavery. Instead, it wanted slavery to be carried out in pagan societies in which slaves from Sub-Saharan Africa "because there was a continual need to replenish the slaves, and because Sub-Saharan Africa was not yet Muslim therefore black Africa [became] an important source for slave of slaves for the Islamic world" (p. 133). I concur with Alexander despite the fact that the Qur'an did not abolish slavery in clear, direct language, its teachings did attempt to raise the moral and material status of slaves and to encourage their freedom which seems to be hypocritical, mainly when we consider the fact that Allah who sent the Quran is said to be Omni conscious or an all knower who was supposed to be clear in what Allah said. This is a bit controversial due to the fact that slavery in Trans-Saharan slavery was practices many years after the writing of the Quran. This is why Clarence-Smith (2006) differs from Abdullah noting that the:

> Qur'an failed to eliminate slavery; and that removing this practice would shake the faith itself due to the fact that the Prophet was totally unaware of the concept of abolition as an idea as well as in practice; and the fact that the whole Islamic social structure with its attendant system was based on a type of slavery associated with the organization of the harem (p. 119).

Recent evidence shows that slavery is still in existence in some Islamic world even presently due to the fact that this practice is cultural and religious to such societies. Oliver (1991: 117) cited in Thompson (2011) notes that there can be no doubt due to the fact the slave trade received a great impetus from the rise and spread of Islam just like it was with the rise of Christianity. Again, it depends on who writes what. Pro-Christian and pro-Islamic scholars tend to defend their faiths even where it is impossible and useless to do so. Ironically, some of those doing so are the progenies of the victims of the same phenomenon thanks to being brainwashed, hoodwinked and indoctrinated to believe more in their neo-religions that employed them to abuse and insult their own people and history. However, despite all efforts, the link between Christianity and Islam to slavery has become gunky to erase. Thompson (*Ibid.*) notes that when Europeans began to access more areas of Africa, slave traders largely avoided Muslim communities during any type of raiding as a courtesy to their fellow traders. So, too, religions have always played chameleonic roles based on a double standard. For example, when Christianity found that slavery was unviable, it changed tacks so as to start fighting the same evil it created and enunciated as it is for Islam. Based on a Latin proverb that *verba volant, scripta manent* literary, words fly away, writings remain. To get abettors in their crimes, Europeans and Arabs tried to link Africans with it. However, there is no nonbiased written evidence to scientifically link Africa with the genesis of this phenomenon. And if there is, it is doubtful due to the fact that much of the history of Africa was written by the same people who enslaved and colonised it. To the contrary, with respect to Christianity and Islam, they wrote their own histories and purported them to have come from God who seems to discriminate against Africans so as to need to be a coloniser that needed to be preached through propaganda and deception (Ekon 2014) just as any colonial penetration of any country.

After briefly tracing the genesis of slavery in the world and Africa, many would like to know why Africans were enslaved at such a big scale but not others. Mhango (2015) argues that Africans fitted the bill due to the fact that they were heathier and stronger than others due to how they were naturally created and adapted as an agrarian society not to mention being hard workers. Secondly, slavery was introduced to Africa due to the individualistic drive and nature of those who looked down on others as inferior creatures to them. Essentially, slavery was authored based on racism that Europe enacted in order to rob Africa so that it can develop while Africa became underdeveloped thereby. Loomba (2015) argues that the British Empire has had a pretty horrible press from a generation of 'postcolonial' historians who incongruously are disrespected by its racism that has been extended, up until now, under neoliberalism as an extension of colonialism in the world. Loomba goes on to link the International Monetary Fund (IMF) to the ongoing neocolonialism. There is no way one can analyse slavery without touching on European racism as Jordan (1812) argues that when Europeans *discovered* Africans the most arresting characteristic was his colour which is the same reason why other races are now favoured compared to Africans who are discriminated against. It is even sad to note that even Africans themselves have fallen in the same notorious booby trap thanks to the role religions played to hoodwink and dupe them. Look at how foreigners who live in Africa are generously treated while the same maltreat Africans. Mhango (2015) cites an example of Jarawa people in Andaman Islands in India who are treated by Indians like animals while Indians in Africa are enjoying more opportunities.

How Colonialism and Religion Are Bedfellows; Who Did What and Why

As it is in slavery, religion, particularly Christianity had a very big role to play during the colonisation in many parts of Africa and Islam in the Sudan, Libya, Mauritania and Saharawi. Colonialism is self-explanatory in that it is widely known due to the effects it has in many ex-colonies as well as colonisers. In simple parlance, colonialism is a foreign and superimposed administration on an occupied entity known as a colony. Therefore, when I talk of colonialism, I simply mean the system under which Africa was occupied and ruled by foreign countries. This does not include internal colonisation. However, it should be noted that colonialism might be foreign or homegrown all depending who is doing the colonising as it currently is in many African countries under illegal governments that have been in power either by tampering with the constitutions or lording it over citizens. This chapter deals with the former though.

The best way of taming anybody is through his or her brain. This is simple. For, the brain is the only controller of whatever, be it known or unknown, that any creature consciously or unconsciously does or perceives. So, Europe had to start with poisoning the brains of Africa through the *word of God* that turned out to help crimes and devilish things. It is at this very juncture Roman Catholic missionaries came into the big picture of corrupting, colonising, and thereby robbing Africa. Although the "his-story" written by European bigots has tried to exonerate the missionaries, their evil missions of paving a way for colonialism have refused to go away or being hidden. Despite biasedly writing dirty his-tory, Europeans failed to expunge the truth that religion was one of powerful tools colonial Europe used to penetrate Africa. In this chapter, I am going to link missionaries with poisoning Africans' brains so that they could, as it came to be, used as colonial machinery instead of becoming freedom incubators.

If it was not for the role missionaries, explorers and merchants or *les merchants de la mort du culture Africaine* played in Africa, colonialism would not have succeeded. So, as noted hereinbefore, missionaries were ones of the colonial agents who were sent to penetrate (*paenitentia* or spying disguised as confession) Africans so as to get their secrets and sell them to their masters back home in Europe. Under the pretext of offering education, missionaries, as any colonial agents, were able to spy and dupe Africans into obedience and mythology that ended up paving the way to colonialism. Despite that, missionaries were strategically different from other colonial agents such as traders, explores and administrators. However, this difference does not exempt most, if not all or any, missionaries of colonial times from the game of colonising (Dube 2017). The so-called explorers, merchants and missionaries were nothing but colonial trinity. Every group had the role to play at different times and levels to make sure that Africans were brainwashed for colonial governments to come in and rob for the benefit of Europe. Woodberry (2002, 2004) cited in Gallego (2010) discloses that some Catholic colonisers, as Italy, banned the entry of new Protestant missionaries to their colonies.

Another thing Europe takes pride in is civilisation. In his-story, the European wrote that he civilised African savages or the beasts of the jungle as they were referred to back then (Kubiesa 2014). One would think that religious people, if they were, such as missionaries would be taken to a swoon upon hearing such insults directed to those they taught that every human was created in the image of God. This means, by accepting that Africans were savage beasts in the African jungle, missionaries were recanting and doubting their God. If God created Africans in is image, he or she too must likewise be a savage beast in the heaven. So, too, when one discriminate against Africans based on the pigment of the colour of their skin, he or she does so against God that Europeans and Arabs came preaching to Africans to end up discriminating against colonising and dehumanising them. Yet, they soldiered on with the project knowingly how inhuman and criminal it was. Based on racist and colonial ideologies, missionaries did not go to Africa to civilise it as they maliciously used to allege. They went to Africa to destroy its culture in order to pave the way to colonialism simply because their belief was that black people were inferior to white ones. You can see this in their dogmatic teachings in which everything white is holy and everything black satanic. Song of Solomon (1: 5), *inter alia*, suffices to show us how being black is evil and punishable not to mention the discrimination black people face. The song reads:

> I am black [*dark*], but comely, O ye daughters of Jerusalem, as the tents of Kedar, as the curtains of Solomon. Look not upon me, because I am black, because the sun hath looked upon me: my mother's children were angry with me; they made me the keeper of the vineyards; but mine own vineyard have I not kept.

The verses above show how being black is a punishment before the eyes of bigots who wrote it as one of European literatures that were used to colonise and terrorise Africa. In racist terms, dark can be used synonymously with African, black, evil, inferior and unpleasant, *inter alia*, to mean the same (Davis 2010; Joseph 2010; White 2010; and Snead 2016). In fact, such an assertion shows the ignorance of the Bible and those who compiled it. First of all, it is against the very teaching the Bible teaches that all humans were made in the image of God without necessarily clarifying as to whose image between man and woman. Were humans created in the image of God or some, especially women were cast from the image of men? Eve or Hawa was just moulded (not created) from Adam's rib (Genesis 2:18–24; Quran 4:1; and Bukhari: 3135). Suppose we say that God created everything in God's image based on cyclic nature of the universe. Secondly, both his-story and the creation of a woman and the condemnation of all females openly show discrimination at its best however justified they might be either by using civilisation, God, modernity or whatever means. These cannot be the acts and word of the true God whom humans have; and will never truly understand. They are the words of the gods that compiled the Bible and the Quran and called such words the words of God while actually they are not. God who shines light and make it rain to every creature cannot discriminate against anything. Such God must be delusional (Dawkins 2016) and the "father of lies" (Ware 2015) which appeals and makes sense.

Interestingly, while whites and their books of authority have despised black colour, innocent birds tell a virtually different story due to the fact that they like black more than other colours except for red when dispersing seeds (Schaefer, Levey, Schaefer, and Avery 2006; Schaefer 2011; and Stournaras, Böhning-Gaese, Cazetta, Matthias Dehling, Schleuning, Stoddard, Donoghue, Prum and Martin Schaefer 2013). When it comes to whiteness, as noted above, things are holy jolly. Roediger (2010) wonders how black people could collectively remain silent about white representations in the black imagination. For example, all angels appear in white. Jesus has never been portrayed wearing a black garb. He is always in white apart from himself being white as if he were a Caucasian but not an Arab. Despite being represented as white, the so-called Jesus had black hair, black bead; and I think black private parts as it is for many. White as represented by Europe, according to the Bible, Leviticus (13:13) means clean. 2 Chronicles (5: 12); Psalm (51: 7); Song of Solomon (5: 10); Daniel (12: 10); Daniel (15: 35); and Psalm (68: 14) among many verses which denote that white is pure. However, apologetics may argue that the language used in the Bible and Quran are figurative, the truth will always hauntingly hunt them.

Due to being brainwashed, there are things we do either consciously or otherwise that are purely symbolic and connotative of racism against black as Europe invented and popularised them. For example, during funeral and mourning in many modern cultures African included, people wear black as a symbol of sombreness and loss while white is donned as a symbol of purity and cleanliness. Further, black has more connotations. In analysing the value of colours, Labrecque and Milner (2012) claim that white is a color with full value while black is a color with zero value, middle gray has a medium level of value, and brown is orange with mid saturation and low value. Sadly however, even the victims of this systemic and universalistic racism, the blacks, fall in the same trap. Moreover, discrimination against black does not end with humans but even animals. For example, Leonard (2011) notes that there is what is known as Big Black Dog (BBD) Syndrome which is the extreme under-adoption of large black dogs based not on temperament or health, but rather on the confluence of a number of physical and environmental factors in conjunction with the Western symbolism of the color black which in Western society is typically representative of evil and other negative connotations. With respect to white as colour, it is everything pretty and worthwhile as Nicholson (2002) cited in Akcay, Dalgin and Bhatnagar (2011) notes that:

> It represents reverence, purity, simplicity, cleanliness, peace, humility, sophistication, joy, precision, innocence, youth, birth, winter, snow, goodness, sterility, death and marriage. It is preferred by intellectuals, by those in the medical profession, and by modern types (p. 44).

More importantly, this racism is entrenched in Christianity as well as Islam traditions. For example, the papal conclave that elects the pope of Catholicism connotes racism. Toman (2004); and Green (2015) testify that the world can know if a new pontiff has been elected or not by looking at the sfumata, or the smoke signal whereby black smoke from the chimney on the roof of the Sistine Chapel shows that the College of Cardinals did not decide on the new

Pontiff. To the contrary, white smoke indicates to those in St Peter's Square that a new Pontiff has been chosen; also see Wüst (2010); Hayes and Hromic (2014); and Manalo (2015). Further, you can see racism in which black is evil in the Halloween that is celebrated in Europe and North America. Almost all Halloween costumes are in black to symbolise threatening nature of the colour. Mueller, Dirks and Picca (2007) note that:

> There have been several Halloween party related blackface incidents documented at universities across the United States over the past several years. White college students have donned blackface and re-enacted images of police brutality, cotton picking, and lynching at such parties, invoking degrading stereotypes and some of the darkest themes in our nation's racial past and present (p. 316).

Racism does not end in the process of electing the pope. Even the product of this process has always produced racist results in that there has not been a black pope to lead the church that prides itself to be universal. Thanks to the effects of Islam and the caste system in India, Vidyarthi (1995) claims that "white is the colour of peace, harmony, goodness and honour, red denotes danger and war, and black is the colour of evil and ignorance." I know how provocative such ideologies are. However, I hope it is more provocative for the victims to embrace the same ideologies for their own peril. Now, one may ask: what does this have to do with development in Africa *vis-à-vis* Europe. There is a link. How much money and time do our people spend either on studying such garbage not to mention spending money on books and literatures that discriminate against them? How many Africans now kill each other because of religious reasons as it recently happened in the Central African Republic (CAR) where Christians and Muslims killed each other? How much property was destroyed not to mention lives pointlessly lost? Ironically, when Africans butchered each other in the CAR, it is Europe that was called in to broker peace instead of being held liable for creating such animosity for its benefits. With respect to religious discrimination, it did not start with black. It goes "back to the crusades and before, turned into racial discrimination" (Grosfoguel 2013: 84). If Europe

51

was able to discriminate against its own people starting with women, what of Africans and others deemed inferior? Swahili sage has it that when one learns how to become a cannibal, will never stop. This is why racism is still rave even today in the age of ground-breaking scientific and social advancements and development. Again, without discrimination, Europe would not have been what it is today. It still goes on. Apart from gender and racial discrimination, look at digital discrimination today (Edelman and Luca 2014) where Africa is now an e-waste dumping yard for old technologies. McIntire (2015) notes that "the United States and the European Union continue to use developing nations, especially those in West Africa, as a dump for their nations' used electronics" (p. 79). Why do they do this? It is simply because that the way they perceive Africans compared to themselves is totally different. Who bothers when turning an animal into a guinea pig or eat on its products? Such humans cannot practically be equal without revisiting the history of such criminality as Europe enacted it.

Religion has many more negative impacts on Africa than positive ones. However, some people argue that religious institutions offer social services such as education and partly health. When you consider permanent impacts they have on the African society, you find that Africa loses much more than it gains. For example, when missionaries came to Africa, they taught people to hate mundane things (wealth) while the same grabbed land. How many thousands of hectares do churches and mosques own in Africa while, in some countries, citizens are landless? Desmond Tutu, retired archbishop of Cape Town, South Africa notes that "when the missionaries came to Africa, they had the Bible and we had the land. They said 'let us close our eyes and pray'" (*Guardian*, 19, August 2003) thereafter Africans found themselves with the bible in their hand and their land gone. Apart from grabbing land in Africa, to crown it all, such organisations in many unsuspecting African countries enjoy tax exemptions under the pretexts of the provision of social services. The story does not end up here. In some countries, presidents cannot take power without holding either the Bible or the Quran so as to be sworn in as a sign of trustworthiness without underscoring the fact that the same harbingers of these faiths proved to be fickle in dealing with Africans as Tutu, indicates above.

Further, missionaries provided education that has never helped Africans to fully liberate themselves. Does this sort of colonised and toxic education help Africa *vis-à-vis* development? Once such leaders sworn in by holding the so-called *holy books* come to power in Africa, most of them misuse public funds funding religious organisations as it recently happened in Tanzania where the government has offered to build the headquarters of the Tanzania Muslim Council (BAKWATA) at the whooping cost of Tshs. 5 billion (*Daily News*, 16 August, 2016) while the same countries has many pupils who study under trees not to mention unpaid teachers. Maybe, the oath of faithfulness is for colonial masters and their ideologies embedded in their religions. The same countries offering such a project still begs for money to top up its budget. Furthermore, the government said that it decided to construct the BAKWATA's headquarters as it's thanks to religious leaders for maintaining peace. Again, you wonder. Is peace in Tanzania maintained by religious leaders or the people? Isn't this a bribe to such organisations if not the sign of partnership in duping the citizens?

I see no peace in religious organisation, especially when I consider the enmity they create among Africans based on denominational ideologies. To me, true and sustainable peace in any country will prevail as long as there is justice but not indoctrination of the *hoi polloi*. I may argue that our leaders tend to kowtow before religious leaders and their organisations simply because they are the products of these religions not to mention using them to hoodwink the citizens in various countries. If the government can build the headquarters of a religious organisation by negating its schools and hospitals, how much money does such a country lose to offering tax holidays to such organisations? Jesus paid tax to the government. Why don't religious organisations, especially Christian ones emulate him? Now, you can see why religious organisations are always rich so as to attract many quacks who appoint themselves bishops, apostles and whatnots in order to rob the general population. This is because Africans were made to seriously believe that mythical stories they read in religious books of authorities were real while they were not.

Take an example where Jesus is said to have fed 5,000 hungry people by praying for a few fish and loaves of bread that multiplied so as to produce enough food so that they ate and had leftovers (Mark 6:30-44). Ironically, for over 2,000 nothing like that has had happened practically at least once to prove such hoaxes.

To cap it all, colonial agents became authorities in their countries. Whatever lies they told ignorant Europeans of the time about the Dark Continent (Mawdsley 2008) as one criminal and bastard that his mother abandoned, Henry Morton Stanley (Newman 2004; and Fiorillo 2010) derogatory referred to Africa, was taken as true despite that fact that what was actually the Dark Continent was Europe (Mazower 2009). To know the type of person that Stanley was, Mutua (2007) refers to him as a historical monster that paved the way for many pogroms committed by the colonial hegemons in Africa. Ironically, despite priding itself to be enlightened, Europe would gulp hook, line, and sinker whatever nonsensical things that any common sense would dispute. Again, how could the Europe of that time bother to reason while it was engrossed in chaotic life of crime and poverty? It is at this time Europe was degrading women like nobody's business.

Based on wrong assumptions, biasness, inexperience, eurocentrism, ignorance and malice, European thinkers of the time redefined Africa by distorting everything to their advantages (Fage 2013; Asante 2014; and Mugovhani and Mapaya 2014). Europeans bigots and quacks went further by denying African the right of having and presenting its own history written and presented accurately. Some of those who wrote the so-called Africa's history had never set foot on Africa's soil or studied anything about it. To get away with murder, they made sure that whatever incriminated them either was given some explanations or expunged from the account of African distorted history. Essentially, the history of Africa Europe wrote was not only Europeanised, but also hijacked with the discretion of what to and who tell what to make sure, as Hegel (1830) cited in Bayart and Ellis (2000) notes, that:

Africa has remained cut off from all contacts with the rest of the world; it is the land of gold, forever pressing in on itself, and the land of childhood, removed from the light of self-conscious history and wrapped in the dark mantle of night (p. 217).

This is why some European bigots dared to say that Africa is like a child who refused to grow. White 2000 notes that, sometimes, when the truth is distorted or hijacked, it becomes difficulty somehow to see the truth distorted by a lie or the truth hidden by a secret or malice. This is what we exactly find when we revisit the history of Africa the Europeans authored. They littered it with blatant lies and bigotries as a way of protecting their position so as to produce what I can call just "a figment of the Western capitalist imagination" (Appleby, Hunt and Jacob 2011: 46) devoid of any verity and originality due to the fact that it was written and presented philosophically but not historically based on its historical context. They did so purposely to prove that their arrival in Africa was a blessing but not a curse for Africa. Basically, European bigots used the lack of written history of Africa as an opportunity to miswrite, misconstrue and misrepresent it. They tied civilisation with the art of writing without underscoring that communication does not only depend on writings but it does also depend on oral and other media where orality has its part to play in imparting and communicating knowledge (Diagne 2008: Thompson 2017). This is because they alleged that they civilised Africa something Mhango (2015) strongly attacks and recants. At this stage, colonialism was not introduced in Africa. Instead, the awareness and information of the existence of such magnificent and virgin continent were relied back to Europe. *Ab hinc*, colonial Europe started its strategies of occupying and colonising Africa. Agents were dispatched to spy, survey and map up Africa for full-fledged colonialism. This was the first phase of the colonisation of Africa that led to inexplicable destruction and exploitation of Africa.

To make sure that Africans were left with no alternative means of survival except being forced to sell their labour, colonisers introduced money economy that gave them the authority of just printing papers and turn them to something valuable. This was not only new to Africans but also an anomaly. Africans had no way they could object this new system provided that they had already lost their power due to having inferior weapons compared to colonisers'. To finish Africa off, they introduced taxes that forced Africans to become labourers in white farms in order to be able to pay tax (Frankema 2010a); also see Furnivall (2014); Acemoglu and Robinson (2010); and Fieldhouse (2012). If you ask what Africans were paying for while there was no any provision of social services which entitle the government the legality of collecting tax, you do not get any logical answer. Nothing stands out. Colonial regimes made sure that they are fleecing Africans by all means possible. For example, the introduction of money economy targeted any valuables such as house, cattle, goats land and whatever colonial administrators deemed fit to be their fair game (Duncan 2012). To make sure that there was no way Africans could boycott or default on this system, they introduced prison corporal and other punishments as the means of enforcing and install this notorious system that has been ongoing ever since. The situation became even worse when post-colonial governments, many managed by Europe-made stooges, retained the same system whereby a cabal of political elites would lord it over the citizens without necessarily being accountable to them except their masters. This is why underdevelopment of Africa has been going even after gaining independence over a half of a century ago. It is because, those privileged to rule did not deconstruct the systems and institutions colonisers established. You can see this on how modern African governments invest. They just copy and paste what Europe has been doing. For example, currently, many countries are investing on infrastructure in order to transport their resources to the European markets without addressing the impasse many poor rural dwellers are in. Even where there is a road or electricity, essentially it is built or created to serve foreign markets. This is why Africa has never created its own markets.

The second and full-blown phase of colonialism started in 1884 (Shomanah and Dube 2012) at what came to be famously known as the Berlin Conference (Mhango 2017c) at which the then European colonisers carelessly and heinously divided Africa like a cake among themselves without being mindful of the rights and structural settings that existed at the time. It is at this very conference, the fate of Africa was utterly sealed as opposed to Europe's leading role emanating therefrom. Since then, Europe has never looked back as far as development is concerned. For, thereafter, Europe secured the rights of exploiting Africa for decades. Since then, Europe has enjoyed the proceeds from this criminal act without the international community interfering to see to it that Africa was redress and its contribution appreciated. To achieve this, Africa needs to do its homework carefully and forcefully provided that decision-making international bodies such as the United Nations (UN) and its umbrella organisations are still colonial by nature and structure. You can see this when a conflict breaks in Africa. Most of those coming to broker peace or helping refuges produced by such conflicts are non-Africans to signify how such bodies are still colonised. The simple logic is that whites are more educated than Africans not to mention that most of these organisations, apart from being headed by whites are housed out of Africa. Refer to how out of UN 8 secretaries-general; 3 came from Europe plus one who is white although he came from South America despite Europe having a small population compared to other continents such as Africa and Asia. Refer to how five countries namely China, France, Russia, United Kingdom (UK) and United States (US) retain veto powers as opposed to Africa as a continent on which many of economies of such countries have depended for a long time. Where is a veto country from Africa?

By using unsuspecting African scientists and gurus, colonial agents explored African rivers, lakes, gorges, mountains, plains and everything they deemed meaningful economically, Europe stole the existing knowledge Africans used to run their affairs without necessarily borrowing from or depending on handouts as it currently is. Provided that European invaders did not have any knowledge about Africa, they were taught by Africans about Africa without crediting such a push that enabled them to occupy Africa. Instead of appreciating the support Africans offered them, these criminals spread many lies to African gurus who tended to believe them due to their understanding that a civilised person cannot tell lies. One of the driving forces for African elites to offer their knowledge is the fact that they believed in reciprocity in that they would offer knowledge and received knowledge from their visitors who happened to be criminal and mean. Although this is always taken as a weakness, the detractors forget that there cannot be any cooperation without two parties opening to each other. Again, it depends on who opens up first. When Africans opened up to help those they deemed to be their visitors, wrongly thought that the latter would reciprocate. It is sad that they did not; and wherever they reciprocated, it was in fully dishonesty.

Primarily, Africans wanted to gain knowledge of their visitors so that they could trade with them competently and fairly. You can see this on how, for example, the International Financial Institutions (IFIs) have always duped Africa by introducing various policies that come a cropper. Sadly though, when any failure happens, everything is blamed on Africa; and African countries do not put the IFIs to tax or make them take the blame for the failure as parts of the process and policymakers (Ferguson 2006). It takes two to tango. Lamb (1986) cited in Lamb (2011) succinctly notes that "assigning blame to Africa's failure has become irrelevant, particularly because there is ample blame for all to share" (xvii). There is no way Africa can be blamed and held responsible for its fantastic failure without equally and openly doing the same to its exploiters, insinuators and violators.

However, in regard to failure resulting from superimposed policies on Africa, the case becomes *ex parte* in that only Africa is blamed for the failures. This has been the way things have been done for the advantage of Europe as opposed to the advantage or interests of Africa. If anything, this sheepishness was inherited since Africa came into contact with Europe which made sure that such an anomaly is internalised and reinforced so as to become a norm. Notably, when these invaders first came into contact with Africa, they pretended to be honesty and humble. Such a comportment deceived Africans so as to trust them thinking they were impeccably sincere the same way Africans were. Therefore, what Africans expected from European was reciprocity but not brutality and duplicity. Again, after knowing and stealing the secrets of their generous hosts, either through duplicity or using betrayers of the society, European criminals started to hit back brutally. For example, after learning that Africans did not have equivalent firepower to theirs such as guns, they brought guns with them; and started wars that caught African off-guard so as to lose in many wars that ensued at the time. Thanks to knowing African classified secrets, European criminals started playing Africans against each other after knowing their weaknesses. Due to the existing competitions and enmities among African societies in which empires fought each other, it was easy for European to get Africans' secrets. They pretended to befriend one party as they posed as an enemy of another in order to get access to their secrets. Once they got secrets from one side, they turned against it so as to side or team up with its enemy. Things worked that way until European invaders were able to take over everything leaving Africans shocked to learn that they were played against each other. It was too late then. Knowing how they stood to lose, African reorganised themselves within fake and weak countries the European created. They fought back and regained their independence in the 60s. However, despite regaining their independence, Africans seemed to have kept on repeating the same mistakes after some post-colonial African countries were played against each other under the then two camps during the cold war namely the East socialist or communist and the West capitalist. It reached at the point where one country was pointlessly divided right in the middle. Angola provides an ideal example whereby two parties fighting for its independence stifled the country to death. The *Movimento Popular de Libertação de* Angola (MPLA) the pro-east and the *União Nacional para a Independência Total de* Angola (UNITA), the pro-west fought a long time battle starting in 1961 up until 2002 (Ferreira 2006) simply because they were backed by two antagonistic forces. In fact, the duo in Angola was fighting hegemonic proxy whose major protagonists were the then USSR and the West. Even today, under unipolar, African countries are still extremely divided along many nonsensical things such as sovereignty, income, size and whatnots so as to keep on becoming weaker and weaker for their peril while Europe is united in order to gain more dominance and prominence altogether. Apart from the division along the cold war, currently, Africa has some intra-national divisions revolving around democracy in which opposing parties threaten national cohesion. Kenya provides an ideal example. In 2007 there happened what came to be known as Post-Election Violence (PEV) in which over 1,000 people died and thousands were internally displaced simply because two politicians from two antagonistic communities of Luo and Kikuyu, the two biggest communities in the country, were battling it out for the presidency. This shows how division has haunted Africa even after regaining its independence. Apart from human loses; Kenya's economy was badly affected. Kihato (2015) notes that:

> Millions of shillings worth of property was looted and burned as ethnic militias rallied behind their leaders: Raila Odinga, the Luo leader of the Orange Democratic Movement (ODM), and Mwai Kibaki, the Kikuyu founder of the rival Party of National Unity (PNU). The violence only ended after a peace agreement between the two leaders in February 2008 (p. 13).

What transpired in Kenya under the auspices of Western democracy is the replica of many African countries. The situation was the same in Ivory Coast in 2002 that divided the country into two parts namely north and south both represented by two leaders namely former President Laurent Gbagbo and the incumbent Alassane Ouattara respectively (Mbeki 2011). Had it not been for its colonial master, France, to decide who becomes president; the country was on the verge of collapsing. Interestingly, Europe is liable for creating such schisms in its African colonies so as to go on many years after gaining independence for its benefit and the peril of Africa. If you look at the two countries cited above, they were all heavily occupied by European settlers. Therefore, they created the systems that would keep on serving Europe even after handing over independence to the home-grown elites who happened to be so blind that they could not see this ploy. This is why they fell in the trap and, by extension; its rulers became the agents of neocolonialism in Africa. Talking about intra-national divisions, Africa still has a lot to do to do away with this toxin Europe intentionally injected into Africa for perpetual exploitation. Demonstrably, there is no intra-national fighting or civil wars in Europe as they are in Africa. All this is because when Europe created fissures among Africans, it united European countries and people so as to be immune of such conflicts. Ironically, when Africans fight each other for whatever reasons major one being power in order to control resources and supply Europe; it is the same Europe they call in to broker peace! This way, Europe gets another chance of controlling the situation to its advantage.

Epistemologically and historically, there is no way one can talk about Europe's development without talking about the underdevelopment of Africa that the former authored after dividing, invading and colonising the latter. Therefore, the development of Europe is based on Europe's criminal past that enabled it to rob Africa. This corpus does not aim at criminalising Europe; neither does it aim at exonerating it from its criminal liability. Instead, the volume seeks; and thereby aims at telling an untold story of Africa; and the way Africa hugely contributed in developing Europe based on research and academic evidence and findings among others. Therefore, an important element that links Europe's development and Africa's underdevelopment can be traced back to slavery or the status or condition of a person whose power is controlled by another for the purpose of owning, exploiting, using and abusing (Allain and Bales 2012); and colonialism (Veracini 2010) and later, neocolonialism, neoliberalism, and imperialism as Europe carried them out and superimposed them on; and executed them in Africa. Imperialism comes from the Latin term *imperium*, meaning to command (Kohn and Reddy 2006). Essentially, imperialism is about one country or person controlling another.

For, under those three epochs herein mentioned above, Europe was able to freely subjugate (Chomsky 2015) and hold up Africa so as to develop itself as Africa became underdeveloped after its ways of life and systems were destroyed in order to allow European ones to take over (Keynes, Pearson, Andrews, Angus, Hegel, and Smith). This is why the concept of Africa's long term and systemic stunt (Nunn 2007, 2008; Jacobsen and Nielsen 2014; and Whatley and Gillezeau 2011) surfaces in this corpus as a hunch of this discourse.

After exploring the history of the harms and ills Europe caused to Africa, this corpus will provide some suggestions of what can be done to pull Africa and Europe out of this impasse based on current realities. The assumption of this volume is that, the world needs to face the reality so that it can change for the better. Essentially, if there will be the will on both sides to see to it that every side is playing its role based on justice and truth, the world is likely to be a good place to live in instead of facing many violent conflicts resulting from the struggle of controlling and extracting resources, a lot of resources, in which Europe has always had a very upper hand. For example, Mac Ginty and Williams (2016) claim that there is a connection between resource-related conflicts with the globalised economy of the world, especially under the free market policies under which it becomes easier for licit and illicit economies to interact. Further, Mac Ginty and Williams disclose that in 2009 the UN estimated that transnational crime generated US$890 billion. Who got what; and who lost what is the question we can ask here. Collier and Hoeffler, (2002) cited in Hoeffler (2008) note that a global statistical analysis of the onset of civil wars suggests that Africa has experienced more civil wars, mainly because the economic circumstances, low income, low growth and high dependence on natural resources; therefore lost more due to the fact that it is the only continent whose resources have always been obtained cheaply by the way of tolerating conflict resulting from resource control. Interestingly, even those who sacrifice their countries for the quest of controlling resources do not actually control anything. They are just straight partner Europe has always used to rob their countries. For some, the ramifications have been to be kicked out of power either by their masters or the people and die like dogs in exile as it happened for the former DRC dictator, Joseph Mobutu or his CAR counterpart Jean-Bedel Bokassa. When we consider the sufferings, deaths and poverty resource conflicts have caused to Africa; and how much Europe made out it, if Africa can seek redress based on *modus vivendi* if not give and take, how much money would Europe pay? Will it still be richer as it currently is? Under restorative justice, Europe was supposed, as it still is, to redress Africa for the ills it committed. Zehr (2015) notes that restorative seeks to address the needs and roles of the victims of crime, offenders and communities rather than legalistic wrath. Instead of being a very odious legal process, I view this as an opportunity for both parties. Even under natural justice, Europe is duty-bound to admit its wrongs; and thereby redress Africa; otherwise all noises about universal human equality and human rights are abhorrent, hypocritical and miasmas. How much can Africa reclaim shall it sue Europe for all miseries it caused, illegal activities it did such as entering without visas, living working in Africa illegally, the water and other resources colonisers used not to mention the civilisation they felled? It is, indeed, billions if not trillions of dollars. Europe needs judicial courage in facing the reality resulting from its criminal past *vis-à-vis* its development and the underdevelopment of Africa. Solum (2006) observes that naturally, "most humans care about their reputations and social standing" (p. 79). There is no way Europe's standing as one of the world leaders in many areas can remain intact and respectable without correcting its past wrongs to others.

Keeping hiding heads in the sands, as it has been or striving to make injustices common things that can be internalised and reinforced, will never do the world good. Instead, it will create a time-ticking bomb waiting to explode. There are so many signs buying into this apart from violent conflicts that are producing many refugees and paupers. The current example is the current wave of refugees from pauperised countries that are trying to make it to Europe for greener pastures. The only way for Europe to survival by putting a stop on this phenomenon is to do justice for Africa so that it can grow economically and retain its people. As I will propose, there is no suitable way like redressing Africa and treating it fairly in international trade. After its people were persecuted in Europe provides a very ideal example of how savagery Europe was to itself and humanity. Innocent millions of people were brutally killed simply because of their pedigree. Therefore, when it comes to the bestiality Europe committed against others, it is not Africa only that suffered this inhumanity. However, the difference is: while Jews were redressed and their plight recognised, it is only Africa that has been left out simply because it is the country of the people whose tinctures are black. After being redressed and helped, Israel is now helping other countries. Africa does not need to fleece Europe the same it fleeced it. It needs justice, as we will see, natural and restorative justice as opposed to criminal or retributive justice. Earnestly, Europe and the international community need to take this matter seriously in order to avoid causing more harm based on espousing more exploitation and subjugation of Africa through extracting resources by all means. The time for the 'winner takes it all' is coming to an end in the globalised world. If Europe keeps on living in the state of denialism, maybe, the rise of China and India may remind it of its responsibility after losing big.

Chapter Three

How Robbing Africa Developed Europe

No doubt that without Africa's contribution, *inter alia*, Europe we know of today would not be as it currently is. It is from this milieu that this volume seeks to lay bare Africa's contribution to the development of Europe, mainly resulting from slavery and colonialism not to mention neocolonialism therefrom. As well, after laying bare Africa's development to Europe, this volume unpacks and makes the case for Africa so that Europe can redress it. Although neither Europe nor any single European colonial power, either out of arrogance, *holier than thou*, malice, decency or naivety, has ever admitted to have held African development back, Africa developed Europe exponentially. Historically and realistically, Africa played a very pivotal role in the development Europe boasts of today. For, without free labour and resources, the Europe we know today would have been unimaginable let alone existing. The fact of the matter is: Africa contributed immensely in developing Europe through slavery, colonialism and neocolonialism. Despite this fact, Europe has always tried to show the world that it achieved its development based on its ingenious drive but not disingenuity as it was displayed in colonialism. History testifies that Africa did not only develop Europe but also saved it from itself; and its enemies. Refer to how the nuclear bomb that was detonated in Hiroshima and Nagasaki; thus bringing the WW II to an abrupt end whereby Europe became victorious over its enemies. Chomsky (2015) discloses that:

> As for Africa, State Department Policy Planning chief George Kennan, assigning to each part of the South its special function in the New World Order of the post-World War II era, recommended that it be "exploited" for the reconstruction of Europe" (p. 39).

This is purely international conspiracy against Africa. If the so-called international community has never seen this as a criminal act, then, there is no way it can be trusted or exonerated from criminal liability when it comes to discriminating against and exploiting Africa. Further, from 1914 to 1918 and 1939–1945 Europe faced wars it called world wars despite being Europeans wars. I think this is because whatever Europe does is deemed international or universalised to show Europe's hegemony. Due to the ferociousness of the war and dangers Europe's enemies posed once again, Europe came to Africa knocking to seek aid. Many Africans were recruited; and thereby taken to fight Europe's war in various areas. Despite this noble contribution, regrettably, the contribution and sacrifice of blood and sweat such Africans offered were never appreciated. It is as if they did nothing to save Europe from itself and its enemies. Up until now, nobody knows how many African combatants actually in the World War I and II were. So, too, even the numbers of those who died has never been known due to the fact that Europe did not bother to document their participation; and where it did, it did not want the actual numbers to be known for fear of disclosing how Africa developed and saved Europe. Maybe, if Europe lost this war Africa would not be what it is today. The number will never be known provided that Europe did not bother to keep their statistics while it did so for other non-African. According to Plaut (2009), at least 1, 355,347 African combatants fought in the war; also see Killingray and Plaut (2012). How much would Europe pay for their deaths, injuries, labour and the sufferings of African combatants had it been today?

How much Africa did lose in terms of manpower that died saving Europe in its horrific and needless wars? How much Europe saved by using African soldiers to fight its wars? How much money would Europe have spent on African veterans had it been today had they gone as mercenaries? How much did Europe achieve after winning the wars? All such questions are important; and they need answers so as to move forward. To get just a glimpse of what happened during these two European wars aka the World War I and II Fischer (2015) reports that "a million people died in East Africa alone during the First World War. Many Africans also fought in Europe, defending the interests of their colonial masters. Today, their sacrifice has been largely forgotten." Who would care or remember African combatants while they were regarded as beasts Europe would manipulate and use free of charge? These and others are the injustices the international community needs to fully and practically address in order to right the wrongs Europe committed on Africa in its process of achieving development.

Many Africans paid with their blood to see to it that Europe is not being occupied by Russians and Japanese among others. So, too, Africa provided the military capability that helped the West to vanquish the entente among Nazi German, fascist Italy and Russia and imperial Japan whose military clout, as aforementioned, was brought to end after the US bombed it with an atomic or nuclear bomb in 1948. As noted hereinabove, the uranium that helped the US to produce this bomb was obtained from the DRC. Without this bomb, maybe, the history would not have been the same.

Africa supplied needed resources such as rubber that was available in the then Congo or the modern-day DRC that was highly needed to run the war. There was no way Europe would run its industrial revolution without having something to dress on the automobiles which became the engines that jogged the industrial revolution. Apart from slaves, with resources such as rubber, gold, diamond (Exenberger 2007) and labour contributed to fuel the industrial revolution.

Also Africa became the good source of income for Europe due to the fact that financial capital gotten by the way of robbing raw materials that were processed and sold back to Africa had a crucial role to play in the industrialization of Europe and later the US.

So, too, Africa decided who was to become a winner in the WW II. Refer to how the bomb that was detonated in Hiroshima and Nagasaki by the US was made of the uranium mined from the DRC (Moore 2007: 4 cited in Mhango 2015). Apart from reconstructing Europe as Chomsky (*Ibid.*) succinctly puts it, by participating in the World Wars I and II fighting along and for Europe (James 2012; and Tucker 2013), Africa helped colonialism to exploit it more comfortably than it was before winning the wars. By fully participating in the so-called world wars, Africans were unknowingly easing the role for their exploitation by those they wrongly thought were pulling together. Despite sacrificing their blood and sweat, Europe still did not appreciate the contribution Africa and Africans

67

made to its security and wellbeing. For example, France felt the pride of recruiting Africans as the way of "rescuing them from barbarism, providing them with the civilizing benefits of military service, and granting them the ultimate privilege of fighting for the motherland" (Keegan 2014: 158). This means, that Africans were the beasts of burden (the same role Africa has always played internationally) whose deaths in this dirty war was a blessing in the eyes of capricious France. Has this stopped to be the take of Europe when it comes to exploiting Africa? If we consider the true meaning of barbarism, what France was doing is more dangerous and barbarous than what Africans did in helping Europe to fight its wars. This is how barbaric Europe has always been when abusing Africa.

Similarly, since the first Europeans' landfall, Africa has always served Europe in many ways economically, politically and socially. Refer to clientele economic and political relationships between Europe and Africa (Médard 2014) which maintained the exploitation even after Africa regained its independence from its former colonisers whose tactics of colonisation were just commuted into the current imperialism, neocolonialism and neoliberalism and other isms.

In writing this volume, I was geared by provocative thirsty of bringing this ignored truth to the fore so that, at least, the culprits and victims could do something constructive about it. This is why; I have tried as much as I can to provide evidence *mutatis mutandis* in order to answer many questions raised in this compendium. To begin with, for example, the West has maintained its lies saying that Africa is the new continent. Ironically, the same criminals, liars and pretender admit that all humankinds originate from Africa. Then you ask yourself: Is Africa really a new continent? How? Simple explanation is that they have always done all this to make Africa look like a baby or a juvenile they can lecture about everything. This is the subdued Truth that was dubiously killed in order to keep Europe being viewed as the harbinger of human development while the truth is that the same is the harbinger of miseries to many millions of people all over the world. This is, especially true when we consider negative effects and impacts of slave trade, colonialism and neocolonialism among others. Such nefarious colonial strategies left its victims antagonised, divided and, above all, pauperised. To unequivocally and practically address such anomalies, I will revisit the history and the impacts of the said ills that colonial Europe committed to Africa, chiefly using it as a typical replica of other victims, in the world that are still suffering from the same problem of being unsung heroes despite playing a pivotal role in developing Europe. Therefore, as the title reads, the major aim of penning down this tome is nothing, as hereinabove mentioned, but to make the case for Africa as far as the development of Europe and the underdevelopment of Africa are concerned. Doing so will help Africa and the world at large to think differently when it comes to why Africa has always been termed as underdeveloped. When the later Dr. Walter Rodney wrote his larger-than-life *magnum opus* titled: *How Europe Underdeveloped Africa*, he took the world by storm for its originality, erudition and painstaking but accurate and objective analysis. Rodney skillfully made the case for Africa to the extent that since then, no scholar, mainly from Europe has ever repudiated his account of event not to mention his position that has weathered the test of time. Sadly though, Rodney did not live to author another, *How Africa Developed Europe*. He was killed by the enemies of development in his native land, Guyana and Africa in general. However, the sparks he started have never faded. This is why—over thirty years thereafter—I feel, as an academic and a victim of colonialism and all evils it ushered in, I am dutifully beholden to proceed from where Rodney left over thirty years ago. Therefore, I must admit from the outset that Dr. Rodney is one of the catalysts that propelled me into writing this volume about how Africa developed Europe which is an antithesis to Rodney's *How Europe Underdeveloped Africa*. This quest was upturned by a question: How could a Guyanese be so passionate about Africa while Africans could not? Rodney was a Guyanese but not an African. Maybe, his blackness and origin contributed a lot in creating the passion for Africa that geared him to write the book that became bigger than him. Otherwise, maybe, if it were not so, he would have researched and written about Guyana. Maybe, like I am, it is because Rodney was more of a citizen of the world than a Guyanese, which would have narrowly confined him; thus disadvantaging him from doing what he did. Unluckily though, since Rodney wrote *How Europe Underdeveloped Africa*, no African academics picked up the baton and mettle to expand on the topic.

Apart from being humbled and motivated by Rodney, I am doing so because Rodney's journey to bring to the fore all evils Africa went through under colonialism has to continue provided that what Rodney eluded on are still the same; or have doubled but not decreased or rescinded. Likewise, as an African, I would like to use my knowledge to give back to my people not to mention to add up to the dialogue. I believe; I am not the only one to do so. Many have tried; and many will do; however in different disciplines, manners and times. Similarly, like Rodney motivated me, I will motivate others who will come up with other nuggets so as to add up. Despite all, the aim will remain the same that the story of Africa's epic underdevelopment and that of the development of Europe must be told due to the fact that the duo depends on each like yin and yang. There is no way one can talk about the development of Europe without touching on Africa and the vital role it played in bringing about; and thereby enhancing Europe's development. Moreover, nobody can tell the story of Africa's underdevelopment without implicating Europe due to the criminal role it played in colonising, enslaving and exploiting Africa that needs to be decolonised almost in all spheres of life (Meredith 2011) which is the duty of all Africans, mainly academics, activists, politicians and whatnots.

We need to define development and underdevelopment in order to assess if truly Africa developed Europe and vice versa. Mhango in Mawere (2016a) argues that Africa's underdevelopment is an externally-inflicted; and partly self-inflicted wounds (Chabal 2016) due to the fact that Africa allowed others to define it; and in so doing, there are many crucial, facts, factors and historical attributes on human development seem to be—either purposely or out of ignorant—left out in the definition of [under] development. So, too, under corrupt and inept rulers, Africa allowed others to define and dictate its policies and politics without underscoring that doing so was another way of developing Europe while under developing itself pointlessly. One you allow your enemy to define, get prepared of being dehumanised and distorted. This is why when it comes to

Africa's development; we need to redefine it based on African benchmarks and interests as it has always been the case for Europe. Importantly, development must be perceived as a long time process but not an event or events differently from the way some thinkers characterise it. Also, development is not a photocopy of others as European thinkers tend to make Africa believe in following Europe's trajectory of development. This characterisation is based on the facts that after gaining political independence, many African countries did not embark on the decolonising and deconstructing the colonial institutions and systems which were in place so as to embark on paradigm shift that would make them turn things around for their advantage. Therefore, despite priding itself about being independent, Africa still retains European version and vision of things as a dominant force that has always blinded and eluded many thinkers and African post-colonial leaders from exploring and interrogating many truths *vis-à-vis* Africa's mysterious underdevelopment while they say their countries are independent. Africa needs to become chary about colonial carryovers it has blindly retained so as to slow down its would-be pace for development based on the deconstruction of everything colonial. Faux (2005) cited in Langmia (2006) disagrees with those who enticingly urge Africa to follow Europe's stages of development for it to achieve development. Apart from such views to be colonial and fallacious, they aim at keeping Africa in the trap that Europe set. China and India are now emerging without necessarily following Europe's script.

As a people and victims, Africans need to deconstruct the meaning and rationale of the independence that, up until now, have never been made clear to Africans, especially those excluded from leadership and high positions in the government. If you ask any African the meaning of independence, you will get different meanings according to where he or she is located in the society. For rulers, independence is for them to access free services paid for by the staggering poor they exploit. This is exactly what colonial governors did. This makes post-colonial African rulers black governors in the state houses that colonisers left behind doing exactly the same as those they expelled did. For example, those who took over from colonisers are still driven in large and long motorcades;

71

they are surrounded by highly armed bodyguards even those who do not deserves them. They are afraid of those they rule. They do not trust them. For they know, just like those they rule do how they do not like or trust them. African rulers do not look like those they rule. For this volume, the meaning and significance of independence can be seen on the citizens. It is inside them. It is in their houses; in their private lives. It can be seen on their tables, in their streets and in their cities and villages. Freedom is not only political but apolitical in that it should be reflected on many things but not only in politics. Freedom is not about the flag and the office of the president. Freedom is power that enables everybody who is deemed to be free to choose. Shklar (2010) maintains that freedom is in the state of mind of people either individually or collectively that involves many things among which can be material and spiritual wellbeing. For example, when I say freedom is seen on the table, I mean the power to choose what to eat but not to eat whatever is available. Why should animals and birds have the power to choose what they eat but not humans if truly Africa is independent? Freedom is about the power to choose the hospitals and schools for parents to take their children and sick people. Markus and Schwartz (2010) note that "choice is viewed as essential to autonomy, which is absolutely fundamental to well-being" (p. 344).

Freedom is not being forced to use whatever dilapidated and poor services rulers offer. Freedom is about wellbeing.

When it comes to freedom or independence of Africa, it is just a few that has ever enjoyed it. It is those that are in power with *carte blanche* to access free services even abroad after sabotaging them at home. This is why African elections are always surrounded with allegations of ballot buying and stuffing and rigging. This is why African elections are more expensive than anybody can envisage. When it comes to freedom or independence of Africa, it is just a few that has ever enjoyed it. Apart from Botswana whose hybrid democracy has, at least, helped the country to move forward, show me an African country that has benefited from such elections or independence. Instead of bringing desired development, many African so-called democratically-elected governments produce self-serving political elites in the upper echelons of power who end up doing nothing but fleecing their citizens and countries. Yet, they call such criminality democracy. Isn't this irresponsible democracy? Such unaccountable democracy is not only expensive but also is corrupt and rotten. For, it enables local elites in conjunction with foreign ones to hijack many countries and turn them into their private estates they can use and misuse as pleased. These local elites have always been accountable only to their masters in Europe but not to the citizens who waste their money and time to vote for them. This being the case, many African democracy have largely produced what Bartels (2016) calls *unequal democracy* among the citizens not to mention among nations whereby the Western democracy dictate poor democracy in Africa and other poor countries by superimposing their will on them. By dictating democratic processes and structures in poor countries, especially in Africa, Europe has another advantage to install the governments it wants to safeguard its interests at the peril of the citizens who shoulder the burden of financing such shoddy democracy. There is no way one can expect Africa to, one day , be at par with Europe that has always dictated Africa's affairs without any reciprocity or deconstructing the current exploitative superstructure. For, in some countries, such a democracy has produced many retired presidents, vice presidents and prime ministers that are making their countries poorer and poorer due to being paid billions of dollars for their retirements and remunerations while they did nothing worthy if compared to how much they scoop and what they did when in power. I wonder about what they are paid for while their positions are political. If it is the job they did, everybody does work but is not entitled to fat perks, up until, he or she dies as it is for politicos mentioned above who enjoy free medical services, trips abroad, gardeners, bodyguards, guards, furniture and other hidden expenses that poor taxpayers shoulder. To me, this is another type of structural and systemic corruption Europe imposed on Africa. It is utterly colonialism, internal colonisation. Had Africa being ruled based on its brand of democracy or whatever you call it, cultures and needs, such colonial leeches would not pauperise it has it has been for over five decades. This mean the Western democracy tied to the Independence of African countries has never freed these countries thanks to colonialism changing shape. It is because they are the keys to ridding public coffers and mismanaging public resources without necessarily being accountable to anybody except being accountable to themselves or those who helped them in maintaining power if not with whom they share power by way of corruption, courtiership, favouratism, nepotism and divisionism. This is the independence at an individual level that leads to a country level. This is the freedom many African immigrants go for to Europe. This is the freedom jobless Indians and Pakistanis go for in Africa while Africans are leaving for greener pastures in Europe simply because their rulers cannot team up with them to enjoy the national cake for fear of unearthing their conspiracy, corruption and greed. It is from the conditions Europe created during; and after colonialism that enabled it to go on exploiting Africa and develop itself while Africa is perpetually sinking in underdevelopment.

There is no way Africa can develop based on European principles that developed based on its *diktats,* however criminal as they are. For example, while Europe exploited and robbed others it colonised, Africa has no place to colonise and occupy so as to acquire the capital needed to develop like Europe did. This being the case, how can Africa copy Europe's trajectory of development and make it while the environment and tools for doing so are not available and viable? Europe has always maintained and convinced others that it attained its development due to its ingeniousness which is wrong. China is now an upcoming superpower of the world that did not follow Europe's trajectory. As for Africa, I would say, there is no way it can reach at world's apex without being reunified so that it can be stronger and influential in world affairs. So, those keeping on cheating Africa that it can copy Europe's model of development are the enemies of Africa so to speak. Every country has its own way of attaining development depending on its condition, policies and homemade enabling environment for doing so. Development is not like the Sun that is only one in the solar system. Even the Sun is experienced differently on earth depending on where someone is located.

Matunhu (2011) maintains that Europe criminally destroyed Africa's civilisation including development course by favouring its own course in order to develop itself in its place as it later happened.

Swahili sage has it that he who makes a drum pulls the skin his way. So, whoever thinks that he or she can develop Africa based on Europe's *diktat* or trajectory must be wrong; and, of course, playing in the hands of Europe for the peril of Africa. If Africa's development were not arrested in order to serve Europe, Africa would be different from what it currently is. Historically, Africa, as noted hereinabove, started to trade with Far East and Middle East many thousands of years before the arrival of Europeans in 1444 signifying the beginning of the end of Africa's development. Refer to how advanced and wealthy empires such as Asante, Mali, Songhai and others were more prosperous and commanded many centers of commerce than Europe did during their heydays (Lovejoy 2011). One can ask: Where did such established commercial centers go? The answer is easy that when European colonisers arrived in Africa, they brought their stooges to take over businesses from Africans. So, too, they purposely destroyed them. Refer to how Africa has many ruins. In the East and South Africa, Indians were introduced to act as middlemen. In Central and West Africa, Lebanese were brought for the pure purpose of sabotaging African businessmen. By then, there were no businesswomen. To make sure that such ticks succeeded, colonial governments refused to buy cash crops from natives as they were then known. Again, you can see how the leading advantage works. Up until now, over 50 years of independence, the economy of many African countries are still in the hands of these stooges colonisers pass on to Africa. Thanks to ignorance and poor education, many Africans still believe that, for example, such colonial agents are better at business than they are without knowing that this is what is called power differentials under which anybody enabled or treated preferentially in anything has the chances of leading ahead of the one who did not get the same.

To make matter worse, European colonisers made sure that Africans are exploited in every aspect and manner. They introduced cash crops, taxes, stooges and low prices for Africa's products. Under such robberies, Europe made a great deal of wealth without investing or toiling except by cheating and committing other criminal acts that ask for the international community to revisit and redress not to mention reprimanding the culprits.

Additionally, Europe established some forced infrastructure (Larkin 2013) in order to easily and quickly drain off African resources by using Africans without paying them. How many people Africa sends to Europe, America, India and elsewhere for higher education simply because there are no institutions to cater for them? To do away with such exploitation, Africa needs to establish its own institutions that will cater for its people and its needs. Instead of sending people abroad, Africa must hire some teachers from abroad to come and teach the same technologies and skills within Africa. For the entire time of over 50 years Africa has been sending its people to acquire knowledges and skills from abroad, it must have already established its own institutions had it been reunited and had some plans to do so. Instead of losing billions of dollars sending its people abroad, some of them do not even return back due to the lack of motivating and conducive environment for them. Had the world had a fair international legal system, how much Europe would pay Africa, first, for forced labour, second for causing deaths that occurred, and for the land that was used without compensation, and, above all, the bulk of resources such resources Europe plundered. Here I have not added many Africans who died in mines, hunting trips, those who were hanged, those who died of frustration, those who were mauled by animals trying to escape from the colonial governments and those who died fighting against the whole criminal project.

We must face it that Europe made it wherever it is now in economic terms by robbing others under slavery, colonialism and now neocolonialism. This is why European countries that used to be poor due to the lack of resources such as Belgium, Portugal, Spain and Switzerland are now richer than almost all African countries simply because they robbed Africa of everything, something that has been on going up until now. This is a very crucial issue to explore and tackle provided that many assertions made about Africa's backwardness and underdevelopment did not propose practical solutions to the problems. This is because, many assertions dreaded or avoided to face and address real problems behind such a situation Africa is stuck in. to make matters worse, such assertions avoided historical facts about how Africa was destroyed and robbed for decades soon after the first contact with Europe.

Due to the failure to deconstruct the current narrative as it was created by Europe, Africa's backwardness and underdevelopment remain an unsolved mystery. Those Africa thought would address the very root causes of its quandaries became a part of the problem instead of becoming a solution. For, instead of taking the problem head on, they slinked into the straightjacket that ended up shaping themselves to becoming agents of colonialism either consciously or unconsciously. For a few who tried to address the cause roots of Africa's problems revolving around Europe exploitation, as I will show later, either were killed or overthrown in order to give room for European stooges who could push the truth under the carpet; and thereby enable Europe to go on exploiting Africa. For example, after acquiring independence, African countries were divided along two colonial masters namely the East and the West under the then cold war politics so as to render Africa's independence meaningless. This in itself was the first major mistake many committed thinking that by taking side with opposing colonial forces, they would emancipate their countries. Colonial masters are the same regardless whether they are from East or West. Those who sided with the East under communism and socialism wrongly thought that they would be safe from the West which was true despite the fact that they were not safe from the East as a colonial and imperial power with hidden agendas and motives. Likewise, those who allied themselves with the West wrongly thought they would reap the goodies the West promised little unbeknownst that they were used against its nemesis. It was like jumping from one type of colonialism to another. Thanks to inexperience and naivety, almost all either failed or were failed by the two forces they were allied with. If anything, this is where Europe invented *coup d'états militaire* as the tools of eradicating the leaders who did not toe the line or changed direction; and thereby take orders from Europe. For example, there are countries that suffered from several *coup d'états* more often than others due to different reasons. For example, a tiny country of Burundi suffered this fate because of toxic ethnicity between Hutus and Tutsis as it was created by colonial Europe while Burundi's neighbour Uganda suffered the same because of the cold war. At this time, Britain cloned and launched Idi Amin who killed innocent Ugandans for eight years while Britain stayed aside and looked. After the situation became worse, Britain recanted him. In Ghana the situation was the same whereby imperial forces did not like to see any *provocateur* in power. Therefore, the first president of Ghana Dr. Kwame Nkrumah was toppled in order to dampen the morale he had created for the total emancipation of Africa from Europe's grip and exploitation. In the neighbouring Nigeria, Europe created regionalism and religion as the major drives for the division and the weakening of the country. In the DRC, as it was in Ghana, the first government was toppled by Belgium in conjunction with the Central Intelligence Agency (CIA) (Mhango 2015, 2016) in order to keep on exploiting DRC's immense resources.

As we will see, this can be blamed on African countries after gaining their independence without knowing the underlying reality of the so-called independence. We all know that Africa became independent in the 60s. However, the truth of the matter is that political independence was more of a hoax than a tool for emancipation given that what was done is but changing the name of colonialism into something else. So, too, what transpired was just changing the guards in which homegrown guards replaced European ones in many countries. To me, independence must embody all aspects of life of the country, a people or an individual. This has lacked in Africa. Almost all African countries live on aid, begging and borrowing from their former colonial master. A country that lives on aid is not as independent as its donors. Mhango (2015) puts it clearly noting that:

> A vagabond is vagabond
> Whether he is in suit or tatters
> A panhandler has no dignity
> Whether he begs out of poverty
> A beggar is a beggar
> Be he educated or ignorant,
> Be he skinny or fat
> A scrounger is a scrounger
> Be he president, or bankrupt
> A beggar is a beggar
> An honourable being should not beg

Sing the song of freedom for him then
It might cure his sick brain
So that he can see the shame
He's always been proud of (p. 17).

Therefore, the first step in defining development objectively even subjectively, we need to set scope and terms. There is no way one can do justice by defining any term based on one side where there are two or more sides. For example, you cannot define the underdevelopment of Africa or the development of Europe without interweaving them together so as to make a meaningful conclusion or proposal. Arguably, development is any action that improves human life. For example, development that is now causing environmental harm to the humankind cannot be conceived as development. In this discourse, development of Europe by Africa does basically revolve around economics and partly social aspects of the lives of the duos in which one is perceived as developed as opposed to the other that is perceived as being underdeveloped. Even in material terms one wonders how Africa can be termed as underdeveloped while it sits on humungous reserves of precious resources. The argument here is supposed to be the rationale and intent used in assessing and defining development. In economic terms, development is about who has more than others which can apply to underdevelopment to mean who has less than another or others. Essentially, there is no watertight definition of development due to the fact that all depends on the intentions and rationales one uses to define and conceive the terms. With the current arbitrary, bias, draconian and rigid system of assessing and defining development, Africa will always miss out. Crucially, the major question one needs to ask when it comes to development must be: Development for whom, in what and by whom? Such a question and its rationale will avert the toxicity of Western-defined-and-imposed development. I do not agree with the holistic take that Europe is developed in everything. This is why I decided to narrow down the definition of development on material or economic gains but not cultural and others. This is because we all know that Europe's economic development was necessitated and enhanced by slavery and colonialism before scientific advancement resulting from the surpluses Europe gained through slavery and colonialism; thus sit back and get time for the experimentation that ushered scientific and technological advancement Europe is now boasting of. If anything, this is a criminal trajectory of Europe's development and Africa's underdevelopment. It does not make any sense whatsoever to say that a robber who breaks into somebody's house; and makes away with all material belongings of the victim is developed simply because he or she now owns the material things that legally belong to the victim. Essentially, this is what Europe did to Africa; and it is the *modus operandi* it used to define development so as to become *mundus cerialis* or universal. To make sense, even at a liminal level, the thug must return the loot and get other criminal rewards resulting from the offense he committed. Importantly, this is where the redress of Africa makes more sense than other hocus-pocus such as aid, debt cancellation, poverty alleviation and structural adjustments that have adjusted nothing except poverty the West has always applied to buy time and perpetuate its exploitation of Africa.

As well, there is no way one can talk about the trajectory of Europe's development without touching on Africa *vis-à-vis* slavery and colonialism among others. This is why seeking to debunk and deconstruct Europe's myths of being ahead of others almost in everything good and meaningful cannot succeed in their journey to seek, actualise and realise Africa's changes and development without re-narrating the very ugly story of slavery and blatant colonialism; and the ways they acted as catapults for Europe's success story enhanced by economic quantum leap generated by Africa through offering its manpower to Europe not to mention playing the role of consuming processed goods from the same tormentor. To understand the underdevelopment of Africa, we need to revisit Africa's past and see how it hugely contributed to the development of Europe.

Demonstrably, the history and story of Africa have always been biasedly told, maliciously misconstrued and purposely misrepresented (Adegbulu 2011) by maliciously removing other important components from the very history. For example, when European colonial agents arrived in Africa, they got a help from Africans that enabled them to *explore* various sources of resources.

80

But they did not admit this in their derivative stories and history about Africa that they would not have successfully *explored* and spied Africa without the help of African gurus and academicians of the time who wholeheartedly helped them thinking they were serving humanity and thereby creating business harmony between Africa and Europe. Further, these *explorers* and spies did not credit African scientists, adventurers and whatnots for their immense contributions which enabled them to learn African science and civilisation. Instead, they credit everything to their adroitness and edge while, in actuality, they learned and scooped everything from their hosts. There is no way a person who grew up in the snow-laden Europe would master the science and secrets on the Equator without any help from those who knew nothing but Equator. The same applies to those who grew up on Equator when they go to polar and cold regions. Everything becomes new from environment; weather to foods something that exactly happened to Europeans when they first set foot on Africa. To cap it all, the same liars alleged that they discovered Africa. How? My argument is emphatically plausible that there is no way anybody can discover anybody; and if such a thing happen the two discover each other otherwise one must be dead. By arguing that Europeans discovered Africa and other places, they mean such places were dead to include those that occupied and lived in these places; and if they were alive, they were but *tabula rasa*. This is why even the argument that Africa, the land of generosity and humanity, was *terra nullius* does not make any sense in whatever way. Making such a claim is inhumanity in itself and the sign of uncivilisation. Quite so, the assumption that Africans were not advanced does not make any sense. How could they live in their continent for millions of years and fail to master it? If there is anything new colonial Europe brought to Africa is nothing but colonialism and injustices such as slavery, corruption, racism and inequality. However, when it comes to the true picture of how Africa was before the arrival of European colonisers, Europe has tried to make everything to be shrouded in mystery while the truth is that Africa was advanced in its own manner based on its aspirations and needs of the time. Again, how advanced was Africa? Lanning and Mueller (1979) in their book, *Africa Undermined,* answer this question maintaining that:

For many centuries before the arrival of Europeans, minerals were produced in Africa by Africans for Africans. The scale of techniques of mining and metal working were clearly comparable with those both in Europe and in the great Eastern civilizations of India and China—until towards the end of the seventeenth century (p. 27).

Not only minerals that were produced in Africa before the arrival of colonisers but also other amenities Africa needed for its consumption and exportation. Nunn (2007) argues that African society was located at high production equilibrium before contact with Europe which is responsible for destroying its systems of administration and production after taking over through colonialism and neocolonialism thereafter. More modern evidence can be drawn from the fact that despite being perpetually and heavily exploited for many millennia, Africans are still able to soldier on.

How Competitive Advantage and Power Differentials Helped Europe

In whatever competition, there must be power dynamics. In the analysis of how Europe became developed; and Africa underdeveloped, power dynamics play a very noteworthy role. In addressing the matter at hand, I found that competitive advantage that leads to leading advantage has a lot to do with the development and the underdevelopment of the duo respectively. Porter (2008) notes that the competitiveness of any country depends on, *inter alia*, interest rates, labour costs, exchange rates and economic of scale which were amiss during colonial times.

Although many academics, activists, donors, particularly European countries have always encouraged Africa to work hard in order to catch up with the so-called developed countries in terms of development, this cannot be without addressing historical realities emanating from Africa's colonial and slavery past. Expecting Africa to catch up with Europe without deconstructing the current international system that refused to address Europe's past injustices to Africa is like putting the cart before the horse. It will not work. As argued above, the simple example is that, you cannot expect a robber and the one robbed to be at par without returning the loot. For, without this, you create power differential that has much impact on the victims. For example, a robber can hire lawyers to cleanse his or her name, hitmen to kill the victim, can buy his way out and, above all, can invest the loot and double his wealth while the victim becomes even poorer and poorer as long as justice of returning his property is not done. This is truly the situation Africa has been in since it was occupied; and thereby colonised. Adam Smith's view on this as cited in Brodie (1989) is clear when he notes that the master, landlord, farmer and merchant have more advantage over a labour or worker who has nothing but his or her labour to sell while the former have property that they can invest in and live on for two years without doing anything something a worker or labour cannot endure. This is the typical replica of power relationship between Europe and Africa.

However power differentials, advantages, disadvantages and the roles they play are not confined to economics only. Brodie looks at economic disparities in Canada based on regions and partly origin. I think this is because the effects of power differentials and their results are interconnected or they go in tandem. For example, Canadian Aboriginals whose land was taken and thereby pushed to the margins after their country was occupied, colonised and later taken for good by European settlers can never compete with the invaders without being redressed. Automatically, their predicament made them poor simply because they were denied their means of survival which is analogous to what has been ongoing in Africa. And once one is poor, all other aspects of life will take the same turn. This is to say; a poor person is neither competent nor competitive; and has no economic or political say not to mention sound capital and standing. This is self-evident when you look at the socio-economic conditions of Canada's Aboriginal people. They are dire and desperate and incompetent compared to those of their occupiers. It is like dreaming about travelling to Mars by bicycle to think that there is a day Canadian Aboriginal will be at par with white settlers if the current setting is not tweaked to practically accommodate and redress them. The same applies to African countries compared to those who robbed Africa. What transpired in Canada has some similarities with what transpired in Africa at the international level. Power differentials are obvious. And what adds salt into a wound is the fact that those who robbed Africa for decades are the ones who define and design everything as far as development (without addressing past injustices) is concerned.

According to Brodie reasoning, anybody with an advantage over another or others, as it the case between Europe and Africa, will always lead and excel compared to those over whom one has such an advantage. There is no way a perpetrator and a victim can be equal in anything, especially when the victimhood resulting from robbery is considered. How can this be possible while one is a gainer and another is a loser? There is no way a horse and a jockey can be equal wherever there is justice. Neither shall the cow and tick be equal. According to Gwinn, Judd and Park (2013), power differentials result into dehumanisation which can lead to collective traumatisation as it is in the cases of Africans and Canadian Aboriginals. Africa, in particular, shows that less power means being less-humans as Gwinn, Judd and Park found in their experiment. Sadly, when it comes to dehumanisation resulting from having less power, indeed, the victims of such a setting prove to be treated as less human. This can answer the question why Africa has always been at home with being given handouts by those who robbed it. Strikingly, wherever there are power differentials through amassing power on some and taking it away from others, even those regarded to be superior in the group face the same consequences of subhumanness, dehumanisation and traumatisation. I think this is why African rulers have never felt any embarrassment when they go to Western countries cap in hand begging.

Power differentials have a lot to do with self-esteem both to a perpetrator and a victim although in different directions, extents and manners. There is no way a perpetrator and victim can be equally self-confident. In the light of Africa, it has always been inferior to Europe not just because it is naturally inferior but because it was made to believe so. This is why Africa has taken its mistreatments and miseries as a God-given reality while, in actuality, they are but are artificial, cosmetic and manmade. To do away with and synchronise the current unequal state of things, we need to deconstruct everything that has to do with development; and possibly with underdevelopment in order to tie the duo together so that they can work together to resolve the conflict. This brings us to how Africa has contributed to the development of Europe almost in everything. Imagine, for example, why Africans have always been recipients when it comes to fashions from the West? Apart from being brainwashed to believe that everything Western is superior and good, they lack self-esteem. To know this phenomenon, compare the speed by which Africans in aping Western things such as fashion, music and even lifestyle to Arabs. Here colonial negative impacts have a lot to do. It is nowadays a common sight to see many young urbanites spending their hard-earned money on torn jeans simply because they are the fashion in Europe. This is contrary to others such as Arabs, Indians and others who still abide by their cultures. For example, despite being colonised, Arabs once colonised Europe for over 500 years while Africans have never colonised anybody. So, too, Arabs, despite being colonised, have their culture protected under another colonial tool namely religion. Many Arabs are Muslims. Therefore, they still enjoy many aspects of their culture such as belief, hegemony, history, names and pride whereas Europe robbed such things from Africans by Christianising them not to mention Islam by islamising them. Maybe, such a culture has insulated Arabs from European cultural contamination and cultural imperialism. The same applies to Chinese, Indians, Japanese and Koreans. Mhango (2015) argues that culture is a booming business in the world. This is why the West and, now China, always export their fashions to Africa while Africa has never done the same due to the lack of self-esteem resulting from power differentials. To prove this, Mhango questions the rationale for Africans to carry Arabic or European names while Arabs and Europeans cannot think about, let alone, carrying African names and ways of life. Even when it comes to cultures, Europeans have always encouraged Africans to fully engage themselves in cultural but not scientific things. This is why an Africa is always associated with drums and music but not invention while there are evidence that Africans discovered many things such as environmental protection even nuclear bomb. Refer to the discovery of the intact remains of used nuclear reactors in Oklo, Gabon in 1972 (Meshik 2005). Astonishingly, when French scientists discovered them, they agreed that they were used at certain time over 2 billion years ago. Interestingly, the scientists found that the said nuclear reactors show the signs of being used and cooled without telling who used to do so and how. Neither French nor any scientists have ever bothered to know who created and maintained such nuclear reactors. Demonstrably, given that such discovery was made in Africa, French scientists referred to them as natural nuclear reactors. Why? Nothing advanced or scientific can come out of Africa. Maybe, they are trying to find biblical justifications to attribute these reactors to Jews as it is in the case of the Great Zimbabwe or Egyptian pyramids that were built by black people (Diop 1989; and Shillington 2012) but ended up giving the credit to Arabs. Their mindsets do not allow them to accept that Africans had their own sciences that sustained them up until they were destroyed after the introduction of slavery and colonialism (Blaut 2012). Ironically, if you ask them to mention other natural nuclear reactors, I do not think they will have something to say.

If the remnants of Oklo nuclear reactors, hereinabove, were discovered in Western Europe, it would have been all over the place that Europe discovered nuclear bombs way far back than any person can imagine. This is not the first time European doomsayers have sought to intellectually discriminate against Africa. When Europeans first saw the Great Zimbabwe and its monumental stone remains, they said they were built by King Solomon as a gift to the queen of Sheba (Holter 2006, 2008; Hubbard 2009; and Chirikure, Pollard, Manyanga and Bandama 2013) to signify that Africans were not capable of building such monuments. This shows academic and historical racism against Africans. Had it not been for the barrier of proximity, I would not wonder to hear that even the Mayan monuments, Mexican pyramids or the Great Wall of China were built by King Solomon. Cavalieri (2013) notes that "whites depicted and viewed black people "as being literally sub-human, mentally retarded, cowardly, incompetent, and often crazed" who can't invent anything." There are so many contradictions in such assumptions. Essentially, for many European colonial agents, Africa was nothing but a dystopia inhabited by the *beasts of the jungle* (Raskin 2012) or sellable beasts of burden (Davis and Zilberstein 2007) but not humans like themselves. Thanks to their hypocrisy and chicanery, when they arrived, they hid their true colour *vis-à-vis* how they viewed their generous hosts. I think; this chicanery still exists today under the so-called international community that has always presided over the pillaging of Africa despite singing the sweetest song of equality, justice and human rights universally. Ironically, through their science, Europeans are the ones who came up with the hypothesis, and finally, the conclusion that Africa is the cradle of human race. If this is true, how did Africans become such *bêtes noires*? This shows how such an assertion is socially constructed just like other evils such as gender and racial discrimination. Ironically, despite such duplicity and folly, they had no name to call the Zimbabwean great stones rather than borrowing the name from the Zimbabweans who built and know the history of the Great Zimbabwe. How utterly naïve such assertion is? How could the queen of Sheba be a Zimbabwean while the history by the same Europeans and their bible says she was an Ethiopian? This is utter nonsensical confusion geared by racism and ignorance not to mention *holier than thou* mentality Europe has always applied on Africa. Essentially, provided that Europe has always used power differential to enjoy its leading roles, even its lies such as those about the Great Zimbabwe are accepted in academic circles while they do not make any sense *ab initio*. Again, why should academics worry if other lies such as the origin of humanity from Adam were accepted simply because they are propounded by dominant grand narrative? I tend to pose this question simply because, if our origin were one, there would not have been any racism, colonialism and slavery. But given that those who fed Africans with such lies know the real truth, they did what they did knowing that our origin is not the same in their eyes and myths.

Bigotry and conspiracy against Africa started; and were systematised many years ago. For example, in the case of the Great Zimbabwe and other scientific findings about Africa either were attributed and credited to others or being rendered to be which crafts, uncouth and primordial while European ones became advanced formulas, modern sacraments or science. If we face it for example, what is known as eating the body of the saviour or Eucharist isn't it cannibalism? How can one be saved by eating somebody's body and drinking his blood even ceremonially? Interestingly, the missionaries and other colonial agents who spread such toxic teachings condemned everything African wholesomely. They did not ask African scientists to prove their science. To add insult to injury, after criminalising and demonising African sciences, they destroyed them by replacing them with theirs. To do away with such bigotries and fabrications Mkandawire cited in Mlambo (2006) suggests that African academics must develop African social science in order to address the challenges they face. I would like to further suggesting that African academics should make a case for Africa to seek forcing Europe and religions to recant their assertions that African sciences are witchcrafts (Geschiere 2013; Middleton 2013; and Weese 2016) and thus sinful. Sometimes, it baffles me how blind and crazy people can be. Is the discovery of salt that Africa did really witchcraft? Though Europe was able to conceal many Africa's inventions, no doubt that the first lake full of salt Natron is in Tanzania within a short distance from where the skull of the first human was discovered, Olduvai Gorge in Tanzania. This lake known was known as wadi Natrun in ancient Egypt (Shortland 2004; and Dotsika, Poutoukis and Tzavidopoulos 2009) whose evidence shows it still exists in Tanzania presently but not Egypt. Didn't Africa discover its own cotton cloth before coming into contact with Europe as Riello and Parthasarathi (2011) testify that West Africa had already invented the use of cotton for spinning clothes? Is it unfair to contend that African slaves who were sold to Europe may be the ones who taught Europeans how to make clothes out of cotton provided that Europe did not have cotton trees? Though many European bigots claimed that African slaves were exchanged with clothes (Riello 2013), had true Africa history been written as it is, chances of finding some incongruities resulting from biases are high. It does not make sense for say Ghana Empire to exchange slave for clothes while it started working on cotton many years before Europe. For example, Maestri (2016) maintains that specialists agreeably found that the wild progenitor of G. herbaceum was an African species, whereas the ancestor of G. arboreum is still unknown; also see Chen Scheffler, Dennis, Triplett, Zhang, Guo, Chen, Stelly, Rabinowicz, Town and Arioli (2007). This shows how those who wrote the *his-story* of Africa failed to cover their tracks. Ellis (2007) argues openly that European take on Africa's witchcraft is problematic due to the fact that it is was the creature European theoreticians created (Broedel 2010) the same way the constructed capitalism and other Western isms they used to colonise and dupe others. To this author, neither religion nor witchcraft can be scientifically proved. Thus, they are all equally the same based that they operate based on beliefs and taboos and other make-believe things. Imagine. Science tells us, up until now, that there is no way a woman can conceive without sexual intercourse. Yet, at the same time, the Bible says that Jesus, if he truly existed, did what are alleged to have done, was conceived without sexual intercourses; he fed the multitudes with the bread and fish he doubled miraculously! Any proves of this? There is none except in belief. Have such acts ever been replicated everywhere? No. they have neither been proved or replicated anywhere and anytime.

Whatever that lacks scientific proofs is as good as witchcraft be it godly or devilish or African. However, when it comes to what is regarded as lack of proof for African science and technology due to the fact that they were surrounded with secrecy not to mention many knowledges being passed orally, *Portfolio Committee on Arts* (2000) cited in Ashforth (2005) note that Africans maintained secrecy for fear that their secrets being stolen by missionaries. Despite that, there is evidence that Africa was not scientifically and technologically moribund or barren. Duignan and Gann (2013) disclose that Africans learn how to mine gold in the middle ages. Despite such evidence, western bigots kept on pummelling the world with farfetched stories about Africa full of lies. To show how racism is internationalised and lies on Africa legalised, Boxlll (2016) cites the definition of Negro or black person to show the mother of all racism against and lies about Africans by quoting the Encyclopedia Britannica (1798) which defines an African as:

> Negro, Homo pelli nigra, a name given to a variety of the human species, who are entirely black, and are found in the torrid zone, especially in that part of Africa which lies within the tropic. In the complexion of Negroes we meet with various shades; but they likewise differ far from other men in all the features of their face. Round cheeks,

high cheek-bones, a forehead somewhat elevated, a short, broad, flat nose, thick lips, small ears, ugliness, and irregularity of shape, characterize their external appearance. The Negro women have their loins greatly depressed, and very large buttocks, which give the back the shape of the saddle (p. 23).

The above definition still goes on without being expunged from such a famous book. Recently, the girlfriend of the UK Independence Party leader, Henry Bolton, Jo Marney uttered racist slurs when she discovered that one royal family member, Prince Harry's wife to be was of mixed race. The *France24* (12 January, 2018) reports that Ms Marney who in popular culture could be described as a "slay queen", said she would never have sexual relations with "a Negro because they are ugly".

Swahili sage has it that the monkey does not see its buttocks. Instead, it laughs at others' buttocks without knowing that they are the same. Maybe, when such bigots fabricated such lies did not know that Africans will one time live in their countries to see how they are *vis-à-vis* what they accused Africans of. Given that I understand that we were all created; nobody created himself or herself, I would not like to go into details or the business of decreating, desecrating and dehumanising each other as to who is deformed, obese, ugly or otherwise. It is sad that European bigots played God by failing to understand the logic of as to why many people on Equator being crated black. I cannot imagine. What would have happened had those thinking are better because of their colour; and how they would look like if God forced them to live on Equator the same way they forced Africa to go working in the cold Americas. I cannot imagine what would have happened had they switched positions during slavery whereby hypothetically Africans would have gone to Europe and enslaved and delivered them to the Equator before subjecting them to such and the same horrendous brutalities like those Africans went through. Swahili sage has it that a spear does not seem to hurt when a pig is the victim, but when a human is, it does. However, good news for Africans is that they can live anywhere despite being viewed as inferior without knowing that the plenty of melanin in their skin is something everybody would like to have (Morrison 1985). Despite such witlessness, the same criminals still aggrandised themselves about being advanced scientifically and civilised while they could not understand a simple matter like this not to mention distorting and misrepresenting their colleague human beings. Suffice it to say, in concocting his-story, the European bigots who miswrote, misconstrued and misrepresented Africa in their his-story, like a monkeys, forgot their own buttocks. When it comes to racist slurs like mentioned above, I like to offer one advice. Those thinking are better than others based on the pigments of their skins, should change their blood groups, anatomy and biological needs and other features all humans share so that they can have different one from those they discriminate against and deem to be inferior to them. Knowing how biological creatures are divided into groups, I do not ponder about even discriminating against other mammals due to the fact that we share many features than anybody can imagine.

I am trying to imagine. What would happen if such garbage and insults were directed to other races or the victims of gender and sexual discrimination? Perceptibly, the international community would not sit aside and look. Again, provided that racism against Africa is indirectly condoned under the so-called international community, who is taxing Britain, for example, to pull such garbage down; and make a formal apology to black people? Africa needs to unite and refuse to be *inferiorised* or discriminated against. When it comes to intelligence, no human society is *tabula rasa* however primitive it may be viewed or misconstrued. Interestingly, despite accusing Africa of secrecy which led Europe to conclude that every African science and technology were superstition, the same Europe has maintained the same when it comes to the exchange of technology. For, despite the fact that there is no empirical way of proving witchcraft, also there are no empirical proofs that the so-called witchcraft is not science and vice versa the same religions are. Andreski 1974: 64 cited in Nørgaard (2008) notes that:

Sometimes, the verbal substitutions masquerading as contributions to knowledge are so inept and gross that it is difficult to believe that the authors really think that they are revealing new truths (which must be the case), and that they are not laughing up their sleeves at the gullibility of their audience (p. 1).

With such abuses and fabrications, I do not think racist white thinkers would do Africa any justice or see anything meaningful in it. So, when we seek evidence to prove how Africa has been abused and misrepresented so as to deserve redress, it is all over the place. Now, what is required is to make a case for Africa to see to it that justice is done through apology and redress. In other words, despite contributing massively to the development of Europe, Africa is still seen through the same lenses humans use when they assess animals' contributions to their wellbeing. Who credits a chicken for nutritious eggs and yummy meat? Who appreciate the ox's hard work? Who credits the cow for its beef, hide, manure and milk? This is the fate those who currently are hypocritically saying all human beings are equal under their democracy, religions and civilisation dubiously and heinously assigned to Africa. Africa needs to stand on its two; and demand that things be rectified based on deconstructive initiatives that will see it being redressed. Like it was the case with feminists, they did not sit down and watch. Instead, they decided to fight tooth and nail for their rights, up until, things changed although not completely. This is the nature of change. It is a process that can take many years the same the problems it seeks to deal with took many years to create.

Through dehumanising and demonising Africa, European first-colonial agents deemed everything African sinful and uncouth without proving their allegations. Nørgaard (*Ibid.*) maintains that "all research ought to begin by raising two questions: What do we know, and what are we going to learn?" (p. 11). Essentially, this is the rationale that is lacking in colonial assertion that African sciences were nothing but witchcrafts. European bigotries knew nothing about Africa. This has been ongoing covertly though in the modern times. This is why historian Lester Brooks (1972: 5) cited in Mou (2014) complains that the media represented Africa in exotic and primitive fashion noting that:

[It is a] a "dark continent," a wall-to-wall jungle full of barking savages, many of them cannibals; "the white man's graveyard"; Tarzan's playground; a perfect place to hunt exotic beasts, except for the torrid climate, murderous insects and snakes; a mecca for slow immolation of saintly missionaries; a land of witch-doctors, Mau-maus, diamonds, throbbing drums and witless, naked, paint-daubed Blacks always on the verge of battle… (p. 19).

He or she who abuses, maltreats, misrepresents and disparages another like this cannot do justice to such his or her victims. Such abuses and misrepresentations become worse when they are done systematically so as to be internalised and reinforced now and then for many years as it has been the case for Africa. Swahili sage has it that *akumulikaye mchana, usiku hukuchoma* or he who shines lights on you during the day, torches you at night. Therefore, in portraying Africans in bad light, European colonisers sought and wanted Africans to prove their allegations as if they are the ones that made them. Once humans are turned into beasts, what follows thereafter is to maltreat; and deny them justice. In law, he or she who alleges must prove. Had such eerie allegations been made today, Africans had nothing to fear but ask those alleging that their sciences and ways of life were witchcraft to prove their allegations or keep up and shut up. If science is anything that is imminently, coherently capable of being interrelated by networks of logical ties based on experience that justifies them (Austen 2010), how did the world took the resurrection of Jesus to be true as if it actually happened while there is no scientific evidence to prove it? Who can, today, justify the fact that Jesus, actually existed while the Jews he is associated with disown him in the first place? While witchcraft as it was concocted by European colonial thinkers was deemed as something archaic and with lack of enlightenment, Institoris and Sprenger cited in Broedel (2010) show that witchcraft was already endemic throughout much of Europe and was increasing daily. Had this been the belief in Africa, what would have been the reaction of Western thinkers to find that African elites believe in witchcraft?

While you are wondering about the above scenario of witchcraft and its approvability, think about Deuteronomy 18:9–12 which posits that:

> When you enter the land the Lord your God is giving you, do not learn to imitate the detestable ways of the nations there. Let no one be found among you who sacrifices their son or daughter in the fire, who practices divination or sorcery, interprets omens, engages in witchcraft, or casts spells, or who is a medium or spiritist or who consults the dead. Anyone who does these things is detestable to the Lord.

Ironically, the book that condemn the ritual of sacrificing sons or daughters to fire, openly say that "for God so loved the world that He gave His only begotten Son that whosoever believeth in Him, should not perish, but have everlasting life (John 3:16). Which sacrifice is devilish and which is godly? You can go ahead and ask: Who cast demons if not Jesus? Who consults the dead such as Jesus, Ibrahim, Joseph, Holy Mary and Mohammad, if indeed, they existed and did what they are purported to have done, among others, if not religious people? Who asks such provocative questions? What was wrong for Africans to implore and invoke the dead to intercede in their problems if dead personalities, as mentioned above, can be invoked in religions? This, by and large, is where Europe duped Africa so as to use it to develop itself.

Chapter Four

How Missionaries Spread Toxic Gospel in Africa

Although Africans were made to believe, not to understand, that the *word of God* or the gospel is a good thing, practically, it is not. This is because of the miseries and double-trouble dilemma missionaries created through preaching the so-called *word of God*. Through the *word of God*, Europe was able to destroy African civilisation, cultures, history and the ways of life. For, the first time, Africa was robbed of its identity through the introduction of European names under the exergies of religion. In this manner, arguably, Africans were treated like dogs. Whenever a person keeps a dog, he/she gives it a new name in order to identify it from other dogs. So, altering somebody's identity under whatever pretexts is an immoral act religions were supposed to know firsthand. This becomes provocative, particularly if we consider the fact that those who altered Africans' identity did it purposely in order to colonise; and thereby exploit them. Although we can take the centrality of identity rightly, once it is altered, the results thereof become something or somebody else from what it used to be. As we will see, the alteration of African identity did not only result into losing identity but also produced other menaces such as lack of self-esteem, self-confidence; and, above all, the lack of self-perception for the victims. This is why it has become a norm for an African to identify him or herself with foreign culture while negating his or her culture and ways of life. In doing so, Africans have contributed immensely to the development of Europe culturally and economically provided, as argued above, that under capitalism, culture is a business. Take, for example, the culture of consumerism. Whom does it benefit if not those whose cultures are adored? The answer is clear that he or she whose culture is adored will create products that the victims will consume (Blasco 2009). Here is where art, fashion, food, and music come in as tools of cultural imperialism not to mention consumable items we currently see in the market of globalisation in which the West makes a killing.

Due to the poison missionaries injected into Africa by destroying and demonising its ways of life, there are some crucial knowledges and skills that Africa lost therefrom. Looking at it holistically, Africa lost in many areas such as religion, science and world view. Apart from, *inter alia*, art, culture, food and music, all African medicinal practices and sciences were felled; and thereby deemed demonic. In doing so, African convicts, who formerly used to use African medicine and other medicinal practices, abandoned them and embraced European ones. This was but a detrimental and suicide move for Africa. Before the destruction of African medicinal knowledge, every member of the society was entitled to free medical treatments whenever he or she became sick. No person would die of any curable disease simply because he or she was unable to pay medical bills as it currently is; after the introduction of capitalism in Africa. As well, almost all members of the society had some knowledges about the herbs found in their areas. Therefore, medicinal knowledge, just like other knowledges, was based on utility but not on business due to the fact that knowledge was collectively and equally owned by the society. There was no way a member of society would die simply because he or she was unable to foot medical bills as it currently is. How could one die of the lack of medicine, if at all, almost every member of the society was trained in many fields including medicine? How could one die while, in the case of the need for specialised treatments, medicine men and women were always ready to serve their people as their duty and a sign of caring and respect to their people but not to be materially paid for their service to their people and society? Wherever there was a need for covering small costs such as specialised treatments, there was wherewithal in that token payments would be made in available items of available resources such as alcohol, black cloth, chickens or food. Tabuti, Dhillion and Lye (2003) cite an example of Bulamogi in Uganda where natural medicine practitioners exchange knowledge free or charge a small amount of money due to being affected by modernity. The same is still a practice is Zulu South Africa where Isangoma or a medicine man just receives token payments for his upkeep but not for making him rich (Beattie and Middleton 2013). These are a few examples that act as the replica of what health services used to look like in Africa before the coming of the Europeans. This is because, for African society, knowledge was not the property of the one who had it. Instead, it was the property of the society. Is there any difference from countries such as Canada and Scandinavian countries where educational and medical services are the right to every citizen? When such an argument is made today some detractors may laugh at it without underscoring the fact that many Africans still live in rural areas without having access to the so-called modern health services. Such lack of services encompasses almost all social services in Africa which depends on donors to fund them with many strings attached.

Interestingly, after Europe felled this advanced system of service provision, Africans started to die of the lack of services that they used to take for granted. Therefrom, Europe introduced its ways of solving medical problems for Africa. However, there are still living remnants of African medicinal knowledge that Africa needs to salvage in its effort to rejuvenate and resuscitate its natural medicinal knowledge that will enable it to do away with exploitative European medical solutions. Underlining rationale is that even the adored and glorifies European medicinal is incomplete. So, too, demonised African medicine is incomplete. Nothing human has ever been complete or perfect. This is why science has always evolved so as to unearth unknown things almost in all areas. For example, Koduru, Grierson and Afolayan (2007) conducted research to find that over 50% of Cape Province in South Africa depends on natural medicine to treat ailment including cancer. While Europe killed African medicinal practices, it went ahead exploiting it by collecting medicinal trees and herbs for processing in Europe and exporting back to Africa. To rub salt into a wound, even in the modern times, Europe still uses some natural African medicinal knowledge in solving many complicated medical problems that it failed to give answers to (Voss, Eyol and Berger 2006; and Eldeen and Van Staden 2007). Again, despite its contribution to boost up Europe's medicinal knowledge, has Africa ever received any credit for it? Gurib-Fakim (2006) maintains that African medicine is the oldest of all; and it is the most diverse of all medical systems. Due to having such diverse medical systems and many medicinal trees, Africa has always contributed a lot to the development of cures throughout the world. Okigbo and Mmeka (2006) disclose that "some African phytomedicines are well known in the international market and so supply economic benefit for the producing countries" (p. 83). Interestingly, many countries producing those medicines are not African countries; they are European countries among other. When I say that Africa developed Europe, this is among the reasons of doing so. Elujoba, Odeleye and Ogunyemi (2005) cited in Okigbo and Mmeka (2006) note that the whole annual market value of phytomedicine is close to $43 billion (more than the annual budgets some African countries). If this is the real situation, how much money has already Europe made out of African medicinal resources since it destroyed Africa's ways of life from colonial times? Apparently, this is not the only venue under which Africa helps Europe. I will show how slave trade, colonialism, neocolonialism and other isms fleeced Africa to the advantage of Europe. Statistically speaking, Africa donates to Europe in terms of medicine more profits than what it receives. Aside, Africa, despite helping Europe to produce medicines, is the consumer of the same medicine whose resources originate from Africa simply because its medical technology was destroyed by Europe. Okigbo and Mmeka (*Ibid.*) disclose that:

> Many African phytomedicines are well known in the international markets and Africa is one of the main world producers of the plants. Examples are Ancistrocladus abbreivatus; a Cameroon plant with Anti-HIV potential, Rauvolfia vomitoria, Zingiber officinale (Ginger), Capsicum annum contains capsaicin, phytostigmine or eserine used to treat eye diseases, a product from Phytostigma venenosum. Catharantus roseus, Madagascar Rose periwinkle is used in management of Hodgkin's disease and Leukemia. The plant Chrysanthemum cinerariifolium produces a class of insecticides. Cinchona yields quinine, a key anti-plasmodial drug for the treatment of malaria. Agava sisalana, a Tanzanian export plant is used in manufacturing of steroidal drugs like corticosteroids and oral contraceptive. According to Sofowora, Prunus africana is exported by Cameroon, Kenya and Madagascar and used for prostate gland hypertrophy. Tamarindus indica is exported by Egypt to neighboring

countries as insecticides (p. 88); also see Msuya (2007); and Laird (2010).

There is no truth in such assertions that Africa was intellectually, scientifically and technologically barren provided that those who propounded such hot air are the same who condoned slavery and paved way for the colonisation of Africa. There is no way science can be like identical twins. For, it originates from the desires and needs for a people or society to solve their problems based on experiential knowledge and time. This is why it does not add up for a person in the Equator to be forced to apply the science of the arctic environment. My experience in North America tells me that many tropical diseases need tropical knowledge the same way polar ones need polar knowledge. This is self-evident due to the fact that, when Africa started to embrace Western solutions, it became dependent and destructive. You can look even at the myth of malaria killing many Africans. Why did it not kill and erase them from the face of the earth before the arrival of Europeans who were hardly wiped out by bubonic fever not to mention malaria itself? I know; some detractors can find such assertions far-fetched without underscoring the fact that when Europeans wanted slaves, they tried at home first to no avail. Thereafter, they only found them in Africa because they were in good shapes. Where was malaria then? Malaria became a problem after felling African medicinal sciences that enabled every family and every person to be educated about the medicine to treat it and other ailments.

Further, to prove how Africa developed Europe, I refer to how Western artificial fertilizers are killing Africa's soil not to mention killings small farmers (Vanlauwe and Giller 2006). Further, the introduction of MacDonald foods and Genetically Modified organisms are now costing Africa dearly due to the cancers they are causing currently in Africa shall Africa not stop them. The report by the Institute of Responsible Technology (IRT) in the *Global Research* (2014) as cited in Mhango (2017) links various ailments such as intestinal permeability, imbalanced gut bacteria, immune activation, impaired digestion, allergic response and damage to the intestine walls to the GMOs or Genetically Modified Foods (GMFs).

Currently, almost all African countries are run on policies either borrowed from or superimposed by Europe or the West. This gives Europe another advantage of leading in policymaking. What show how Africa is going to keep on developing Europe is the fact that GMFs imported or introduced in Africa come from Europe. This is not good news. Such foods, apart from having health ramifications, are cheap. Cheap foods curtail agricultural development in Africa so as to have negative impacts on the economy of the country (Diao, Hazell and Thurlow 2010) due to the fact that no farmers will risk spending the little on fertilisers and other agricultural needs while they are able to get cheap food with cheap quality. Apart causing economic problems, the importation of the GMF causes health problems. So, too, food dependence doubles insecurity for a country internally and externally. Food can be used as a weapon (Jarosz 2009; and Patenaude 2010) shall conflict break. Internally, wherever there is food shortage, there can be chaos. Externally, a foreign country can use food in suffocating the government so as to create unrests resulting from food shortage. European countries can use food shortage as means effecting regime changes; or it can be used a political weapon for the *status quo* to cling to power as it happened in Zimbabwe (Bratton and Masunungure 2008) during Mugabe's dictatorship. All this shows the centrality of food for a country and its people that now Africa lacks as a continent.

It does not make any sense whatsoever for the continent with the most fertile soil and varieties of natural foods to be fed genetically manipulated foods. Even if we consider Africa's population compared to heavily populated continent of Asia, it still has the means and wherewithal to feed its people, if Europe and other countries stop exploiting it. Further, currently, the rates of High Blood Pressure are high in many African countries such as South Africa not to mention obesity simply because they have divorced their natural foods and habits. Raschke and Cheema (2008) note that:

The NCD (*Non-Communicable Diseases*) epidemics currently sweeping sub-Saharan Africa have been directly attributed to the nutrition transition, whereby traditional foods and food habits have been progressively replaced by the globalised food system of the multinational corporations (p. 1).

Further, consider long and negative impacts the introduction of the GMF will cause on Africa in the future. Again, why GMF are introduced to Africa? First, it is because of lazy and visionless leadership that has always acted as an agent of colonialism if not an extension in Africa. Secondly, it is because African natural foods are felled in order to give room to the GMFs the West uses to make money and control Africa in its drive for neocolonialism as espoused in neoliberal policies championed by the IFIs and some greed, gullible and visionless African leaders.

Apart from suffocating African farmers with cheaply and massively produced food Europe produces and dumps to Africa, under colonialism, Europe made sure that it destroyed African agricultural systems by introducing its own all aimed at sucking Africa and developing Europe. For example, Europe introduced what is now called as cash crops or crash crops (Mhango 2015) in which African small farmers produce items that they cannot eat and sell to get money to buy food instead of producing foods. In doing so, colonisers purposely phased out food production in order to create hunger that would force Africans either to sell their labour or produce the so-called cash crops in order to survive. For the first time in their lives, Africa witnessed a manmade famine but not the ones they were used resulting from weather fluctuations. It took them many years to believe that a human could author miseries for others simply because he wanted to make money. For, the first time, colonialism, and later capitalism, started to sink in so as to alert Africans to start planning to fight them.

Apart from wasting a lot of energy and time, African farmers have become poorer and poorer despite cultivating the so-called cash crops massively without getting any meaningful cash to run their lives. As if this is not enough, African farmers are made to believe that if they produce more, they will become richer while the truth is: the more they produce cash crops the poorer they become. While this is ongoing, European countries add more pangs to the plight of African farmers by robbing their resources such as minerals. We will cite an example from Tanzania where minerals worth billions were stolen for over 20 years while the Tanzanians were suffering and sinking into abject poverty by day. The governments used to tax farmers and encourage them to produce more while it allowed precious minerals–that would have plugged the gaps–being stolen massively; simply because a few corrupt political elites were bribed in vending their people and resources.

To crown it all, Africa has recently become a major food importer as if it does not have fertile land or manpower to produce its own food. This is because many African countries have invested in cash crops so as to kill food crops to end up depending on the countries to where it exports these cash crops for food supply. Take, for example, Ivory Coast, a world leader in cocoa production but still is one of the larger rice importers in Sub-Saharan Africa, but its imports of 10,000 tons per year (Minot 2010) simply because its farmers cannot eat cocoa. This is replicated in many African countries whose economic backbone is agriculture. Africa imports food simply because its farmers were encouraged to produce cash crops they do not eat. They cannot eat flowers, tea, coffee, sisal, and pyrethrum. The situation becomes even worse due to the fact that such crops have only one market that is the West. To rub salt into a wound, many markets for African cash crops and other resources are in Europe. This means, Europe has more advantage in trade due to controlling both markets and sources of supply which is strange in fair and truly competitive business. Ironically, when it comes to goods Europe produces, all markets are in Europe. There is no way one, for example, can manufacture a Boeing in the US; and allow the market to be established in Europe. Exploitation does not end up here. Europe still dictates the policies on how to trade with Africa. To do so, it introduced the so-called free market which has been the major push of neoliberalism. Under such policies, Europe has preyed on Africa (Galbraith 2008) by simply allowing corrupt governments– many have been in cohort with it–to prey on their people for the benefit of a few stooges it installed in power while the majority of citizens cascade in manmade poverty needlessly. Apart from using corrupt and inept governments, Europe has always invaded African countries economically even in simple things that Africa can do by itself. For example, if you want a rental facility nowadays in many African capitals, you will have to pay Knight Frank Company, a western company, which is now a leading player in real estates in Africa.

Essentially, what Knight Frank and other western companies do open offices; and benefit from the already established African real estates while local companies are starving due to the lack of capital and connectivity compared to their European well-established competitor. Even if African companies try to establish their office in Europe, they will never be allowed due to hard laws and regulations of doing business there. The same goes with McDonalds and other food-vending Western companies. Such companies have introduced dangerous fast foods to Africa so as to starve African food producers not to mention causing health problems to Africans. Ironically, if one opens an African-food vending company in Europe, he or she will never get as many customers so as to expand and have a name internationally. This is because African foods are not preferred by Europeans the same ways Africans do to European foods thanks to being culturally colonised to believe that everything European is modern. Further, it is evident that "many people residing in urban areas are unaware of the health benefits of indigenous African foods" (Raschke and Cheema 2008: 7). Therefore, many still prefer European foods to local ones. This is because they are cheap and easy to get without necessarily wasting time preparing food at home. To some, thanks to their ignorance and desire for fake modernity, are promoting European subsidised farmers as they butcher their own. Steyn, Labadarios and Nel (2011); and Feeley, Kahnn, Twine and Norris (2011) argue that fast foods are the major cause of obesity in South Africa, the country that is now grappling with the growth of an obese society after the government allowed western fast food companies to operate in South Africa. The dangers fast foods pose do not only result to obesity and other health risks, but also fleece African economically to make Europe rich by killing local agriculture. In their research, Ellwood, Asher, García-Marcos Williams, Keil Robertson and Isaac (2013) note that "our results suggest that fast food consumption may be contributing to the increasing prevalence of asthma, rhinoconjunctivitis and eczema in adolescents and children" (p. 7). While all these diseases are claiming the lives of many innocent people in Africa, the governments turn a blind eye provided that a few corrupt government officials get their cuts in this criminality that is on the rise in Africa. What makes the situation worse for Africa but economically an opportunity for Europe is that when people become obese, they add a burden to the already dilapidated social services in the country. As for Europe, it gets another opportunity to supply medicine to such a country wrestling with obesity and other diseases resulting from consuming fast foods. On top of fast foods, Africa has recently opened doors to foreign supermarkets that, in the main, sell foreign produces that are locally produced such as apple, wheat, flower and beef. This is another advantage Europe is enjoying in Africa at the detriment of Africa thanks to having what I call monkey-see-monkey-do, corrupt sitting-duck and do-nothing governments. There is no way foreign firms can be allowed in Europe to do such a thing. Chinese are known for their entrepreneurship. They tried to penetrate Chinese foods in Europe without any success compared to how now Europe is doing in Africa.

Knowing how precarious such as situation is, Europe sees it as an advantage of deciding how much it pays for such crops. Mhango (*Ibid.*) suggests that Africa must produce what it eats and eats what it produces in order to avoid facing the plight of a chicken that eats what it does not produce and produces what it does not eat. Who does not like a chicken, especially its eggs and meat? This is Africa Europe designed and would like to remain as it has always been for the development of Europe. Currently, in some African countries, European produces have made headways into. This means, small farmers are slowly being suffocated; and thereby phased out of production. By importing and buying European produces while stifling African farmers, Africa is contributing enormously to Europe's economic muscles. What makes matters worse is that a poor and small African farmer is now competing with established and subsidised European farmers under the so-called free markets that neoliberal policies espouse.

Furthermore, FAOSTAT (2011) cited in Rakotoarisoa, Iafrate and Pachali (2011) notes that in 1980, for example, Africa had an almost balanced agricultural trade when both agricultural exports and imports were at about USD 14 billion, but by 2007 its agricultural imports exceeded agricultural exports by about USD 22 billion (p. 1). This is the situation that Europe has enjoyed helped by the International Financial Institutions (IFIs) to see to it that Africa depends more and more on imported foods but not home produced. The small country of Gambia provides an ideal example on how Europe has kept tabs on Africa. To do it successfully, it introduced neoliberal policies that offer Europe freedom to invade African markets without allowing Africa to do the same without any meaningful parity or reciprocity. The Gambia used to subsidise its farmers. But in 1986, the International Monetary Fund (IMF) imposed Structural Adjustment Programmes (SAPs) that scrapped off subsidies to Gambian farmers. Such a move resulted into importing more rice than before (Moseley, Carney and Becker 2010). By forcing the small the Gambia to stop subsidising its farmers, the IMF gave it a rope to finish itself. Therefore, the importation of food goes hand in hand with the importation of policies not to mention medicine, machinery, fertilisers and recently the GMFs from Europe. While the Gambia was pushed to its economic suicide, some rich countries were doubling their subsidies to their farmers even where they had promised to reduce them. Unfortunately, due to the lack of voice in the so-called international community, no country could stand against such annihilating policies made in Europe. For example, Stiglitz (2010) notes that US president George Bush, in 2002 doubled agricultural subsidies where by four years thereafter just 27, 000 well-off cotton farmers shared US$ 2.4 billion a year in a program that violated international trade law and hurt African farmers (p. 199). If a few cotton farmers could be awarded such a huge amount of money, how much other got in other crops; and how much Africa suffered?

Indeed, when it comes to the gospel that Christian missionaries preached, it is nothing but mephitic and poisonous one. Vivid evidence is in what I have discussed in this chapter to come to the conclusion that what Africans thought were salvation, ended up being Europe salvation as opposed to Africa's crucifixion that has been ongoing, up until now, without any efforts made to alleviate or arrest it. It is worth noting that Jesus came for his race but not for

Africans if we underscore how African suffered under Christianity. Jesus said "I was sent only to help God's lost sheep--the people of Israel" (Matthew 15:24). This is the same way the so-called international community came for the white people. Are Africans and other non-Israelites really in Jesus mission? Now, how were they brought into the big picture? Once again, Europe decided to hijack Jesus' ministry in order to use it to rule the world for its development. Therefore, by creating Christianity that Jesus did not create or sanction, Europe was able to corrupt the world under the pretext of pacifying it.

How Europe Furthered Colonialism in Africa

There have been so many dubious versions of the history of Africa. For example, Africa was told that it needed democracy to develop. However, what happened is absolutely different and undemocratic. Interestingly, for many years, such versions did not come from Africa. Instead, they all came from Europe which is liable for destroying the same history of Africa. Ironically, despite the fallacies and follies in Europe's version, the world has always taken them to be true while they actually are but hogwash. The case of Josephat Njuguna Karanja, former Kenya's Vice President when he was doing his doctorate in the US, testifies as to how imported education can be toxic so as to make those who received it more of zombies than academics. Amutabi (2013) discloses that, in 1961, when Karanja sought a scholarship from Rockefeller Foundation (RF) which in turn sought confidential report on Karanja to gauge if he was for liberation of his native country or would be a stooge that "would look the other side as his fellow countrymen were oppressed and harassed, left, right and center" (p. 1). This is an affront to Africans and those who accept such lies fanned in order to keep Africa at bay for the perpetual exploitation of Europe. However, there came many compromised Africans who vended their countries despite being seen as enlightened in European ways.

To control and colonise Africa eternally, Europe has controlled and dominated Africa's minds be they in arts and science. Such intellectual control has sired Africa's dependency and sheepishness

106

almost in everything but not intended democracy and development. And sadly, such conspiracy against Africa has never changed. Every society has its *crème de la crème*. Through educational and other institutional assistance, Europe has always pretended to care about its victims by providing scholarships in order to produce stooges that would safeguard its interests in Africa and wherever colonialism was introduced. You can see this in the former presidents such as Dr. Hastings Kamuzu Banda (Malawi) Jomo Kenyatta (Kenya), Felix Houphouet-Boigny (Ivory Coast) and Joseph Mobutu (DRC), *inter alia,* as opposed to the likes of Julius Nyerere (Tanzania), Dr. Kwame Nkrumah (Ghana) Kenneth Kaunda (Zambia) and Abubakar Tafawa Balewa (Nigeria) among others who rebelled against their colonial sponsors either to end up being killed, overthrown or shunned. To make the business of fleecing Africa for the development of Europe easy, Europe made sure that almost all of its stooges in power were above the constitutions of their countries. This turned them into demigods that were not accountable to anybody except their masters and themselves not to mention being autocratic and good human rights violators. Europe protected such regimes in order to avoid being overthrown. This is why the fleecing of Africa went on swiftly for many years and without any resistance from the citizens. This is why many, if not all, vending stooges either died in power or ruled for many years without being overthrown as it was the case for noncompliant leaders. Additionally, this might be the reason, among others, why many African corrupt rulers fleeced their countries and stashed the loot in Europe where they were guaranteed temporary secrecy and security which evaporated after exiting office.

Provided that most of African corrupt rulers were educated in Europe, whatever crimes they committed against their people did not bother them provided they made their masters happy so as to keep them in power. Has this changed? No, it still goes on whereby some bright African youth are offered scholarships to end up being indoctrinated; and thereby becoming stooges for the West. Amutabi (*Ibid.*) argues that whenever any Africans who were viewed as progressive and radical, were loathed and never got funded. Who would fund the people he or she knew would become stumbling blocks to his or her exploitative project?

Another face of this mental imprisonment and manipulation can be view on the fact that Europe has never willed to exchange science and technology with Africa the same way it is currently doing with the Middle East and other emerging powers. Take an example of Dubai. It is now touted as the citadel of development in the modern Middle East. Why? It is simply because Europe decided to export its technology there. I think two things are the reasons why Europe preferred to develop Dubai, Hong Kong even Singapore but not Africa. Firstly, these countries share the same predicaments that, besides Dubai, others do not have natural resources that the West needs. Secondly, as for Dubai, the West knows how its resources, oil will either one day be exhausted or will not be on demand thanks to hybridisation of engineering that is now producing electrical vehicles. As for Africa, two things stand out. Firstly, it is the mistrust that African resources such as coltan, copper, diamond, iron, gold among others will be on demand for a long time from now thanks to the dependency the technological advancement has on them. Secondly, thanks to colonial racism, helping Africa to develop means the end of Europe's exploitation of Africa. Thirdly, mistrusts come from Europe's criminal past against Africa in which there are fears that Africa may demand redress or choose another exploiter in China or India and whoever evolves as a superpower of the world. Further, the Middle East is now boasting of having advanced universities compared to Africa that is older than them almost in everything. As for Africa, it has never been allowed to have even a single such advanced center of high learning. Nothing new that the Middle Eastern countries did that Africa cannot do shall it be allowed to benefit from its abundant resources and given the place it deserved internationally. Apart from Dubai, Australia that was found by British criminals (Clark 2006) provides another ideal example. Who knew that a country found by criminals would excel almost in everything? Australia is one of the richest countries on earth despite its dark history. This shows how criminality pays as it has been for Europe. Australia made it to the list of rich countries simply because it is Europe's add-on. If you look at Australia's environment and weather, they are the same as those of Africa save that Australia is a white country and Africa is not. There is evidence to suggest this.

Despite toiling for a long time under brutal exploitation, some African countries have recently performed well economically at the time European economies were tanking. The possibilities that Africa can perform even outperform others are immensely many. If Africa survived the 200-2008 credit crunch better than most (Bayne 2016), what else can stop it from performing like; or outperforming others? While Western countries were shaken to the core, African economies were intact. Once again, Africa came to the aid of Western economies. To assuage the loss the credit crunch caused, Europe extended loans but not bailouts to Africa so that it can assuredly get more money in the future with which to plug the gaps the credit crunch caused. Circumstantially, this is the loophole through by which many Western countries make more money. They extend loans to African countries whose debts swell by the way of predatorily servicing the debts (Squires 2004) which is known as evergreen loans (Aluko and Arowolo 2010). The question one must ask is: To whom are such capricious loans evergreen? The answer is obvious that it is the lenders who are in the West. This predatory profit-driven system (Niemi Ramsay and Whitford 2009) is very good at making profit. For, it does not need the banks to keep the money, workers or insurance as it is for normal banking systems. While this rapacious loans are known as greener pastures, for Africa are but future financial starvation.

Essentially, the way African economies survived the credit crunch needs to open their eyes and become a lesson for Africa that it still has its own ways of survival even amidst adversity from the West. To do away with the credit crunch, Western economies invented bailouts that were not extended to African countries. This shows how Western financial policies are built on shaky foundations. Had it not been the advantage in amassing loots from colonies and making policies internationally, chances for Western economies to shrink even more were high. This shows how resilient Africa can be despite being at the receiving end almost in everything. Likewise, if one looks at how Africa is expanding in terms of infrastructure currently, shall Europe stop fleecing Africa under the so-called international community, it is likely to turn things around for the better. What is importantly needed to be done is for Africa to clearly state its case *vis-à-vis* Europe's criminal past. Africa needs to be invited to the table internationally when it comes to police formulation. To do so, Africa needs to initiate the process by agitating that it be recognised for its resources as it has been for the West with its technology. Neither resources nor technology can be advanced in the absence of the other. They both symbiotically depend on each other. If anything, this is the secret-cum-weapon Europe has kept a secret so as to keep on exploiting Africa. Africa needs to show Europe that it knows this trick; and it is not going to make do with it anymore.

Apart from economic or material domination and exploitation, Europe has benefited from Africa intellectually. This is the ploy it has always used. For example, when it comes to African *crème de la crème* of all kinds, under brain drain (Mhango 2017b) Africa stands to lose while Europe stands to keep on gaining more and more at the detriment of Africa. Take, for example, Africa's literary gurus such as Ngugi wa Thiong'o, Wole Soyinka and the late Chinua Achebe. They were all lulled out of Africa to go to the West to teach African literature in Western Universities. Why? It is simply because the West did not like to allow them to establish themselves in Africa where they would spoil other Africans. So, too, to make sure that they were not staying in Africa, Western stooges in power harassed them so as to force them to take bait. The situation is still the same even today. Despite hollering about human rights, Europe has never reprimanded African stooges in power who stifle academics by not paying them well or listening to them. Instead, it has been an onlooker when most of them are persecuted or frustrated. One thing that makes the West keep quiet is the fact that once it attracts such academics, it uses them to teach its academics that end up becoming experts on African issues without necessarily spending money and time to study in Africa to qualify. This is a very cheap way of creating a pool of diverse knowledge that helps Europe to always be ahead of others. There is no way Europe would have kept tabs on Africa without knowing its secrets. As aforementioned, formerly, Europe used colonial agents to access Africa's secrets. Currently, it is using Africa's academic *crème de la crème* to access them and create more experts on Africa that are not Africans themselves. The flipside of this is the fact that whenever Africa needs anything about Europe,

110

European experts are consulted. And when it comes to African issues, the same Europeans experts not African are consulted. Soon, China and India will do the same in order to safeguard their interests in Africa. When will Africa create its own pool of knowledge so that it can safeguard its interests not in Europe, China or India but at home?

When it comes to how African stooges in power persecuting academic, Kenya provides a living example. When academics like Dr. Willy Mutunga, professors Ngugi wa Thiong'o, Micere Mugo and others were persecuted at home, the West offered them asylum instead of bringing the government to book for gross violations of human rights. Essentially, this has been ongoing for a long time. Instead of helping such *crème de la crème* to establish themselves in their countries, the West has always given them the rope. To make matters worse, Africa has refused to learn and change. This is because, for many years, Africa has been ruled by Western stooges or their protégés, sons or handpicked consiglieres as it is the case in many African post-colonial regimes who would not allow any positive change aiming at emancipating Africa happen. Europe created elites who eat first but not last as leaders as African traditions dictate that the adult, leader or parent should eat last after children have eaten. Such people cannot think about common Africans. If they do, they will lose the unfettered positions they have in exploiting and vending Africa. These are trustworthy servants of Europe who abuse and destroy their social services to end up being treated or going for medical services in Europe. These are greedy and sick creatures who sold Africa even more to Europe. We still have African *crème de la crème* who still pride themselves to have been educated at prominent Western educational institutes such as Cambridge, Harvard, London School of Economics, Oxford, Massachusetts Institute of Technology (MIT) and others. If you compare the traitors mentioned hereinabove with people like Nelson Mandela, Patrice Lumumba and Thomas Sankara who were not the products of Western oxymoronic setting, you find that they were more progressive than those. Prah cited in Mlambo (2008) maintains that such mentality reinforces inferior and appendage status for African academics, in a world simply because most of the prestigious institutions of higher learning are in the West, where most scholarly journals are based and where most of the financial resources for research originate. Africa needs to deconstruct such dependency as it embarks on its new adventurous journey of redefining itself through Afrocentricity which Hoskins (1992: 252) cited in Kumah-Abiwu (2016) defines as the endeavor that will enable and enhance it:

> To go back to the dawn to human history in order to de-Europeanize/detoxify/demystify/debrainwash their subconscious mind-set of this invisible drug called Eurocentric miseducation….with the correct knowledge, information, and interpretation of the rich, glorious and dynastical history, scientific inventions, humane communal modus vivendi,….and unmatched intellectual acumen of their African ancestors (p. 170).

There is no any stumbling block for any society or people like hijacking its *crème de la crème* as it is in the case of Africa. For, doing so makes the society either redundant or ignorant of itself. Because, through the *crème de la crème*, the society is able to tell its story through academia, media and whatever that represents the society. This is why governments fund, education, especially universities and other high-learning institutions. When it comes to Africa, despite having its *crème de la crème*, it is not utilised, underutilised or exploited by Europe. This is what Africa has been going through since many African countries gained their independence. There is no African country whose *crème de la crème* does not look up to Europe without questioning the rationale of the lack of reciprocity in this manner. Politics is the same in Africa. Almost all African governments, apart from depending on Europe almost for virtually everything, look up to Europe even for guidance. Refer to how the West has always sent observers to African elections without any reciprocity. Further, refer to how the verdict Western electoral observers make is regarded to be more important than home observers who are made of, regional or local Non-Governmental Organisations (NGOs). Basically, there is no strategy apart from divide and rule (Adan 2015) that Europe enacted in Africa that worked as the mental rape of Africa's academic and political *crème de la crème*. For, after brainwashing, draining and corrupting post-colonial African political elites, Europe sealed Africa's fate. For, they are the ones that mismanaged, and still do, instead of managing, and vended Africa's people and resources instead of guarding and liberating them. They became like blind, greedy and rabid dogs appointed to guard the meat. They will either devour or infect the meat. This is very important to underscore. For, it is political elites who preside over corrupt governments in Africa. As the sage has it: birds of a feather flock together, corrupt, greedy and myopic African political elites namely among who the rulers are the ones responsible for appointing other elites or personnel to serve in their governments. As well, their governments are responsible for appointing and employing citizens to [mis]manage the country. All workers in the country are under their watch. Such personnel are charged with managing all business of the country such as guarding borders, airports, and natural resources, *inter alia*, and they enter contracts with foreign investors among others. With corrupt governments, those under their watch take advantage of systemic rot to illicitly amass wealth as the citizens suffer. This is why many of African rulers vend their people for the exchange of nonsenses such as expensive cars, drinks, suits, yachts, mansions, scholarships for their children and concubines and their illegitimate children, trips abroad and other lossmaking and narrow ventures. This is because they were made brainless and heartless once they were offered the bait that they greedily and myopically bit and swallowed. Instead of receiving education, they received ignorance in the name of education. Instead of coming out of school with skills that would enable them to make their countries prosper, they came out with only criminal skills of robbing and vending their countries. I will show this when I discuss African corrupt and venal rulers who robbed their coffers of billions of dollars and stashed in Western capitals to end up being taken when they die or being overthrown. Such criminals and self-seekers invest heavily on nonsenses such as building big mansions, churches and other white elephants; all paid for by the paupers they have always pauperized. Mhango (2015) provides three examples of such toxic investment in the DRC where the former dictator Joseph Mobutu turned his bush village into a city; in the Central African Republic (CAR) and Ivory Coast where former dictators of the two countries Bokassa and Felix Houphouet-Boigny respectively burnt billions of dollar financing cathedrals while their people were dying of curable and preventable diseases not to mention other services such as education, clean water and security. Ethiopian king Haile Selassie used to keep and nourish lions (Riccio 2012) as his pets while many Ethiopians were dying of manmade hunger and poverty. Up until he was overthrown, Selassie was hailed as a very successful leader simply because his dirty linens were not yet to appear in the agora.

How Fake Elitism Perpetually Ruined Africa's Economies

When it comes to controlling Africa, Europe made sure that it controls Africa in all aspects of life so as to be able to keep on exploiting it. Apart from economic and political control, Europe exerted its control socially by using things such as religion, fashion and media. As mentioned above, religion was a good conduit of colonial venom that paved the way to full-fledged colonialism in Africa. Missionaries were hidden spies (Županov 2006; Raftopoulos and Mlambo 2008; Falola 2009; and Adegbulu 2011) who reported back to their home governments about the behaviours and secrets of Africans so that it could be easy for their home countries to use whatever weakness unearthed to occupy and rule Africa. The word of God was used to soften Africans to easily and unconsciously succumb to colonial agendas and drives based on lies and manipulations as colonial covert and dominant forces. To easily and perpetually exploit and undermine Africa, Europe introduced fake elitism as tool it used create classes among Africans whose precolonial elitism did not create classes. Therefore, the creation of fake elitism produced mistrusts and schisms among Africans so as to end up being brutalised, colonised and exploited. In doing so, a few fake African elites supervised the exercise that saw their being robbed for the development of Europe and the underdevelopment of Africa.

Since time immemorial, societies had elites who were viewed as the beacons of these societies based on their merits and contributions to the society. However, there are three types of elites in this category namely, political, academic and hermaphrodite ones to mean those

114

used by the first group to exploit their countries as opposed to the second group that oppose the betrayal of Africa. This is why such elites were; and are still allowed to rule countries nearly in every aspect of live all over the world. Regardless of how a society is highly developed or otherwise, no society is run by laypeople. Instead, virtually all societies and countries are ran by elites. If there are anything the world political calibration shares is nothing but the roles elites play in the business of the state and society altogether. Knowing the important roles elites play in any society, colonial powers decided to create them for Africa so that they could be used to indirectly rule Africa on their behalf as it came to be. Almost all post-colonial African presidents were Western trained except for a few such as Ahmed Sekou Toure (Guinea); Sam Nujoma (Namibia); Nelson Mandela (South Africa); and Kenneth Kaunda (Zambia) who however, had some traits of Western education due to the fact that education, virtually in all countries, was provided by missionaries.

However, when we compare the current crop of compradorial and oligarchic elites, we notice a very huge difference in the formation and application of elitism. For example, African precolonial elites were specialised in some areas that gave them more responsibilities to the society than others were not known as elites the term we use today. But soon after Europe colonised Africa, African elites were phased out to give room for colonial elites; purposely created to serve their master, colonialism. To the contrary, this new crop is different from precolonial African elites who were totally different when it comes to serving the society. Smiths, healers, priests, traders, kings, chiefs and others were charged with the duty of seeing to it that everybody was getting services. Everything, everybody owned or had, was used for the service of the society but not otherwise as it currently is whereby elitism either serves and individual or the masters who clone the very elites. So, when it comes to how Africa developed Europe, even today, it is still ongoing under brain drain (Docquier, Lohest and Marfouk 2007; Baine and Rapoport 2008; Dustmann, Fadlon and Weiss 2011; and Docquier and Rapoport 2012) in which African elites free their home countries seeking greener pastures in the West. This danger has two facets namely the lures from the West and frustrations from African political elites who see others as a threat to their grip on power. Africa needs to stop this trend; failure to which it will keep on developing Europe as it helps to increase or double down underdevelopment itself. Muula (2005); and Mhango (2015) propose some measures for Africa to take among which is to creating conducive environment for its experts to return back after graduating from various universities in the West which is now lacking. Among the proposed measures are the amendment of the constitutions of African countries in order to get competent leaders who will attract African academics and skilled persons to return back home. Mhango reasons that there is no way Africa can develop with recycled-rulers who ceased to think many years ago. Muula proposes the establishment of some institutes which will offer some skills locally instead of sending Africans to Europe or other countries to end up remaining there after graduating.

To draw a line between the current elites and their seemingly precolonial African counterparts, it is better to define the term elite in order to prove how Africa developed Europe. Essentially, apart from being a new term to Africa, elite group consists of all who's who in a group who enjoy the beauties and the cake the group makes. Most of such elites are political elites who control everybody and everything including academic elites. In this volume, the group means both a group and a country. The group of political elites is more powerful than any group of elites in any African country minus the army which is not elite naturally. The online Free Dictionary defines elite as "a group or class of persons considered to be superior to others—and of course considers itself—because of their intelligence, social standing, or wealth" (page not provided). To the contrary, many African precolonial societies that were egalitarian by nature (Pelican 2009; Dueppen 2014 and Gluckman 2017), elites were not regarded as being superior to others. Instead, they were respected for their services and skills which did not differentiate them from other members of the group. For example, any elite was one in many; in that he or she fulfilled whatever responsibility and still remain the same. The African pre-contact doctor could become a musician even a hunter without necessarily creating any rift between him and other members of the society which is different today elitism is seen as something Martian. However, there is no a watertight definition of elite or elitism. Thurlow and Joworski (2006) simply define it noting that "it is usually conceived of as a structural, social category describing those who rule or lead through instrumental, political power" (p. 103).

Arguably, the term elite started to surface in African vocabulary after some Africans went to school run by missionaries and later governments and other government or went to Europe for education the trend that still goes on even today. You can see this on how European or American trained personnel are more valued than homemade ones. All this can be attributed to colonial carryovers colonial Europe left behind to haunt Africa forever. When Africans who went for education to Europe came back home, they were treated differently due to the belief that they had acquired white man's secrets (Thiong'o 2015) they could use to fight and defeat him conditionally that they should not follow them. It is unfortunate that modern elites, despite learning the secrets of the white man, have followed his *diktat* instead of using the secrets they garnered to liberate themselves and their countries. For, it is the same people that are now vending Africa many years after colonial flags were pulled down. Instead, they used the secrets or knowledge they got from the white man to replicate what they were supposed to fight.

Fischer (1993: 22) cited in Huchzemeyer (2004) elaborated the roles elites played in Africa using the "theory of technocracy", which talks about "a governance process dominated by technically trained knowledge elites," who "replace or control democratic deliberation and decision-making processes...with a more technocratically informed discourse" (p. 339). This informs us that our democracy is controlled by a clique of a few informed individuals that uses the citizens as they deem fit provided that they are not disturbing or tilting the international balance of power. The control does not end up there. Even those local political elites are controlled by their former colonial masters for their benefits but not of the countries they rule and misrule in many cases.

To the contrary, when the white man got Africans' secrets extracted from converts, he took and used them against Africans so as to hold them at ransom for many decades for the benefit of his people. Also, he used converts who were castaways in African society. For, at the time, no decent person would be converted to Christianity or become a born again. The white man used Africa's secret to develop Europe we know of today. We know white man's secrets. What are we doing to use them to liberate ourselves from beggarliness, dependency and poverty colonialism brought to the land of extremes as a decent people? Hopkins (2014) maintains that colonialism disrupted Africa's state of harmony, cohesion and development based on shared values that were replaced by artificial unity (the formation of colonial states) backed by forced and ruthless exploitation which reduced indigenous people to a degree of poverty they had not known in the past.

Can we keep on blaming a white man for hijacking and exploiting us while we know everything that our own brothers and sisters, the black colonisers sold us to their masters? Although saying that blaming white man for everything is not a way forward, it does not exonerate him from the mess he created for others through using local elites. So, too, it does not alter the fact that Africa developed Europe in many ways; and it has gone on doing so up until now.

Every country has elites who manage or mismanage it depending on if they meet the expectations of the mass or how one assess and evaluate them. My experience vis-à-vis Africa is that elites have mismanaged Africa. The evidence is clear that Africa has always been at the receiving end almost in anything meaningful internationally. Mwaura (2005: 6) cited in Alemazung (2010) has no good word, especially for political elites whom he calls traitors with dubious and fictitious patriotism they use to benefit their Western masters who ever since they left Africa have gone on exploiting Africa through using them. This is contrary to what Africans fought for during the struggle for independence. Alemazung (Ibid.) adds that Africans fought colonialism in order to reclaim their rule of law that colonialism felled to end up getting just the same whose difference is only colour. Strauss (1999) argues that the so-called elite is nothing but capitalistic division of labour which though is not equal and equitable, especially if we consider the fact that the elite is regarded and it regards itself as superior to non-nonpareil members of the group or those excluded from managing the country and enjoying its cake. You can call them those who eat without sweating and dipping their hands in the dirty. Ironically, despite committing such a crime, such criminals are still accepted and revered not just because they do good things but because they have a good thing, wealth however dirty it is. Despite their disservices killing many Africans thanks to diseases, ignorance, poverty and other miseries they have created, the West has never treated them as criminals responsible for mass murder. Instead, the West has always been in bed with them in robbing Africa for the development of the West or Europe.

Some call elites the rainmakers, shakers and movers of the society due to the high life they live while those oiling the cog of the economy toil and live like dogs. Form (2015) argues that even elites or those who do blue collar jobs are divided or stratified according to what one does. He cites an example from the army of Israel in which blue collar soldiers acknowledged to receive hegemonic status of the combat soldiers. Division, differentiation even exploitation goes down as far as becoming gendered in that females receive less status compared to their colleague males. The division and superiority and inferiority go as far as affecting almost every aspect of the group. For example, those doing clerical jobs feel they are better positioned than those who do mechanical jobs. So, too, such schism goes far deeper so as to affect how we perceive our professions. For example, when I was in school, those who studied science felt they were more intelligent than those who did art. Essentially, this is the juncture at which division goes deeper and deeper so as to create unnecessary enmity among the members of the group for the benefit of those who cloned them or the ones who introduced the system that moulded them. Those doing clean jobs feel that they contribute a lot to the income of the group compared to those doing dirty jobs. A clerk feels superior to a janitor or a street sweeper without underscoring the fact the group needs their service equally. The division goes on whereby elites from the so-called developed countries are regarded to be superior to their counterparts from poor countries. Even females from rich countries are viewed as superior to males from poor countries. Even their institutions undergo the same division whereby the president or prime minister of a rich country is perceived to be superior to her or his counterpart from a poor country.

Such assumptions affect the functioning of the group in that those employed in certain positions tend to not value each other's activities. You can see this on how military personnel perceive themselves compared to the so-called civilians. This is nasty in Africa where military people think they have a bigger role to play in the countries, protecting it against enemies even when such enemies are fake and artificially created to maintain the *status in quo*. Differently from the so-called developed countries in which the duties of the armies are, *inter alia*, to protect the country, invent new technologies such as in the US and defend democracy. In many African countries, it is different. The military is there to protect the government even when it requires suppressing dissent voices. However, to get away with murder the military says it protects the constitution which a single individual who commands and feeds it can tinker with it and get away with it as it currently is in many African countries under tin-pot dictators. Yet, countries which squander public funds on keeping such suppressive military and police forces are referred to as democratic countries simply because they go to polls and end up rigging elections. This has been a chronic disease in Africa.

Who are the elites? They include all those who perform what is famously known as blue collar jobs. They range from politicians, professionals, businesspeople, priests and the like. The marriage between political elites and military elites has kicked out professional elites in many African countries. What makes them the force to reckon with is the fact that this group has justified its monopoly on the territory with exclusive power of employing even force under their jurisdiction (Jackson and Rosberg 1982) which gives them the power of mismanaging their countries as they deem fit provided that the interests of their foreign masters are securely safeguarded. This is why many corrupt African governments have never been obligated to run their countries democratically and justly as it is in the West. To make things worse, due to the exploitative and systemic arrangement that the *hoi polloi* take as normal, such governments are able to do as pleased even if doing so is contrary to democracy and the will of the people. Such illegal governments receive international recognition in that other countries even the democratic ones; still do business with them on behalf of the people they have hijacked. Citizens need to be educated so that they can argue or force their governments to downsize their armies so as to save money that should be channelled to other important sectors such as the provision of social services. William C. Thom cited in Herbst (2004) maintains that Africa state armies are on a decline which is good for the economies of many African countries should they expand the trend of downsizing their armies and governments.

Additionally, Herbst argues that the expansion of state armies was geared by the cold war which is no more. Although the cold war is history, many African rulers still use the same armies to remain in power illegally. What makes the situation abhorring is the fact that such rulers, who cling to power illegally, still refer to themselves as democrats while they actually are but autocrats and despots who are supposed to be behind bars. Even if you hear what they say about democracy, you end up in dismay. By definition, democracy is supposed to hinge on the concept of the government of the people by the people for the people (Weinstein 2008) to mean being owned by; and the ones that empower the very people those running it pretend to defend and work for while they actually work for their stomachs. We need to ask a very bold question: which people between the majority, minority, elites and the *hoi polloi*? Do we question this definition to see if we fit in it as excluded people? Are the real people fully involved in running the said government? Does the said government meet their expectations? The government of the people by the people for the people has always used as an exclusionary tactic of duping the mass to believe that they are in the big picture while they are not. I do not think if the sweeper whose work is not recognised or the one who goes so many months without receiving salary owns such a government. Such is not one or any of the people proclaimed under the mantra of the government of the people by the people for the people. I do not think if such a person likes the said government. For such a person, the so-called democracy is a hoax that one needs to fight tooth and nail to see to it that he or she is empowered by being allowed to hold to account those in power duping others. Nyongo (1990) cited in Fayemi (2009) ties democracy to the deterioration of economic conditions due to the lack of accountability. This has been a story of Africa where rulers are like gods who are unanswerable to anybody except their egos and their masters abroad. Here is where local and foreign elites get married to ruin African countries.

Soffer (1969) argues that the behaviour of the twentieth century's democracy is unreasonable and unpredictable. For, it gave birth to the new liberalism and elitism that ever since have monopolised democracy and economy of the world. In this volume, we will restrain ourselves to the African case in which democracy seems to have failed so as to end up being the agent of underdevelopment instead of development in all aspects. With the exception of Botswana (Mill 2012), there is no African country that can pride itself to being truly democratic or uncorrupt.

Due to the undemocratic nature of African politics, democracy has never made politicians accountable. For example, politicians talk about creating jobs but not service. They do so knowingly that they want people to work so that they can reap where they did not sow. Again, do they work themselves to meet citizens' expectations? What are legal mechanisms to deal with those who do not make good of their promises? As noted above, African elites have hijacked the citizens of their country. Due to the role they have always played the economies of African countries are not doing well not just because they are exploited by the West only. It is because much of the income these countries generate end up keeping elites in government. Look at the percentage of the money many governments spend on keeping their bureaucrats you will agree with this argument that local elites are more of a problem than their foreign accomplices. And I am so comfortable in my own skin to make such an argument.

While elite division becomes an obstacle for development in Africa, in the West things are different. Nobody bothers with anyone's job except the income one makes. Before the coming of the European evil scum of the earth from far and wide, Africans did not discriminate against each other based on what a person legally does. It was as it currently is in the West where what matters is a job by not the type of the job one does. Despite helping Europe and the West in general to fleece Africa, local elites still are paid by those they fleece but not the beneficiaries of their crimes. This is another aspect in which Africa has gone on developing Europe under fake democracy

Europe exported to Africa. Take, for example, how money is spent annually in African countries. The biggest chunk of this money goes to elites but not taxpayers who in many African countries are poor farmers. For example, Tanzania's budget for the fiscal year 2012/2013 was Tshs.15, 191.944 billion out of which Tshs. 10,664.105 billion was allocated to the running government operations while only Tshs.4, 527.839 was allocated to development (*www.mof.go.tz*). Can such a country develop really while a big chunk of its income ends paying bureaucrats; not to mention servicing predatory debts Europe extends to African countries? The situation is the same almost in all African countries. What the budget above does is immoral. Again, since the introduction of colonialism, morality was put aside. The African that we knew many years ago before colonialism was introduced is long gone.

Morality was the central beacon that used to lead African society. Morality was so much revered and worshipped so much that it ended up bringing Africa down, especially if we revisit the introduction of colonialism to Africa. This is why there was no division between the nonpareil and *hoity toity*. The irony and tragedy are that those Africans who saw colonial agents coming did not view them in their true colour and motives. The hosts did not know that those they thought were like them had some ominous intents and plans in their missions, to destroy their society so that they could later subdue and exploit forever for the development of Europe. Further, the hosts viewed the invaders as humans like they were while, actually, they were not. Creating new Africa based on moral qualities but not illegal achievements can help it to forge ahead. It is its morality that will enable Africa to confront Europe seeking to be redressed for the contribution it has on the development of Europe. Indeed, it is Africa's morality that will enable it to tell Europe to its face that its development is the creature of crimes that created and caused the underdevelopment for Africa.

Chapter Five

How Democracy Is a Double-Edged Sword

Nothing seems to have *hyperhypnotised* Africa like European democracy. To make it appeal, democracy was tied to development (Persson and Tabellin 2006; Demirel-Pegg and Moskowitz 2009; Wesserman 2010; Wanangwe 2016; and Leslie 2017). If truly democracy goes hand in hand with development, it proves that Africa was more democratic before the arrival of European colonisers than it currently is. For, when European colonisers arrived, they found a very robustly functioning society that offered them what they were looking for. There is no evidence to prove that Europe taught Africa everything. For example, when Europeans came to Africa, they found that some other ancient African empires, kingdoms and states had already established business with Asia and the Far East (Liu 2010). Evidence shows that Africa had already established trade links with India and Asia many years before the first contact with Europe. Engle (1976); Francis (1984); and Kanungo (2004a) cited in Dussubieux, Kusimba, Gogte, Kusimba, Gratuze, and Oka (2008) trace such links to the first century BCE.

However, despite having such powerful kingdoms and empires which must have had their democratic settings and systems, things changed after their civilisations were erased. For, after being colonised and fought for their independence, Europe decided to offer independence to African countries. After offering independence to African countries after colonising and dividing them, Europe decided to leave something behind that would busy and divide Africans even more. Knowingly, Europe introduced democracy that was a typical replica of its own not to mention being new to Africa. Democracy is not a bad thing; if it serves the interests of those using it to govern their countries. Again, democracy is not supposed to be dictated by one side to the other. Oke (2005) cited in Imhonopi and Urim (2012) notes that:

Democracy, whether liberal, African or modern includes a fundamental recognition of popular sovereignty, equal opportunity for all, majority rule, representativeness, minority rights, right of choice between alternative programmes, popular consultation, consensus on fundamental issues and more essentially periodic elections (p. 72).

I think the above quote summarises nicely how and what true democracy is supposed to be. There cannot be any sense of a true democracy whereby one part of the world dictates or funds another without any mutual reciprocity as it currently is between Africa and Europe. There is no logic whatsoever in what is ongoing as long as Europe keeps on treating Africa undemocratically in its drive of wanting Africa to *democratise* Africa. *Prima caritas incipit seipso* or Charity begins at home; Latin adage has it. Europe and its so-called the international community need to treat Africa democratically so as to teach it how to do things. Europe needs to teach by deeds but not by empty words. Truly, there is no way Africa can keep on being taken for granted by accepting unequal democracy with the aim of exercising equal democracy at home.

Now, how did post-colonial African governments fall in the trap of Western democracy? The answer is simple. Due to being ruled undemocratically for many years, African post-colonial government thought that now they could become developed like their masters without underscoring the hardship this ploy may pose to newly-independent countries. They forgot that true democracy cannot function well in poverty due to the fact that it will be funded by foreigners as it has been the case in Africa. Poor countries cannot guarantee human material rights. By being able to fund democracy in Africa, Western countries have an upper hand in its institutions and policies. Like freedom, democracy cannot be imported (Toplak 2011). It is enhanced by the desire of the people to have it. This is why it is wrong for Western countries to dictate African countries as to when they need democracy. They forgot that the *modus operandi* and the time Europe used and took to reach where it was then were different from their circumstances. For example, one of the tenets of Western democracy is human rights among which is the right of deciding who should rule based on laid down procedures which in this sense are European. They forgot that democracy, just like any doctrine is a cultural thing that aims at serving a certain purpose or purposes and "cannot be captured in one model that fulfills exactly the same functions and provides the same meanings across the societies" (Lindberg 2006: 29). If you ask African rulers the essence of democracy, they will tell you that it is about the government elected by the majority. There are questions about the so-called majority. What type of majority? What types of issues that the majority is to consider in order for it to become the majority? Where do they put the rights of the minority? Were the ruling elite prepared and ready to be accountable to their constituencies and peoples? Were their institutions self-reliant and self-sufficient to practices democracy? Did they have economic and financial bases to support democracy? Did they have the general will and wherewithal to nurse and nourish this new democracy? These are among the questions ruling elites and their citizens did not ask, ponder on and provide right answers to up until now. Kenny (2007) cited in Toplak (2011) notes that "free elections and democratic leaders cannot increase the level of political freedom by themselves, if the society is incapable of benefiting from these achievements" (p. 78). There cannot be democracy, sound and true democracy, without justice socially, economically and politically. There cannot be healthy democracy without self-reliance or fulfillment of people's needs. The lack of right answers to democracy gave Europe yet another chance to rule Africa indirectly by making sure that democracy is used to its advantage.

After introducing the concept of democracy, let us now look at some important issues pertaining to democracy, specifically its definitions and meaning. The major question I ask is: Who defines what based on what and for whom or what when and where? Nash (2005) maintains that "researchers and practitioners require a definition that recognizes the incompleteness of our concepts, generates a level epistemological playing field, and enables hypnosis theories to "reach" (p. 265). This means that academics, especially African ones, need to question the definitions they apply in whatever field[s] in crafting their definitions. If we apply such a rationale, let us say in questioning the definition of democracy to mean "power or rule of the people" (Mhango 2017d) what do we get? Saying that democracy is about the people is vague. Which people? For, etymologically, the word people in ancient Greece or *demos*, means white native adult male resident of a polis (Ober 2008: 3 cited in Mhango (*Ibid.*). However, this definition has been academically universalised. Held (1987: 3) cited in Enslin and Horsthemke (2004) maintains that "democracy' is notoriously difficult to define: 'the meaning of democracy has remained, and probably will always remain, unsettled" (p. 553). Therefore, whatever definition attributed to democracy still needs to be redefined and interrogated. This shows how other societies whose grand narratives are not dominant were excluded so as to end up with a narrow Western definition of democracy borrowed from ancient Greece. Didn't this mangled definition cause power differentials under which males got advantage over females so as to keep on dominating in democratic processes? Isn't this the reason why men have always been enormously voted in top positions in governments such as presidency all over the world than females simply because the vague and patriarchal definition of people has been used without being deconstructed? There is a belief that democracy is the rule of the majority. Well, suppose such majority is reached simply because one dominant group based on gender, tribe, community or block has the majority. Is this still the rule of people or some people as opposed to others? This has been a blind take of Africa when it comes to democracy. You can see how the so-called majority is not the majority by its meaning but just the majority predominantly based on certain undemocratic criteria. For example, in countries where tribal voting is an in-thing like Kenya, Gikuyu–the biggest tribe–has produced three presidents out of four the country has ever had. This is not a majority of Kenya but a tribe with many voters who team up with another tribe with substantial votes that enables whoever cobbles them together to have an advantage over others. Apart from Kenya, Cameroon provides another ideal example. Since it was divided between Anglo and Franco camps in after the WWII, Cameroon has been boiling slowly. The division of Cameroon created the schisms whose results are two antagonist and distinct parties, English and French whereby the former has small population compared to the latter. Therefore, in this politics of separation (Anyefru 2011), whenever elections are convened, the majority Francophone carries the day so to make the Anglophone feels that its rights are trampled on even in democracy. If the definition of democracy is not deconstructed in such countries above, the chances of being ruled by one community or part of the republic are high. Arguably, there is a logical need to deconstruct or redefine the definitions that have always been taken for grant to be accurate while in actual fact they have a lot of shortfalls.

There is no dispute about the use of the word people despite the fact that people is ambiguous naturally. What is clear is the fact that rule is about people but not animals simply because people or humans have the power of elaborate ways of communication that can be learned and taught easily. Despite that, there still is an ambiguity on the term people. Which people? Who decides who the people are or must be in certain rule? Who is included; and who is excluded? I can answer this question arguing that the people intended here are the ones upon whom powers of deciding who rules them are mutually and temporarily conferred based on consensus resulting from negotiations and consent of the members of the country or group guided by their constitution, goals, interests, justice, procedures, traditions, aspirations and needs. This said, democracy is supposed to be unique to every people based on their choice. Enslin and Horsthemke (2004) maintain that "democracy is essentially 'embedded', i.e. a local, indigenous phenomenon. Its manifestations differ according to social and cultural context. African democracy is distinct and unique" (p. 545); which makes sense without using the lenses of superiority and duplicity that Europe has always superimposed on others. This is why England has always been ruled by the monarch; and still is a democracy. What difference does England or Norway has from Buganda Kingdom (Wiredu 2008) or Luba-Lunda Empire? The answer is simple. Europe killed African democracy, just like other aspects of the society in order to give room for its own brand of democracy that serves it but does not serve Africa. If democracy is supposed to be unique but not homogenous due to the fact the needs of countries and traditions differ according to time, this brings us to natural African democracy that existed before the introduction of flimflam and harmful Western democracy.

The issue of the superimposed Western democracy brings us to another thorny issue namely tribalism as a colonial invention (Lonsdale 2014) that was introduced in order to antagonise and set African against each other aimed at weakening them for perpetual exploitation. Tribal acrimony is one of the things that have cost Africa greatly economically, politically and socially. For, after being set against each other, Africans started wasting a lot of time and resources in addressing tribal fake needs such as fear, insecurity and prosperity. Instead of standing together as they were before Europe divided them, Africans dangerously stood against each other. However, this does not mean that Africans did not have their tribal differences. They were there; but they were exacerbated by the poison Europe injected in the society all aimed at exploiting Africans easily and perpetually as it later occurred. After introducing the divide-and-rule; that resulted into divide-and-conquer strategy (González 2009), Europe destroyed the harmony that existed among precolonial Africans; and thereby used them against each other; thereby obtained their secrets and used them against both. Instead of using their time and resources to develop their societies, Africans spend them finishing each other. Nothwehr, (2008: 5) cited in Sanou (2015) notes that "tribalism is the attitude and practice of harboring such a strong feeling of loyalty or bonds to one's tribe that one excludes or even demonizes those 'others' who do not belong to that group" (p. 95). Such a definition is different from an organic Africa tribe which meant a group of people with many commonalities such as sharing the same land, language, identity, aspirations, mores, taboos and sense of nationhood which do not necessarily involve the othering or demonising others. Most of African tribes had many more positive ties among themselves before Europe poisoned their organic ties. However, after colonial Europe reinvented them, African relationships became toxic so as to help Europe in conquering, occupying and colonising Africa. Essentially, the division of Africa either tribally or nationally is the only reason why Africa is, up until now; the major reason that forces and requires Africa to stand and claim its redress from the evils colonisation and slavery caused it. Division is the weapon Europe invented that had kept it safer from any claims resulting from its criminal past. This was

130

not applied only on Africa but also on other colonies such as the Indian subcontinent that was divided in acrimonious states such as India and Pakistan in order to weaken them and keep them at bay. To crown it all, Europe brought in another big gorilla namely democracy that has kept many internal forces wrangling with each other over power without necessarily addressing historical evils such as colonialism and slavery.

As I shall prove later, Africa is ruled by the mixture of Western forms of expensive democracy and destructive dictatorship all aimed at producing prefects who can supervise the plundering of Africa. Aristotle cited in Bartels (2016) pins democracy down asking: "what difference differentiates oligarchy and democracy is lack of it" (p. 394). And this is practically true to Africa where disproportionate democracy has been in place as dictated by Europe. If you look at those competing for powers, you will find that they are not paupers whom are told that the country belongs to. Kenya's example cited in the prior chapter does well show this. Cilliers (2010) maintains that democracy has failed to replace neopatrimonialism in Africa which is not only an antithesis to Western democracy but also an irony and a sign of a double standard and hypocrisy. Ironically, while Europe has always made Africa to believe that it is the means by which to deliver justice to the majority, in Africa, it is just atypical system that is there to make Africans believe that they are now at par with Europe politically while they are not. Democracy for Europe is the means by which the majority is able to call its rulers to account. This is because democracy has different meaning and uses between Europe and Africa. Essentially, in the name and pretext of democracy, Africa received a simple and paternalistic form of governance based on anarchical democracy but not normal democracy (Chomsky 1992). However, Leonard (2008) notes that:

Economists, traditionally heavily represented among those opposed to paternalism, hold three mistaken beliefs about paternalism. They are: one, the belief that paternalism must be coercive, two, the belief that paternalism is avoidable, and, most important, three, the belief that people make choices that are better, by their own lights, than the choices that would be made for them by paternalists. Each of these traditional beliefs is a misconception or false (p. 356).

Further, while Europe has always forced some noncompliant regimes in Africa to treat their people *democratically*, it has never replicated the same for Africa. Currently, Africa still has many undemocratic countries or superficial democracies whose leaders are in power after either rigging the elections or amending their constitutions to stay in power democratically and illegally. If, indeed, what Europe wants in Africa is democracy, it would not tolerate such despots. Again, provided that such despots offer to protect and safeguard Europe's interests in Africa, democracy does not matter at all. Take regimes such as the ones, *inter alia,* in Angola, Burundi, Equatorial Guinea, Gabon, the DRC, Rwanda, Uganda and Zimbabwe with their fake, illusive, pretend or virtual or face democracy (Uwizeyimana 2012) that is open to everybody. However, due to serving the interests of colonial powers, nobody bothers to tell them that they need true democracy so as to do away with mockery and superficial democracy. It is only Burundi and Zimbabwe that were shunned and squeezed simply because they either did not toe the line as far as safeguarding Europe's interests in Africa is concerned or do not have any resources that Europe seeks in Africa. In Africa, democracy is but a white elephant based on political hoax due to the fact that it has never delivered anything meaningful except political vainglory if not a colonial or political marginalia. Like religion, apart from being received blindly, democracy has become like the opium for Africans. Nobody questions the cost of democracy simply because African political elites benefiting from the current design of democracy were taught that democracy is always expensive. Why if, at all, Africa lived harmoniously without it? Citing the example of expensiveness of democracy in Nigeria, Imhonopi and Urim (2012) note that "granted that democracy is expensive everywhere, but the cost of running the Nigerian democracy has become simply an obscenity" (p. 75). Arguably, the obscenity of Nigeria's democracy is but the *typical replica* of democracy in Africa as a whole. To make matters worse, Africa's democracy is not only expensive but intrusive. Show me any credible, free and fair elections conducted in Africa without the supervision and tutoring by Europe. Do African countries send their electoral observers to European elections? If they do, do they have any say about the said elections the same European ones have on Africa?

Apart from dictating Africa's democracy, Europe funds it without necessarily telling openly what it wants to achieve apart from hegemony is nothing but resources and the perpetuation of the colonisation of Africa. To show how Europe gains a lot from dictating democracy in Africa, it has always been comfortable and ready to help in this lossmaking investment that has failed to change the lives of many Africans since it was introduced as we have seen above. He who pays the piper calls the tune. By dictating and funding Africa's democratisation, Europe has successfully been able to contain Africa for its advantage. There is nothing agonisingly tantalising in Western democracy like the money poor countries blindly and unquestionably spend on elections. Whenever there are elections in any African country, money is spent like nobody's business. Politicians spend millions of dollars on advertisements, bribing, flattering, and scheming without necessarily to have the duty to tell how, when and where they made such millions not to mention what they buy. Again, Van Biezen and Kopecký answer (2007) the question on what politicians buy during their campaigns noting that there are common forms of corruption in party politics that involve financial donations to political parties and politicians in exchange for favorable decisions, such as building contracts or granting of licenses which is rife in Africa.

After looking at how the situation is in Africa, we can now question: How is the situation about the same in Europe? Politicians spend money within the limits of transparency and accountability. They are legally duty-bound to show how the money they spend on elections was made and where it comes from shall it be donations. When it comes to Africa, any thieve can rob the paupers and fund his or her election campaigns without any worry or requirement to show how the money so spent was made or where it came from and why. Circumstantially, many unfit African politicians, who corruptly make it to power, are bought by their Western funders, mainly big corporations and investors, in enabling them to buy their paupers they later sell to the same funders.

Ironically, while all this criminality goes on, the teachers of democracy from Europe turn a blind eye knowingly that by getting corrupt and venal rulers, it will be able to use them to rob Africa as it has always been. Some European countries extend even loans to countries conducting elections without necessarily bothering about how the money is spent or how it will be paid. When it comes to the dividends of democracy to the voters, nothing substantially has happened in Africa with all such many dictators and thieves in power. Regarding the beauties such as justice, equality before law, good governance, rule of law and development, there is nothing to show after democracy failed miserably. Diamond (2015) ascertains two anomalies of democracy namely its failure to control corruption, abuse of power and visible decay in governance that is now easily seen in what was thought to be the best-governed African countries, such as South Africa among a few in Africa. Due to this, Diamond sees democracy in decline or recession but not acting as a panacea for Africa's problems as Europe has always made Africa to believe.

Demonstrably, such practices, done in the name of democracy, enshrine systemic corruption and plunderage in Africa. Once, again, intellectually, this puts Africa in peril provided that trusting such definitions without doubting and questioning them has made Africa intellectually moribund so as to keep on being a recipient from Europe without any intellectual hybridity or reciprocity in which the duo must negotiate definitions and meanings.

Europe introduced Western democracy to many African countries under the slogan that it is an important component of development and human rights under neoliberalism. Despite being beautiful, there is one thing African countries have never underscored. Western democracy is very expensive; and it is ineffectual in many African countries. If you look at countries with thriving development in Africa according to European standards, they do not reach even ten. And when it comes to development, it is arguable that they are not developed as envisaged. If there is anything that the West succeeded in doing is nothing but enhancing Europe to keep tabs on African governments be they democratic or autocratic. For, poor African countries depend on the same masters to finance their elections which give the donors an upper hand to tamper with their affairs. Take an example of Kenya. In 2017, it conducted general elections that consumed over $1 billion (*Daily Nation*, July, 17, 2017). What can such a poor country get from such elections? Interestingly, despite burning such big bucks, many countries return the same thieves in power. As for Kenya, after sinking a billion dollars in elections, its presidential results were invalidated by the Supreme Court due to what it held that were "illegalities and irregularities" (Maraga 2017). Thus, Kenya was forced to dig deeper into its empty pockets and burn more money to buy democracy in which two same figures were at each other's neck seeking power by representing their families and communities as I have indicated above in chapter one that Kenya's democracy revolves around families and tribalism. What is the upshot behind such an event in which more millions of dollars were burn in the fight between just two families and two communities?

My personal experience of growing up in socialist country under the president who used to say he was a benevolent dictator shows that sometimes there are things we need first before democracy. I will compare two countries namely Tanzania and Kenya. Kenya, stronghold of capitalism and Tanzania a stronghold of socialism, at the time, show the paradox of democracy. All countries were under the dictatorship of their first presidents, Jomo Kenyatta and Julius Nyerere respectively. While Europe praised Kenya for being developed simply because its capital Nairobi looked like European capital compared to dilapidated Tanzania's capital, Dar es Salaam, Tanzanians were proud of having free and full access to land as opposed to Kenyans who were landless in majority thanks to the land be owned by local and foreign petit bourgeoisies. While Kenyatta believed in foreign investments, Nyerere believed in local one by putting the means of production in the hands of citizens. Now, many years since the founders died, if you compare who are better between Tanzanians and Kenyans, Tanzania are doing a way better than Kenyans simply because they were afforded the opportunity to own land while Kenyans ended up becoming labourers in farms of foreigners and a few elite who grabbed land after gaining independence. Currently, while a Tanzanian poor farmer is able to produce much of his or her food supply, in Kenya, South Africa and other countries with many landless people, a labour produces what he or she does not eat and eat what she does not produce aka chicken life mentioned hereinabove. Take, for example, a labour who is working a flower or pyrethrum owned by a foreign investor. Such a labour toils every days and nights thinking about food but no other things simply because he or she has no land to work on and produce what he or she needs first. Such a person lacks gearing (Kirzner 2010) which is important in any economic development. Among all things, Europe has never wanted African countries to have their own gearing as the means of improving their economies and the lives of their citizens. For, doing so will deny Europe the consumers not to mention the dumping grounds for its cheap produces.

Thanks to their poverty, many Africans are forced into the *cul de sac* that forces them to go knocking on the doors of donors looking for money to burn into non-productive business of politics not to mention corruption (Raymond Choo 2008). Interestingly, when it comes to dishing out money, donors do not hesitate when projects aimed at being funded are lossmaking ones such as elections. When it comes to what can act as economic gearing as it happened in Zimbabwe where its dictator repossessed white farmers' land to offer to landless Zimbabweans, the donors shunned him. Mugabe seized the opportunity resulting from the Lancaster House agreement 1979 that expressly provided that landless Zimbabweans would be given land that would be made available through willing-seller/willing-buyer formula soon after Zimbabwe's independence (Mamdani 2009). They knew. By providing citizens with land to even produce for their subsistence needs, they will not contribute to the economies of Europe. With land, they will not sell their labour to white farmers who turned them into labourers that had no any other means to survive but succumbing to ever exploitative labour market. Again, the fact that many Zimbabweans were; and still are landless is agonising. Those who got pieces of land, at least, they have something to live on and for. This is because, land, for an African, is not only just the means of production but also a vital part of him or her. Sometimes, I wonder. How can wild animals in many parks have land to roam free on but some humans do not have any. For landless people, the independence of their countries is incomplete and meaningless. For, freedom must be seen on ownership of property as means for survival but not on a flag. A landless person does not only have nowhere to produce but selling his or her labour but also where to be buried when one dies. As for Zimbabweans who got the land, however poor they may be defined, they are be able to produce their own foods on top of owning land which in African culture is more than an asset or means of production. Although I do not support Zimbabwe's expropriation of land due to the fact that it was based on discriminatory and illegal setting, I think, for African countries with land problems must address them if, indeed, they want to move forward instead of wasting a lot of money building infrastructures and other things to emulate or copy Europe while the biggest chunk of their populations are in abject poverty. No person can eat democracy. After all, if you look at the said democracy, you wonder to find that those espousing and funding it have never treated Africa democratically in their *democratisation*. Essentially, what is referred to as democracy is more of a ploy or trap to force African countries into lossmaking projects and spending so that they can always seek loans in the West; and thus, live with them hanging in their necks. Due to the chicanery of Western democracy, in addressing the shortfalls and burdens of Western democracy, van Biezen and Kopecký (2007) conclude that things became worse due to the fact that there is 'no state subventions' and 'no regulation of party finances' occurs most often in Africa" (p. 245). Interestingly, despite being dingily immersed in corruption, political parties still garner millions of dollars from public coffers by the way of subsides! Reasonably, the money that goes to political party with the aim of enshrining corrupt and expensive Western democracy would make more sense had it gone to subsidising poor farmers who are in the majority in Africa as they wallow in abject manmade poverty as it was enacted by Europe to keep Africa at bay.

How Organic African Democracy and Development Were Ignored

> *"Our principles then are democracy which in our main language Setswana is rendered by IIPUSO ya batho ka batho", or rule of the people by the people, and development which we translate in Setswana as "ditiro tsa ditlhabalolo "which means literally" work for development", a significant rendering as I am sure you will agree. Our third principle is self-reliance which is variously expressed on Setswana and illustrated by numerous Setswana idioms of long-standing and our fourth principle unity, which is also expressed in Setswana by a number of words and idioms, each with its particular shade of meaning,"* Sir Seretse Khama, (1970) cited in Mhango (2016c: 144).

The quote above, *inter alia*, shows how democracy is not a new concept in some African societies; thus it was not supposed to be imported from Europe. To reach such a conclusion as the above one, surely, such a society must have been developed though in its own light. For, without any intellectual and conceptual development, the Tswana would not have been able to establish such a system based on what seems to be more meaningfully advanced than the current imported democracy; that currently exists in Africa. In importing democracy from Europe, Africa was supposed to do so *mutatis-mutandis* but not *Est quod est* as it has been the case for Africa. Like other relative concepts such as, *inter alia,* civilisation, culture mores and freedom, however different it may look and be construed, democracy is a relatively world phenomenon. It is universal just like those concepts are however in different contexts. Therefore, those arguing that Africa had the vacuum of democracy either are buying into *his-story* the European concocted about Africa; or do not know what democracy actually means. Democracy, just like a government and other concepts, depends on how a certain society perceives and uses it. Hence, when an argument is made that Africa had democratic elements, it should not be treated as glorification or romanticising Africa. However, the difference is in language use. When we talk about some concepts, they evoke different meanings and understandings in different societies. For example, when one says wealth, as a concept, it means many things in one. Wealth can be material and immaterial things; all depending on the user. For a communalistic society, wealth is more than material things as opposed to a capitalistic. Even the concept capital, as well, evokes different perceptions and meanings. What is capital? In economic terms, Victor (1991) cited in Hinterberger, Luks and Schmidt-Bleek (1997) notes that "there is no single theory of capital to which all economists subscribe" (p. 5). The concept differs from one school of thought to another. This convolution is the one that provokes dialogue, researches and analyses. Capital can be natural, ecological, political, and social; and many more depending on how certain people conceptualise it. If one concept can mean many and different things in one field of social science, what is wrong with democracy having the same in different cultures and societies?

When it comes to whether Africa had its brand of democracy before the arrival of European colonisers or not, Kanu (n.d year) maintains that:

> Democracy is a cherished African value, which existed in pre-colonial Africa as a pattern of African administration. It avers that democracy was already in Africa before the encounter of Africa with the West, and thus, that Africa is not a passive recipient of democracy (p. 1); also see Fayemi (2009).

Kanu and Fayemi offer an example of Yoruba community; and how democratic was homegrown. From their analyses, I found that Yoruba system was more elaborate and sophisticated than homegrown Athens' from which the so-called modern, however it is not modern, originated. Chemhuru (2010) notes that African natural democracy was non-party; and it was more successful than the superimposed one, Africa currently has, is. Under human empowerment theory, Alexander and Welzel (2008; 2011) cited in Alexander, Inglehart and Welzel (2012) argue that "democracy is an empowering institutional feature that should be antedated by empowering conditions at the social basis of democracy" (p. 56). I gather from studying African natural democracy that was not only empowering but also cheaper and more doable than the current one is. Also, democracy was not alien and conditional like the current one is. Even when the new brand of democracy was introduced in some African countries like Zimbabwe, precolonial leaders were the ones who popularised it based on their experience emanating from precolonial democracy (Makahamadze, Grand and Tayuvanago (2009). Two examples above prove how democracy is not a new thing like computers and airplanes in Africa. What creates mix-ups is the fact that when Europe introduced its brand of democracy considered the power of the majority while eliminating other important things such as consensus in dealing with whatever matter the society is faced with regardless if the decision is reached based on the majority or logic. When it comes to what is natural African democracy, Giuliano and Nunn (2013) define it as "an ancestral ethnic group as having a tradition of democracy if the appointment of the local headman was through either formal consensus or informal consensus" (p. 87). In Zimbabwe, such headmen were known as *vashe* or *induna* while in Nigeria there were different levels such as Alaafin, ogboni, bashorun etc.

Again, how could Europe truly embrace African brand of democracy while its intentions of invading, occupying and colonising Africa were to succeed and meant to portray Africa as a society of *real beasts in real jungle African jungles* (Raskin 2012) whose colonisation and vending was legal before human laws? And democracy does not end up with African only. Out of Africa, for example, Feldman and Martinez (2006) cite an example of Islamic democracy in modern Iraq which does all things other democracies in Africa do such as elections, the rule of the majority and allowing opposition. For, Iraqis, if Islamic democracy meets their aspirations, it makes sense the same way natural African democracy used to do to Africans before it was felled by European colonisers. Essentially, any administrational structure makes sense in the milieu of those using it. This is why it does not make any sense for Africa or the world to be forced to buy into Athens' model of democracy whose application and rationale are different due to the nature and time the said democracy was applied. This democracy did not evolve from the blue. There were enhancing causes and enhancing environment. This is because the aspirations and needs of the Athens' society are different from those of Africa and the world today. Even though what democracy in Athens sought to achieve may be the same, its applicability is totally different due to the fact that those who decided what the concept people means were totally different from those who decide the same today. Like other relative concepts, democracy is not a new concept in African political psyche and traditions. What makes African organic democracy, as the concept, different from the Western one is only Western mindset and superimposition based on Western *holier than thou* mentality whereby everything to make sense must either be defined by the West or be compatible to its creation and take. As you can see in the quote above, for Tswana people, democracy did not only mean the rule of people but the rule that could enable such people to be self-reliant. This is an antithesis to the modern-time democracy in Africa whereby almost all African countries are dependent on Europe for financial support and political tutorage with all matters to do with democracy. If the current world order would be just, methinks, democracy would accommodate this element in order to enable all countries on the world to be self-reliant so as to have self-esteem. And, indeed, had this ingredient been added to the menu, the room for one country to exploit another would be history. Once again, this shows how Africa is not barren, as it has always been deemed and regarded to be, when it comes to international affairs. If Athens, a village at the time, was able to contribute its version of democracy to the world, why is it impossible for the whole country of Botswana to do the same? Again, Botswana is an African country. And, sadly though, for Europe, nothing good and great can come from Africa except its resources.

Apart from Tswana, the neighbouring South African Zulu nation offers more evidence about the fact that democracy is not a new concept in Africa. In Zulu, or isiZulu, democracy is *intando yeningi* (Alberts and Mollema 2013) or the will of the many or majority. What difference does this have from *vox populi vox dei*? Apart from Zulu, there is an African uniting philosophy that is found in all Bantus namely Ubuntu or humanity to mean the equality of humanity universally which is purely democratic. Further, Msila (in preparation) cited in Bush (2007) argues that Ubuntu is rooted in African precolonial society and it espouses the ideal of interconnectedness among people that has links to democracy based

141

on the 'ideal democratic tenet' that contribute to 'a world of moral stability. This is very true based on the fact that under Ubuntu, everything is done based on consensus (Louw 2006) aimed at achieving the harmony of the society but not the majority or minority say. Ubuntu is more advanced than modern democracy provided that it concentrates more on moral uprightness of the person and the society (McAllister 2009) in order to do justice to all members of the society namely Bantus or humans universally which is different from Greece democracy that was adopted from the small *polis* whose view of *demos* was gendered and narrow in that it knew only the citizens of the *polis* of Athênai (Evans 2017) as opposed to Ubuntu which is all encompassing *vis-à-vis* human dignity, equality, justice, rights and existence globally which is still new to Europe.

When it comes to felling African systems, it was done to make sure that European exploitative and capitalistic systems irreparably destroy (Arowolo 2010); and thereby take over from African egalitarian systems. However, it should be noted that when colonial powers and their agents arrived, apart from destroying African already-established systems, they denied their existence so as to create a vacuum that Western systems of managing public affairs replaced for the benefit of Europe. Mimiko (2010:640) cited in Arowolo (*Ibid.*) maintains that Africa had its "sophisticated systems of political rule" with strong democratic foundations long before coming into contact with Europe; and these systems were relatively developed and advanced. Due to this sophistication, Europe felt threatened. Therefore, to get what it wanted, it had to destroy them and cause chaos and confusion that offered an opportunity that Europe seized and ruled Africa after deceiving and invading it. What Europe did to Africa is no different from *coup d'état*. It is a *coup de continent* which amounts to *anathema maranatha* or a big curse. The difference however is that a coup can be put down or be brought down through mass actions. This did not happen for Africa. Also, a coup is always carried out by the group of people who are legally citizens of a certain country which, at least, makes sense wherever there is bad governance such a group seeks to dispose and replace as it was in Burkina Faso in 1983 under Thomas Sankara or recently in Burkina Faso for the second time and Zimbabwe.

Actually, what Europe committed in Africa is beyond comparison. Call it thuggery or anything like it. For, when thugs invade someone's house kill, maim even rape, rob and destroy everything so as to leave everlasting pains economically, financially and socially. This is exactly what Europe did. It killed our kings, chiefs, and ways of life, economy, institutions and wellbeing while it retained the same in Europe. What will happen if today someone overthrows and kills all kings and their institutions in Europe? Obviously, everything will crumble. If anything, this is what happened to Africa after its leaders and institutions were felled to give room to European ones. If you ask a British today why the United Kingdom (UK) is still under the monarch in the 21st century, he or she will tell you that the monarch is the symbol of the country. Despite being expensive to maintain, British have made sure that monarchy goes on as the way of maintaining their cohesion and traditions through being a "pinnacle of an aristocratic social hierarchy" (Dickinson 2008: 12). Again, when it comes to African kings, queens and chiefs whose roles and significance were no different from their European counterparts, national cohesion or national identity and symbol did not make any sense. How could Europe care about African national cohesion while its mission was to destroy the very same nation so as to occupy and colonise it? The same has been ongoing even with the modern African states that have never meant anything to Europe except to be impetus that Europe can exploit and use as pleased under the so-called the international community. You can easily see this on how African leaders are not respected by European counterparts simply because they are from Africa. This is why sometimes I wonder say when I see the Prime Minister of Israel or the leader of Palestine are received in Western countries with more respect that the leader of the DRC. Yes, just imagine such small and dependent countries are valued more than the country that has contributed hugely to make Europe rich and developed than any country on earth. It is like a criminal who hijacks somebody and his family. After successfully doing so, the criminal may kill some of unwanted or potentially dangerous members of the family, disturb their ways of life so as to starve and suffocate his victims. Interestingly, this siege took many years before

143

coming to an end. I, therefore, strongly concur with Mimiko due to the fact that Europe built on these systems in the running of the colonies. There is evidence strongly suggesting that many colonial governments in Africa were run by Africans supervised by colonial agents. Had there been no developed and advanced systems–it is obvious–that colonial aims would nosedive. Essentially, after colonising Africa, European colonisers used the same Africans and their systems to smoothly run day-to-day business.

When it comes to how mature and sophisticated African systems were at the time Africa came into contact with Europe. Claessen and Henri (1987: 210 cited in Mhango 2016c) cite an example of the empire of Dahomey whose administrational setting was so much complicated that it awed Europeans in their first encounter. Although the denial has gone on, many African empires were so sophisticatedly arranged that no administrational vacuum existed. Another example can be drawn from the kingdom of Buganda. The teleology of Buganda kingdom shows that it has no difference from the European kingdoms of the time (Uwizeyimana 2012) or the modern-time British kingdom thanks to having the finest-culture that the world has ever known (Jackson 2015). For, when European colonial powers arrived in Uganda, they were shocked to find that Buganda's administration was more like British one. There was a king (Kabaka) on the top followed by the Prime minister (Katikiro) and the parliament (Lukiiko) (Apter 2013) which are the emblematic institution of the state in modern British kingdom. Many Western thinkers tend to argue that Africa did not have democracy which is a little bit weird if we underscore the fact that there is not difference between the former and the latter in this matter.

For the matters of clarity, Apter goes on to list down the position that existed in Buganda administration from the King or Kabaka, prime minister or Katikiro, Bajosi, Bakungu and many more whom either the king appointed or were elected by their people to represent them in the parliament. Isn't this democracy if at all British government is democratic despite having the same formation? To prove that democracy is not a new thing to Africa, Buganda kingdom has a motto saying that ""that the country is its people and the common people are the majority and the rulers are the minority"

144

(Summers 2014: 30); also see Tuck and Rowe (2005). Apart from having thriving democracy, Buganda had all important instruments of the states. Summers (*Ibid.*) succinctly notes that:

> Their loyalty was not simply to clans or king, or to some stereotypical tribe, but to an identity with modern substance and symbols that included a parliament, courts, police, and other bureaucratic institutions, along with elections, a flag, and a national anthem, within a region that was a regional administrative and commercial center (p. 27).

Once again, this shows how the so-called modern systems of administration are not new to Africa. Instead, in some kingdoms, it was engrained on human psyche. This is why there are no records that show Africa once borrowed systems of managing its affairs from anybody at any time before being colonised. Again, after everything was felled, Africa started to heavily depend on exploitative neoliberalism and aid from those who exploited and destroyed it; after being forced to do so. This has been ongoing ever since. And essentially, this volume seeks to deconstruct such a tendency and dependency so that Africa can tailor its own policies of managing its affairs.

In a nutshell, democracy is not like a fashion that can be imported. Once democracy is imported, as it has been the case in Africa, apart from becoming expensive, it remained foreign funded by foreign powers that use it for their interests as opposed to the interests of its hosts. Every society is supposed to have its administration and management models and systems based on its environment and interests. Helgesen (2002) discloses that imported democracy has failed to accommodate the community-shared values which are based in natural political order based on the culture, mores, needs and aspirations of the society.

Chapter Six

How Africa's Underdevelopment Became a Myth to Save Europe

In trying to tackle the above heading, we will start with a question as the foundational hunch and a window into the issue at hand. The question we are asking is: Is Africa truly and desperately dependent, poor and underdeveloped as its detractors have always ridiculously defined it? This question is crucially mind-boggling so to speak. However, the answer to the question why Africa is underdeveloped may differ from one person to another, of all; Africa needs to provide not only an answer but also an accurate answer. While many academics have tackled the problems resulting from the so-called Africa's underdevelopment, much remain to be seen *vis-à-vis* providing the accurate and pragmatic answer that will be employed to do away with such a manmade impasse. The move to move Africa out of the Western-defined underdevelopment academically speaking needs to start theoretically then pragmatically all based on dynamic human nature. Mawere (2010) argues applying the theory of evolution to pin down the fact that the purpose of life for any human has never been static. Again, if this is the real situation, why has African been vacuously deemed, unfairly categorised and permanently been viewed as a static continent while human nature dictates that human life is always dynamic whether consciously or otherwise? Why do Africa's doomsters and prophets of doom contradict this logically, simple, clear and understandable human nature? Is there any malice against Africa all geared by the quest of exploiting it forever as it has been the archaic and colonial view of it? Arguably, Mawere's argument, apart from being powerful, is true and provocative, especially for those who have always underrated Africa so as to relegate it to their manmade underdevelopment. This is where the importance of formulating a definition that reflects the reality of things is needed. This is where the quest of questioning Western frameworks and thinkers who formulated the current definition of development is important, largely for Africans who, in a sense, are the victims of this very categorisation based on colonial standards and criteria as espoused by Western thinkers.

It is, therefore, from this milieu that this chapter seeks to challenge the so-called Africa's underdevelopment that has ignored its root causes emanating from colonialism and slavery that Europe carried out on Africa for many decades. The chapter will show how such a conclusion is maliciously concocted in order to make Africa believe that it is naturally dependent while, to the contrary, it was pauperised by Europe for its own development. In so doing, I question the legality-cum-rationale of those who assign such a tag and role to Africa without underscoring some other vital elements in reaching such a conclusion; which, in all honesty, lacks credibility; especially for the victims of such international conspiracy against Africa. Hereunder, I explore some aspects of defining Africa as an underdeveloped continent while it is richly endowed and sits on immense resources such as rivers, people, markets, minerals, gas, oil, fertile land, and forests, among others that have always benefited unthankful Europe.

How Who Defines What, How and Why Negatively Impacted on Africa

"... 'romanticism', though it continued through the nineteenth century and very much influenced social and economic theorists and politicians, is tangential to the doctrine which I will call populism," Kitching (2010: 2).

The quote above summarises all three elements this chapter is going to delve in *vis-à-vis*, political and socio-economic facets of Europe's development and the [under-development in Africa. As Kitching nicely asserts, development has been doctored, romanticised and essentialised not to mention being monopolised by the one side, the West, that superimposes its *diktat* on others as it ignores its unfair trajectory that enabled it to achieve such level of *development*. Although the terms development seems to largely depend on biased and controversial Eurocentric and materialistic definition[s], however narrow, romanticised and highly propounded and protected, it is now a universal phenomenon despite its weakness of superimposing them to all countries of the world to follow Europe's trajectory, (Kitching *Ibid.*) without highlighting the importance of manner in which it was attained, time and history of the victims of the terms. Friedmann (1967), for example, argues that the general underpinnings of the theory of economic development appear to be a fundamental requirement for greater autonomy rather than as an end in itself. This means that development is not supposed to be monopolised or superimposed on others. Instead, development needs to be defined clearly as oxygen is defined. So, too, development is not supposed to be narrow, tyrannical and prejudiced. It is supposed to be as attractive as beauty, happiness and wealth are. Looking at the type of development Europe has always envisaged, espoused and superimposed on Africa, its definition based on theories and practices show some missing links. Where is the autonomy, for countries whose development is defined by others? Thanks to populistic academic psyche, there is no way I can avoid scooping from other definitions however academically poisonous they might be. Therefore, I cannot avoid or ignore them for my peril. In this chapter, I address the history of Africa based on cultural imperialism and religion as the agents of [under] development for Africa; and agents of development for Europe; mainly from the time colonialism and slavery were introduced to Africa, up until now, under neocolonialism. I will try as much as I can to icepack my assessment which is very hard to do.

First of all, the term development is relative; and needs to be qualified by answering the question: Development or underdevelopment in what? This chapter seeks to address three facets of African continent namely, economically, politically and socially.

Secondly, whatever definition one uses is situational and inferential due to the fact that there is no agreed meaning or definition of the concept.

Third, when it comes to development, as an ambiguous, relative and insufficient term as it arguably is, we need to redefine it in order to give the readership the tool with which to understand what is postulated or propounded. For the purpose of this discourse therefore, development means, *inter alia,* the attainment of high standard, quality or level in anything someone does or pursues provided it is legal and acceptable for the benefit of humanity and the person him/herself. Philips (1977) maintains that there is no satisfactory definition of development that does not imply capitalism even in the most technological definition not to mention the same to be the case epistemologically and culturally. Phillips goes on arguing that, to the contrary, underdevelopment is wrongly and biasedly viewed as an original state of things simply because it has to be measured based on the lenses of the so-called developed countries that appointed to themselves the status to themselves in order to bully and exploit others based on utopian struggle to attain development.

Fourth, differently from others, my definition of development revolves around the improvement of human wellbeing but not material attainment. I live in the so-called developed country, Canada. Whenever I see how animal rights are protected however manipulatively, I suspect term, chiefly when I remember human beings who are left out of this development. One would candidly say that if humans are sincerely serious in protecting animals' rights, would stop eating and taming them. I, sometimes, wonder how animals can have more rights and expensive rights than humans in some areas of the world. One day, we were casually talking about animal rights. One Aboriginal boy told me that animal rights' activists pretend to protect animal rights while they abuse them by keeping them as pets for their exploitation, gratification and satisfaction without necessarily underscoring that they naturally were created to live and roam free in the wilderness as they 'abuse and trample on Aboriginal people's God-given rights as the true owners of this land invaders call theirs. This assertion stimulates the discussion in point based on development or otherwise whether it should hinge on humanity or materiality resulting from quintessential human coloniality and individuality.

Even when it comes to development of Europe as opposed to the underdevelopment of Africa, sometimes, I feel left out, especially when I remember how children in Africa are taught to care about environment. Here I see in public places where people abuse utilities such as water and papers to indicate that they are either selfish or do not know that doing so causes harm to mother earth. Sometimes, people are too lazy and too ignorant to grasp little things which have huge impacts on the world such as frugality, collectivity of humanity, morality and whatnots. Furthermore, when I consider how people consume stupidly not to mention throwing a lot of food to trash, I doubt the whole concept of development and civilisation. The *Globe and Mail* (1 October, 2012) reports that Canadians waste approximately 40 per cent of food, or $27-billion worth annually, according to the *Value Chain Management Centre*, an independent think tank based in Guelph, Ontario Canada. And just over half (51 per cent) of that gets tossed from households. If a country with small population of approximately 40 million throws away such a humungous amount of food, how many tons of food the so-called developed countries push to the trash annually simply because they do not care about others; leave alone chronic and unnecessary consumerism? Apart from Canada, Vaughn (2011) notes that when it comes to committing the offence of food destruction American families are among the worst offenders due to the findings which show that an average family of four throws out $600 worth of good food every year, and that 14% of that is food that has not expired or even been packaged (p. 4). Statistically speaking, the scale of food destruction is sacrilegious by all standards. Lipinski, Hanson, Lomax, Kitinoja, Waite, and Searchinger (2013) disclose that the *Food and Agriculture Organisation of the United Nations* (FAO) estimates that 32 percent of all food produced in the world was lost or wasted in 2009 (p. 5). Despite such criminality and recklessness, those committing this crime still pride themselves to be developed. What are they developed if they cannot underscore such a simply but crucial matter?

The above hedonism tells us what Europe has always done without the regard of Africa that it exploited for decades; not to mention currently, when the same Europe has introduced GMO foods to top up the loss it has already caused to Africa by destroying its soil and its small farmers through the introduction of artificial fertilisers (Vanlauwe and Giller 2006). Apart from causing soil degradation, artificial or chemical fertilisers cost Africa a fortune. Sanchez and Swaminathan (2005) cited in Lal (2009) disclose that Africa loses, at least, US $4 billion in fertilisers. However, there are some authors who think the introduction of artificial fertilisers is the way to go for Africa simply because it doubles production (Sanginga and Woomer 2009) but not problems as it has already proved to be. Despite such dangers, as opposed to the gains, Europe still makes a killing by selling the same poisonous stuff to Africa under the ploy of developing Africa. What type of development is this if we face it? While developed countries are throwing food to the trash, the report by the World Bank issued in 2012 discloses that Africa had as many as 19 million people living with the threat of hunger and malnutrition in West Africa's Sahel region. Good news is: the same report said that Africa can feed itself and generate an extra US$20 billion in yearly earnings if African leaders can agree to dismantle trade barriers that blunt more regional dynamism. However, FAOSTAT (2011 cited in Rakotoarisoa, Iafrate, and Paschali 2011) notes that, in 1980, Africa had an almost balanced agricultural trade when both agricultural exports and imports were at about USD 14 billion, but by 2007 its agricultural imports exceeded agricultural exports by about US$ 22 billion (p. 1). Again, how could one blame our people in the so-called developed world while neoliberal policies as Europe enacted them encourage them to consume ravenously as a sign of development simply because European businesses can make more dollars? Consider this. Fast foods claim many lives in this part of the world. Yet, the governments do not ban them simply because the companies selling such poisonous foods pay taxes.

No doubts that some of Africa's quandaries resulting to the so-called its underdevelopment that the exploitation by Europe caused can, *inter alia*, be divided into two categories. The first causes can be attributed to colonial legacies almost in all spheres of life namely economic, political and social in which Africa is culturally, geographically, historically and racially discriminated against so as to be easily exploited (Mhango 2015). Since 1884, when Africa was divided into small and feeble states, as noted hereinabove, its precolonial economic systems became extinct. Africans who used to live in collectivistic society were exposed to individualistic ways of life whereby every new country created at the Berlin Conference 1884 started to act solo for its peril and the peril of all. And whenever such a country needed partners in whatever encounter, it looked at its former colonial masters but not neighbours and sister states. This exposed African countries to more exploitation that their former colonial masters, and now emerging powers, are using to exploit them even more. You can see this in the economic and political models African countries applied and employed after acquiring their political independence. After being curved out, African countries were divided along their former colonial masters whose languages, cultures and interests they took and applied in their countries for their peril. Further, after gaining their independences in the sixties for many, almost all African countries were additionally divided into two camps namely the West or East camp during the Cold War. Moreover, after the end of the cold war, Africa is not out of the woods yet. It is still divided along its sovereignty; which every country clings on for fear of losing out to others. Ironically, despite knowing the danger of their divisions, African countries have failed to reunite Africa to the tune it was before the Berlin Conference (Mhango *Ibid.*) simply because they are still labouring and the colonial carryovers. By maintaining colonial divisions, Africa seems to suffer even more economic and political setbacks under the unipolarity than it did under the cold war period; in which the former Union of Soviet Socialist Republics (USSR) and China used to support some countries in deterring the influence of the West that supported countries on its fold and vice versa. Currently, such aid is no more forthcoming however hazardous it was for Africa due to the fact that it was given to serve the interests of the donors but not recipients. Corsetti, Guimaraes, and Roubini (2006) refer to this as a 'moral hazard', principally when he deals with how aid has cost Africa greatly. After the cold war came to an end, aid, now, is tied to neoliberalism whose drive is democracy for development however illusory it may be. Presently, Africa is under multiparty democracy that its former colonial masters superimposed on it. Economically, Africa's countries have always depended on Western countries in the relationship in which Africa plays the role of natural material supplier and consumer of processed goods from the same countries it supplies its natural or unprocessed resources. To make matter worse, China and Russia that used to support some African countries simply because they were in their camp, are now scrambling for Africa with the West; all aimed at keeping on enjoying its cheap resources.

As argued above, despite Africa playing a vital role of being a raw material supplier and processed goods consumer, is it really underdeveloped or poor? How so with such abundant resources? Why those defining development do not include untapped resources or vibrant cultures that Africa boasts of having? For, development or underdevelopment is the product of socio-economic and political culture of the people or society. Porter (2000) observes that "economic geography in an era of global competition involves a paradox. It is widely recognised that changes in technology and competition have diminished many of the traditional roles of location" (p. 15). This means that traditional roles that have been felled by global competition based on hegemonic neoliberal policies guarantees the exclusion of such roles in defining development based on core (Europe) and periphery (Africa) (Tickner 2013). Such characterisation is obvious in that development is, mainly defined based on geographic locations in that the core is seen as more developed than the periphery. This take is not empirical due to the arguments above but it is socially constructed as it aims at reinforcing hegemony and colonial understanding as realities while they actually are not. For, if you look at the so-called Western countries, you find that some are in north others are in West. To get away with murder, such countries are either defined under the axis of North-South or West-East if not the First, Second and Third worlds. There cannot permanently be the first, second and third world in everything. Somebody can be first in something while another can be second or third and vice versa but not orthodoxly first or last as it is currently.

How [Under] Development is and Whose Needs Matter?

Whether Africa is underdeveloped, thus dependent or not, all depends on the definition, lenses and means one uses to reach at such a conclusion. So, too, it depends on who is making such an evaluation; and why it is done. Therefore, in evaluating Africa's *underdevelopment*, one can get many different answers depending on what is included or excluded in the evaluation. In this chapter, I am addressing the centrality of basic human needs by delving and dwelling on whose rights are accommodated and whose rights are forgone *vis-à-vis* Europe and Africa respectively in order to gauge who is developed and who is not.

Arguably, the question whether Africa is truly underdeveloped or not is more a dichotomous matter–that needs us to look at both sides of the coin–instead of wholesomely making such a wanting conclusion; while, purposely avoiding or ignoring root causes among which is the role Europe played in attaining its development that resulted into the underdevelopment of Africa. Ignoring such a historical reality makes the whole regimes of human rights a hoax and meaningless if not a white elephant. For those who maintain that Africa is comparatively underdeveloped know the reason[s] among which is the one that Rodney (1972) maintains that it is exploitation, but not evolution, in the main, Europe created and benefited from without even admitting it so as to do something about it. So, arguing that Africa is poor because Europe is rich is not a farfetched reason due to the fact that the successes and failures of the duo are interrelated and interconnected in causals; and, possibly solutions; shall justice be done, particularly for the victim. Indeed, Africa was made poor–something that has pointlessly gone on up till now–so as to be deemed as underdeveloped as opposed to Europe's development thereof.

However, when we critically and honestly interrogate the components, criteria and the true meaning of development based on human basic needs (Maslow 1970: 25 cited in Pittman and Zeigler 2007), sometimes, we see very different realities (Seidlhofer 2009) in different ways and rationale which fundamentally affect our conclusions and answers to the problems altogether. For, despite sharing needs, human beings have diverse needs; all depending on their cultures, time, priorities and, above all, choices. Even the way they make sense of things is totally different. For example, Europe's needs after plundering Africa for many years are completely different from Africa's. While the latter needs to make right all wrongs the former committed to it by revisiting the history of this criminality; the former needs to admit its criminal liability; and thereby redress the latter. Importantly, one of the basic human needs is security based on essential amenities as needed and required by all human beings equally globally. All human beings have the same basic or primary needs such as clothing, food, shelter and dignity. What differs is the priority about how to get them and in what sequence. We all need dignity, shelter, right to identity, food, clothing and the likes equally. Despite security being a self-explanatory concept, when it comes to how to achieve it, culture and history, *inter alia*, play a very important role. We achieve and understand security differently based on our aspirations, assumptions and needs. For example, people from collectivistic societies expect to get the guarantee of their security in every aspect of their lives from the society while for people from the individualistic societies, security is a personal matter as opposed to collectivistic societies in which the same is more a collective societal than personal matter. Even the ways the two perceive security are totally different. This concept of security is invoked in order to show how people from two culturally-antithetical societies above evaluate security; and thus, development, very differently. For the member of hunter community in the Kalahari Desert in Namibia, security means everything that contributes to the survival of the entire group as a whole while, to the contrary, in the Western societies, security can be guaranteed by having a gun, an account or accounts in the bank, freedom from others' benefiting from or interfering with whatever an individual purchases, owns or robs from others as it was in slavery and colonialism which Europe used to make Africa insecure economically, politically for its security, as I have proved above, based on the results of these two crimes. So, while security is the quest for all groups, its actualisation and realisation are completely different. In a group of hunters or a collectivistic society, security is actualised and, largely depends on and the interconnectedness and interdependence of the group while in the latter, it absolutely depends on one's independence. Likewise, development and underdevelopment can be viewed differently whereby, in the collectivistic society moral attachment, social capital, trust, sharing, connectivity and interdependence are means and guarantees to development just as they are in the realisation of security as opposed to the individualistic society in which security is a private matter.

More so, in collectivistic societies, development or lack of it is more a moral issue while in individualistic societies it is a material matter. Therefore, the angle this chapter takes *vis-à-vis* the underdevelopment of Africa as opposed to Europe's development resulting from Europe's plunder of Africa is fundamentally based on the history of the duo; and the archaic nature of the international system governing development and the *realpolitik* of the current world that tends to ally with individualistic culture as opposed to collectivistic culture. Ironically however, when it comes to exploiting and robbing Africa, individualistic Europe adopts collectivistic behaviour by working unitedly to keep tabs on Africa. In doing so easily, the same Europe forces Africa to act individually by dealing with African countries severally. This is why this corpus encourages African countries to keep their collectivistic culture and nature in pursuing justice from Europe. Further, the victims of international conspiracy, bias and Europe-engineered underdeveloped need to question, with all determination, the yardsticks used to defining and assessing Africa's underdevelopment without necessarily considering its causes or history behind it. The need to question the logic of choosing some components of development while ignoring or excluding others that inculpate Europe is vital shall we aspire to treat one another deservedly; and thereby do justice by forcing Europe to return or pay for what it robbed Africa. The dialogue resulting from such questioning and negotiating how the process is conducted will eventually help us to get a fitting definition for whatever concept we apply in the process of ranking countries almost in everything.

There is no way Africa that contributed comprehensively to the development of Europe–and still does–can get out of the manmade economic underdevelopment and impasse it is in without deconstructing the definitions, rationales and systems by which categories, conclusions and ranks are reached. For development or underdevelopment to be meaningful and make sense, all stakeholders need to be involved in the process by deciding the terms and parameters to be used in analysing and defining what they would equally want to call [under]development. We need to know what people, specifically the victims know about these two concepts; and their inputs about how they deconstruct and define them instead of letting Western think-tanks and policymakers alone to decide for others. In this matter, there is no room for one-size-fits-all way of addressing the paradox of Africa's underdevelopment and Europe's development altogether. As you will see later, I wonder to find that, in rating development even materially why, for example, untapped resources such as minerals, lakes, rivers, and wildlife are excluded. This is a material side. Again, it also baffles me more, perhaps even you, to find that nonmaterial assets such as cultural richness are excluded in development rating. Why rating is a big and real deal in this respect? It is simply because of the trauma and privileges attached to it based on location one finds him or herself. For example, Europe and the West in general have used Africa's underdevelopment to bully and exploit it under whatever circumstances. Rogoff (2003) observes that generally and historically, "development is a cultural process" (p. 3) that revolves around the relationship between human and nature (Siraj-Blatchford 2009). Importantly, the question we need to ask is: Who guides and supervises this process; and what criteria are applied in actualising this process of development? For over five decades, Europe has been guiding, supervising and superimposing the process of development in Africa through various tactics such as aid, policies and structural altering and tweaking to no avail. This means that Africa needs to take over the process through exploiting and revisiting its history based on how it was exploited and misled by Europe. This is where the centrality of addressing all historical evils that Europe committed in Africa becomes a tool of emancipation and delivering justice. For, there is no way Africa can develop outside its culture by depending on foreign and superimposed cultures and policies. For Africa to apply and depend on Western culture to develop is as impossible as for a lamb to strive for development by depending on lion's culture or *diktat*. It does not work; as it will never work.

Arguably, once one's culture is destroyed, replaced or subjugate not to mention to be colonised or violated as it was under colonialism chances of attaining desired development are extremely slim. Due to the centrality of culture in development, there is a need of revisiting and unearthing cultural imperialism that Europe exercised over Africa. Africa has been blamed on its underdevelopment without looking at the other side namely Europe that caused it. Rogoff goes further warning that "human development has been based largely on research and theory coming from middle-class communities in Europe and North America" (p. 4) under the current dominant grand narrative that has undeservedly self-appointed to be the diviner of the modern world the position it uses to shield Europe from paying for its sins it committed on Africa. Such a research cannot help Africa to achieve development; and thereby enjoy parity with Europe without necessarily considering the manner in which Europe attained its development. For, time and circumstances do not allow this to happen, especially if we consider how Europe made its development capital by the means of exploiting Africa. How will the concept look like shall Africa be allowed to contribute its inputs based on its culture, history, needs and aspirations?

Although we tend to take the concepts of defining things for granted without interrogating them, the definition[s] plays a vital role in conceptualising; and thereby getting things rightly or wrongly pinned down. If there is anything that Africa got wrong is nothing but to allow Europe to define it almost in everything. Africa has, for many years, been defined by Europe in every aspect. Europe defines Africa as to how it should eat, live, sleep and work without necessarily the latter being given the opportunity either to define itself or define the former. Even when it comes to Africa's economic or political performance, all depends on Europe. I am not quite sure if the statistics about the growth of Africa's economies come from them but not from the IFIs–that, by and large, represent the interest of Europe or the West. This is where the nexus of colonialism and the advantageous position for Europe to lead emanate.

Essentially, a definition, as a concept, dictates how we understand or misunderstand whatever thing or concept that is defined. This is why it has been possible for academia and other players to biasedly or erroneously define the underdevelopment of Africa without necessarily incorporating the development of Europe due to their interrelated causal circumstances and roots. Therefore, it is crucial to interrogate the definitions we use, who defines what, why and how such a thing or concept is defined so. Moreover, we need to have a sort of negotiation about the definitions we use without privileging some to do this for others while denying others the same privilege. The definition is a roadmap for us to conceptualise whatever concept we come across. Therefore, before accepting the definition[s] as it is the case between Africa's underdevelopment and Europe's development and their root causes. We need to subject every definition to some scrutiny and tests to see if it meets and suits what it defines for the benefits of its consumers. As well, when we make a claim that Africa is [under-]developed, we must specify in what ways; how it became underdeveloped, who caused what; and how such a conclusion[s] is reached. For, it does not make any sense, especially for the victims of the current paradigm of [under-]development, for example, to say that a car or house owner is more developed than the person who owns a herd of 100 cows. Development is like beauty which is always in the eyes of the beholder. It is supposed to be unbiasedly evaluated based on somebody's needs, understanding and culture. This is why African traditional fishermen view modern trawlers as useless—due to causing environmental harms resulting from overfishing—compared to their canoes despite catching a few fish compared to the trawlers that are not threatening the future of the world *vis-à-vis* fish supply. What is viewed as development or advancement and betterment in the eyes of one person can be viewed detrimentally different in the eyes of another. This is why Europe and the international community have never practically seen anything wrong in invading, occupying and colonising Africa.

Furthermore, you can see in the concept of taking care of elderly people between the so-called underdeveloped and developed countries. While it is squarely the duty of their children to look after elderly people in Africa, for example, it is different in the so-called developed countries where elderly people are provided with almost all material amenities minus spiritual or moral ones while in Africa is vice versa. What the two societies are doing in this matter is seen as development in the eyes of one and otherwise in the eyes of another. All systems of looking after the elderly persons have its, flaws, strength and shortfalls. What is evident here is the ignorance of the fact that in the two groups, the former provides less material support though it provides more moral support while in the former it is vice versa. The elderly persons living in an air-conditioned house with all

160

amenities minus visitations or human attachment from her their children are materially better but morally worse. So, too, the elderly persons living in a shack with less material support but with abundant social support are morally better but materially worse. In other words the duo is equal save that in ranking the former is seen as doing better than the latter. The bottom line here is simply that we need to negotiate these difference based on both aspects of human needs based on the culture, desire, needs and whatnots of the person in question instead of generalising everything as it if the lenses from the culture we use are the identical and analogous.

However, when it comes to assessing which society is doing better than another, the latter is ranked higher than the former. You can go further; and look at how human rights and animal rights are priotised between the twosomes. Due to its development achieved by the way of fleecing Africa, animals in Europe have more rights than humans in Africa; and this is taken to be normal. Currently, much more emphasis is on protecting endangered animals in Africa than humans. Testifying before the US Senate in 2009, one victim of rape in the DRC Chouchou Namegabe cited in Victoor (2011) notes that:

> The women ask WHY? Why such atrocities? Why do they fight their war on women's bodies? It is because there is a plan to put fear into the community through the woman, because she is the heart of the community. When she is pushed down, the whole community follows. We also ask, Why the silence of the developed countries? When a gorilla is killed in the mountains, there is an outcry, and people mobilize great resources to protect the animals. Yet more than five hundred thousand women have been raped, and there is silence. After all of this you will make memorials and say "Never Again." But we don't need commemorations; we want you to act now (p. 55).

Essentially, based on experiential account by the victim above, it seems that the will even money for protecting animals is palpably available but not the will to stop exploiting Africa. Once again, this is where the assumption and concept of the savage beasts in the African jungle resurfaces as to inform us as to why the plight of

161

women in many African countries facing violent conflict has never been taken seriously by the so-called international community. Had such victims been European or non-African, the situation would have been totally different. Currently, there are two conflicts that seem to busy the world a great deal more. The conflict in Syria and Myanmar (Holt, Jebodh and Gilbert 2015) seem to be given more priorities than the conflicts in the CAR, Darfur (Sudan), the DRC and South Sudan. Ironically, the latter started many years ago before the former.

When it comes to development, the incorporation and inclusion of human needs, understanding of the needs and concepts are essential among which are the right for justice for Africa and the duty for Europe to redress Africa. A simple example can be drawn from two people namely a doctor who gets much money because of his professionalism and the artist who makes much more money than the doctor, especially in the so-called developed world due to their skills. This claim shows how different things can bring material things however when it comes to rating countries, art and culture are excluded. Arguably, there is no way a people can be [under] developed in everything; otherwise such a conclusion is arrived at/through what Escobar (2011) refers to as the "'colonisation of reality' in which some representations become dominant; and thereby shape indelibly the way in which reality is imagined and acted upon" (p. 5). This is where the complexity and relativity of development as defined by Europe lies. On this note, I propose the inevitable decolonisation of the way the world has been doing things under the current dominant grand narrative in order to do away with the effects of intellectual colonisation and domination Europe has always used to exploit Africa so as to develop while Africa become more and more underdeveloped because of it. I see the current dominant European grand narrative as a culprit for many crimes and evils Africa has suffered. Escobar concurs with Rodney (1972) arguing that the so-called underdevelopment of Africa is basically historical but not real or evolutional. There is no way Africa's former colonial masters could entertain historical factors while they know doing so will expose their ploy that they would like to have internalised by their victims so as to keep on depending on them pointlessly. In others words, we need to 'decolonise reality' based on today's actuality; and the tools we can use *inter alia*, is the decolonisation of education which I argue elsewhere that it is toxic so as to need the process of detoxification. When reality is [mis-]construed, depending on hidden agenda by the one representing it, chances are that hegemonic views are likely to dominate others just as it has been the case in defining the [under] development of Africa without associating it with the development of Europe. It does not make sense to refer a continent with ancient civilisation as underdeveloped while, to the contrary, young civilisations such as Europe whose–successes resulted from crimes such as slavery, colonialism and neo-colonialism they committed against those they categorise as underdeveloped–are referred to as developed countries. This is developmental injustice that the victims need to fight. Allowing such tendency whereby development and underdevelopment are defined and rated by the culprits is so detrimental to the so-called underdeveloped countries. It is like allowing a convict to decide what should happen to those he or she offended. The safest way for such a person to be free is to condemn his victims. And all this is possible due to the propaganda machinery neocolonialism has always put in place to safeguard its interests as opposed to those of others in this concoction, reinvention or the creation of otherness (Statszak 2009). As it is in international commerce, the West has always acted as one group against the so-called underdeveloped countries due to its chronic othering tendency championed by neo-liberal policies and neo-colonialism.

In essence, arguably, development or underdevelopment is a relative term. Furthermore, development is supposed to include many aspects such as history, civilisation, culture, aspirations and achievements in many areas. Logically, it does not make any sense, for example, to say that Europe is more developed than Egypt, Sudan or Zimbabwe whose civilisations are older than Europe itself as a continent. Development is supposed to be dichotomous, linear and perpendicular by nature in order to accommodate various variables of human society. And the job of defining development is supposed to be inclusive by nature whereby all stakeholders should negotiate and agree upon which definition[s] to be used based on their understanding, culture, mores, needs, and intentions. For example, while South Africa under former Apartheid regime was viewed as economically and technologically more advanced than its neighbours such as Zambia and Zimbabwe, the latter was more advanced as struggles for liberation and human rights were concerned. Again, the West that supported such criminal regime ignored such aspects simply because it had the wherewithal to define the duo based on its alliance and interests. To achieve this, we can apply Self-determination Theory (SDT) which Deci and Ryan (2010, 2011) claim to be an understanding of human motivation and human evolutionary history that require a consideration of innate psychological needs for competence, autonomy and relatedness. As you can see, relationship and autonomy appear in tandem. Therefore, in defining and making sense of Africa's underdevelopment, we need to accommodate these natural human drives towards self-preservation in their environment. Deci and Ryan make a good observation by emphasising psychological human needs as opposed to physiological ones to indicate how psychological needs are more prominent to humans although they are all needed however at different levels. Whether this is true or not, depends on how one looks at these two aspects of needs namely psychological and physiological. So, too, it depends on the culture one is coming from. This is obvious that we are talking of qualitative or more inner needs than outer needs. Here I am talking of nonmaterial as opposed to material human drive all based on one's choice and motivation of doing so.

There can be development in different aspects and areas *vis-à-vis* a particular country or society. Therefore, it misleads to make generalisations as far as development is concerned as is currently the case whereby some countries, that are well off materially, are deemed developed even when they are poor in moral and nonmaterial aspects as I will further indicate. Sometimes, you wonder to find a country with many suicides or deaths resulting from obesity in the high ranks in development. Before putting such a country in high ranks of development, we need to know what is causing such a phenomenon. To add insult to injury, some of these countries are rich economically. Again, when it comes to rating the levels of development, malnutrition is considered while obesity–that results from overfeeding–is not. What is the consequence of the two? I would argue that countries with the absence of suicidal traits should be viewed as doing better than those grappling with the phenomenon even if these countries are economically poor. For, however developed countries boast of having advanced medical services, developed countries facing suicidal problems, need to think twice due to the fact that suicide is mental health matter that many poor countries do not have. Their culture that prevents suicide is their asset just like any other material assets like money and medication.

Economic development should also accommodate justice development. For example, currently, South Africa is viewed as an economic highly developed country in Africa. However, the same South Africa has a big gap between the haves and the have-nots compared to Zimbabwe. What makes South Africa underdeveloped as far as human equality and economic justice are concerned is the fact that the enjoyment of its natural resources revolves around colour whereby the majority indigenous South Africans are poorer than their white-minority counterparts who, in essence, are the products of colonialism that Europe introduced to Africa. May and Govender (1998) note that poverty is not confined to any one race group, but is concentrated among blacks, particularly Africans: 61% of Africans and 38% of Coloureds are poor, compared with 5% of Indians and 1% of White (pp. 2-3). The situation is the same in the so-called most advanced nation on earth, the United States (US), at the same period, where systemic bigotry is on the rise thanks to having rigid and archaic system of apartheid. Dlaker and Neifeh (1997) maintain that the poverty rate for Blacks in 1999 was still about three times the poverty rate for White non-Hispanics (7.7 percent) (v). In terms of economic development, there are some countries that are materially developed but morally underdeveloped or decayed. In addressing the dichotomous nature of development, Weingast (1995) observes the paradoxical nature of the government might be strong in protecting economic rights of its people. Yet, the same may be strong in confiscating properties from their citizens. This is the nature of many governments in the world that are built on Western philosophy. You can see this in the 2007 US during credit

165

crunch when the government spent public money in bailing out lossmaking private companies despite opposition from the citizens who ended up becoming losers simply because the government used its muscles to rob them. Bailout is nothing but corruption based on capitalistic cronyism. Rosas (2006) observes that:

> The hefty costs shouldered by taxpayers and the obvious moral hazard incentives that accompany bank bailouts make it important to understand the conditions under which politicians rescue banks, whereby corporates reciprocate by sponsoring politicians during the campaigns (p. 175).

Corruption in politics has been ongoing for many years all over the world. Again, when it comes to defining corruption by countries or governments, the so-called developed countries are not blamed for such a vice. Had bailout been introduced by Africa, it would have been termed as communism if not socialism; thus needed to be stopped forthwith. As it is in collectivistic versus individualistic behaviourism[s] and mannerism[s], whatever is good for Europe is good for the world; and it is legalised even if it is illegal as we have seen in the cases of slavery, colonialism and neocolonialism. The reason is obvious that Europe is the one that dictates the terms and the definition of the vice. Therefore, it plays *holier than thou* as it has been since colonialism, neocolonialism and neoliberal policies controlled and swamped the world under the so-called international community and its instruments such as the IFIs among others. In whatever aspect of social science, it is wrong to generally categorise countries as developed or otherwise by excluding or ignoring some other vital aspects such as the effects of whatever categorisation on human wellbeing. Human beings are not like machines which need only repair and supply of energy such as electricity or gas. Instead, humans, naturally and equally, need more than material needs. What differs basically is the degree of appreciating or ignoring such significant things. For example, collectivistic societies of which many are found countries ranked as underdeveloped put more premiums on moral things than the individualistic societies whose premium is more on material things than moral ones. Societal cooperation, interdependence and relationships are more important than wealth. And once such things exist in the society, they are regarded as wealth of a sort while in the individualistic such things are insignificant. Tung (2008) argues that it is wrong to assume that culture and society enjoy homogeneity. Thus, individuals from such societies present a very different self-conception depending on independence and interdependence. Such an argument can show how two different societies namely collectivistic and individualistic conceptualise development. For example, for individualistic societies, freedom and security depend on the power an individual has in consumption while in the latter, freedom is not as important as interdependence is in which providing services to others is more important than consumption. So, too, in an individualistic society, personal freedom and security have more importance than in the collectivistic society in which the freedom and security of the person depend on the freedom and security of other members of the society. Therefore, it holds water to argue that, in defining and rating development, such differences need to be reconciled instead of allowing one society to define everything to its advantage based on its standards which is detrimental to the others.

To well provide humans, both material and moral aspects, need to be accommodated in formulating the definitions or categories of advancement, development and underdevelopment. Künzle and Reichert (2011) note that we need to understand that "an object comprises a set of actions and a set of attributes" (p. 4) which factors every definition has to abide with; and thereby accommodates in order to avoid biases. Arguably, in defining anything, important attributes must be a general rule without any exception. For example, you cannot define the behaviour of the governments that, as indicated above, act controversially, lineally or vertically only without interweaving all aspects of its behaviours in order to come up with a balanced, informed and inclusive definition. Such a take invites us to interrogate the development of Europe and the underdevelopment of Africa critically and equally by entertaining and including other missing aspects and attributes such as the history of colonialism and slavery and the effects and impacts they had on Africa's underdevelopment. To take a leaf from Africa, while Western countries have almost everything material any human needs, the situation is contrary in many African countries. Ironically, when it comes to, for example, the prevalence of happiness, the so-called underdeveloped countries outshine the so-called developed countries. According to the *BBC* (13 July, 2006), "the Pacific island nation of Vanuatu is the happiest place on earth, according to a new 'happy planet index." The *BBC* goes on noting that, while Vanuatu claimed the leading in happiness, the UK was languishing in 108th place, below Libya, Iran, and Palestine. Given that humans equally need and seek material and nonmaterial things in order to live happily, how come the aspect of happiness is excluded from evaluating the development of any country? I am talking of happiness or *joie de vivre* or joy of life depending on how a subject experiences and enjoys it. There are many more things to talk about that must be included in defining and evaluating the level of [under] development of any country. For example, why should those who define development or otherwise not consider the peaceability of countries of the world so as to discourage wars resulting from struggle for controlling resources in poor countries in which governments and warlords seek the opportunity to supply the resources to the West and other rich countries in order to become personally rich quickly? Researchers found that the causes-cum-secrets behind Vanuatu's happiness were rooted on the culture of the people based on harmonious coexistence and interdependence which largely lack in the so-called developed countries. Vanuatu's lead turns Western misleading assumptions based on material wealth that happiness is about making choice based on economic muscles (Zautra 2003 cited in Veenhoven 2008) to their heads. As argued above, even in the quest to achieve development, people have different priorities. For example, while individualistic-cum-materialistic Western countries consider material wellbeing as a vital part of development, some countries, especially collectivistic prioritise moral wellbeing before material wellbeing. It baffles to note that a country like the US–with such cities and communities sharply segregated along races–to feature high in the list of the so-called developed countries.

Further, we need to consider non-material things in the logic of development definition due to the fact that African countries cannot compete economically under the current regime of economies in which rich Western countries created an exploitative system that only benefits and serves them at the peril of poor countries like those found in Africa and elsewhere. Apart from this, African pre-modernist economy was butchered when neoliberal policies became the policies of the world chaperoned and championed by the IFIs. How can we expect Africa to provide sound health services as one of the criteria to achieve Western-defined development while, for example, its Traditional Medicinal Knowledge (TMK) was butchered and replaced by Western one? Africa depends on medicines from abroad after losing its own. The consequences of this can be seen on the so-called modern life whereby Africans are dying of obesity–which seriously affects life expectancy–resulting from bad habits they copied from Western countries. Refer to the introduction of MacDonald and other fast foods to Africa under neoliberal policies. Habitually, Africans would not become obese due to the fact that their lifestyles were themselves curative thanks to doing manual activities as opposed to the West where machines took over almost everything. Caballero (2005) argues that there is the high energy demand of manual labour resulting from daily-survival activities that makes it difficult for people to achieve a net positive energy balance so as to gain weight. Again, the situation has now changed dramatically after African ways of life were destroyed. Caballero (*Ibid.*) goes further observing that:

> In more urbanised developing countries with a higher GNP, food scarcity may no longer be the driving factor behind energy intake. Instead, the availability of cheap, energy-dense foods (including those from street vendors and fast-food restaurants) may facilitate the consumption of more calories (p. 1514).

The deluges of cheap-fast foods and GMFs are in fact not an accident. As indicated above, Western companies such as MacDonald, Subway, KFC, Chicken Chef and many more are now making inroads to Africa to make quick bucks at the expense and peril of Africans. Thanks to corruption, dependence and ignorance by African leaders and intellectual domination by the West, despite knowing the dangers such foods pose, nothing is done to address them. Many Africans are blindly taking fast foods and Western lifestyles as modernity while they actually are not, but poisonous. The dangers such a trend poses are higher than anybody can imagine due to the fact that Africa has–ever since the introduction of cultural and political colonialism–always copied almost everything that has to do with modernity from the West. Due to this toxic and exploitative relationship, Africa has never produced anything the West could consume or copy except its resources. Ironically, such is the same player that rates world countries in development. Do you think can there be anything good from Africa apart from its resources and consumption market?

The scenario presented above clearly shows how many terms we use tend to be controversial and wanting. Considering this fact, therefore, I may argue that Africa's underdevelopment is an inflicted-cum-self-inflicted wound due to the fact that it allowed others to define it; and in so doing, there are many crucial factors on human development that seem to be–either purposely or out of ignorant–left out in the definition of [under] development. Allowing the development of Africa to be defined by others offers an opportunity for them to ignore many important aspects that are supposed to be included in the definition of development. Sometimes, I wonder to find that a dazzlingly multicultural society like Africa to be referred to as undeveloped. Essentially, this is what colonialism and hegemony are all about. What do you expect when you play in your enemies hands expecting her or him to [re]define you? It has never made any sense for me as a thinker to concur with those who draw propagandist conclusions that Africa is poor and underdeveloped which is without considering what made it poor and underdeveloped not to mention ignoring its immense resources and rich culture and its peaceability. How if Africa sits on hugely vast resources? Again, when you allow somebody else to define you, he or she will define you according to his interests, terms and wishes. Gordon (2016) cites an African proverb saying that "until the lions [prey] produce their own historian, the story of the hunt will glorify only the hunter." Arguably, there is no way the story of the prey can make any meaningful sense without being corroborated with the factual and true rebuttal story of the prey as opposed to the story of the predators. Therefore, it is sacrilegiously scandalous for Africans to keep on believing that the story of their poverty and underdeveloped after over fifty years of shedding colonial chains can be accurately told by his-story on Africa written in Europe. It defies logic for Africans to accept their poverty and underdevelopment without questioning the development of Europe that Africa, pre-eminently enabled to take place. You do not need to be an ace economist to comprehend that Africa has always been mistreated almost in every sphere of life in order to be easily exploited due to its disunity and divisions as the colonial masters superimposed; and thereby, reinforced them so as to be internalised by Africans either through ignorance or manipulations carried out by their own governments run by their own people. Before concurring with any definition, we need to ask many questions such as what is the definition all about, what agreed-upon criteria have been used and why. Being at home with being defined by others is as good as committing suicide intellectually, economically, politically and socially. It is the only dog and other pets that allow humans to define them but not humans.

As argued above, Africa suffers from twofold causes of what is defined to be its underdevelopment in which there are some external and internal factors leading to a misleadingly generalised conclusion. Thus, it is our aim to address both causes namely external and internal ones. Englebert (2000a, 2000b cited in Nunn 2007) observes that "imposed post-colonial institutions explain a significant proportion of the underdevelopment of the countries of sub-Saharan Africa" (p. 2) based on and geared by their hidden agendas. This is why the fact that there are some inadequacies that are arbitrarily applied on defining Africa based on the imposition makes more sense. It is true; especially if we underscore the fact that Africa's successes and failures have always been defined and measured by Europe or the West by using the International Financial Institutions (IFIs) such as the International Monetary Fund (IMF) and the World Bank (WB) among others imperialistic tools of reinforcing modern imperialism (Grocott and Grady 2014). Instead of drawing the conclusion on whether Africa is truly poor and underdeveloped or not, we need to underscore the causes and reasons of such a predicament-cum-impasse based on Europe's interplay and history of exploitation of Africa. For the person who used to be rich, but later became poor after being robbed by thugs, his or her history of impoverishment does not become accurate if the acts committed by thugs are expunged from it. Everything that happens must have the reason[s]. As argued above that development is a relative term. So, too, the causes of Africa's predicaments are relative in that some are internal while others are external; however external ones have profound negative impacts on the internal ones due to their gravitas. Henceforth, it is our duty to trace the causes of Africa's underdevelopment even though the said underdevelopment is controversial. This take is important. For, it is aimed at avoiding romanticising everything the Europe has produced as it has been for the so-called modernism as opposed to the pre-modernism that has always been romanticised as a magic bullet even where it is a stumbling block as far as the true history of Africa and the world at large is concerned. There is some underdevelopment and development in both Africa and Europe under whatever lens is used just like in any mortal society. Importantly, we need to consider such causes of poverty, thus underdevelopment in real terms but not factious ones; whereby other crucial aspects of the society–that would hugely contribute in defining true development truly; and thus true ranking–are ignored or purposely excluded.

In analysing Africa's underdevelopment, we need to avoid being brainwashed (Ferim 2012 and ROŽŇÁK (2016) or brain-corrupted. For, if we labour under such phenomena, we will be easily cowered so as to fail to stand what is obviously right in that there was no way Europe would have made such strides in development without Africa's. Patnaik (2005) notes that despite the elimination of "colonial drain", ex-colonies kept on paying for the consequences of their history even after gaining independence. In other words, it does not make any sense to rate any victim country in development without considering the consequences of its history in the first place. So, too, for whoever that wants to appropriately address the *underdevelopment* of Africa, must first and foremost address this external factor based on historical and current concocted realities as far as relationship between Africa and its former colonial masters is concerned, especially on defining development. This is crucial due to the fact that many so-called developed countries, Europe in particular, achieved development by robbing Africa. Essentially, it takes two to tango. The question we need to ask ourselves is: What has Africa done; and still does to do away with such suffering from historical consequences? How much has Africa lost to Europe for such a period? As urged above, the first and foremost, suitable step out of this impasse is for Africa to define itself instead of allowing its exploiters and enemies to define it as it has been since the introduction of colonialism.

Chapter Seven

How Aid Became another European Hypnotic Tool in Africa

For many years Europe has made Africa to believe that it cannot live without aid. This is contrary to what Africa used to be before colonialism. Africa was self-reliant; and used to live free of aid. However, currently, many African corrupt and inept rulers believe that they cannot survive without aid. For, through aid, such rulers are able to rule their countries. Actually, without aid extended by their masters in Europe and elsewhere, however conditional it is, they cannot pay their armies, government employees and sustain their and families, friends and courtiers' expensive lifestyles despite collecting taxes from their poor citizens. Ironically, Africa sits on immense resources so as to become one of world's richest and superpower *vis-à-vis* resources. Yet, it has the poorest population. Why? First, Africa lacks priorities and right vision. For, when it comes to development, Africa is still at the receiving end. The IMF and the World Bank (WB), as colonial agents and institutions, have made sure that Africa is perpetually bullied and exploited. Loomba (2015) cites Joseph E. Stiglitz, Nobel laureate and once Chief Economist at the WB maintaining that the IMF's methodology in dealing with developing countries has no border with a colonial ruler. What else can we add if such words are coming from the horse's mouth? Through their colonial drives, the International Financial Institutions (IFIs), as they are referred to despite being purely and imperialistic organisations, have made sure that Africa remains colonised, especially through using local colonisers and bad policies that have never added up to Africa. Thanks to such neo-economic colonialism, Africa is viewed as underdeveloped either measured by its own standards or neo-imperialistic ones.

Whether Africa is developed or underdeveloped or not, considering factors such as corruption, bad governance, bad services, big governments and the like, sometimes, underdevelopment definition entices based material-underdevelopment considerations.

To the contrary however, when it comes to humanity, Africa still has something to offer. Mhango (2015) argues that Africans who were enslaved in the Americas contributed a lot in the highly touted industrial revolution due to the fact that they produced surplus that enable colonial Europe to sit down and invent; which is obvious; if we consider the size of the number of slaves who worked without any payment for many years in the Americas. Mhango goes on to put the number of Africans who were shipped to the Americas at the range of 9 to 12 million without including many more who died at sea on their way to the Americas or those who were shipped to other places. Essentially, slave trade derailed Africa as far as technological and innovation are concerned. Bairoch (1993: 8) cited in Nunn (2007) concurs with Mhango noting that "there is no doubt that a large number of negative structural features of the process of economic underdevelopment have historical roots going back to European colonization" (p. 139) and slavery. For, the Africans who were shipped to the Americas were energetic and young people who would have produced more for Africa if they were not shipped to the Americas and elsewhere; not to mention resources colonialism robbed Africa for a long time. Nunn goes on arguing that the trans-Atlantic slave trade alone saw approximately 12 million slaves exported from Africa whereas another 6 million were exported in the other three slave trades (p. 142). Such findings expand the number of the victims of slavery. Nunn (2008 cited in Nunn 2011 and Wantchekon) maintains that the slave trade, which occurred over a period of more than 400 years, had significant knock on and negative effects on long-term economic development for Africa and Africans while, to the contrary, the same trade had positive effects on Europe that resulted to its development as opposed to Africa's underdevelopment.

If we consider the dangers slaves faced and the ordeals they suffered and went through, chances are that over 50 million Africans perished at sea, mainly if we consider how rudimentary ships, dungeons and the handling of slaves were. Another element that must be considered is the length of the journey. Remember; boats or ships that ferried slaves had no doctors or medical services on board. When a slave fell sick, the solution was to throw him or her over board. This was the then slavery. When it comes to the fact that Africa lost energetic, intelligent and healthy population, the same is repeated in modern slavery whereby African academics go for greener pastures in Western countries. The United Nations Educational, Scientific and Cultural Organisation (UNESCO) cited in Oyelere (2007) puts the number of educated Africans in the diaspora at 300,000 of who 10% are PhD holders. This is not a small number for a poor continent like Africa. Interestingly, while such *crème de la crème* is rotting in the diaspora, Africa has a big deficit of the same. I say that many of these are rotting in the diaspora due to the fact that many end up driving taxis or doing menial and lowest-paying jobs that do not correspond with their qualifications which is another type of exploitation. Europe knows too well. It will go on benefiting from exploiting such African professionals thanks to the corrupt systems it created in Africa as it is manned by its stooges in power. Therefore, out of necessity, despite knowing the ramifications of what they are doing to their continent and themselves, African scholars and professionals that are suffering in Europe have no choice. Once, again, Africa is developing Europe. Take this example. Many fake money makers from Europe go to Africa and are awarded high-paying jobs as experts even if some have less qualification. Naicker, Plange-Rhule, Tutt, and Eastwood (2009) note that the United Nations Conference on Trade and Development has estimated that each migrating African professional represents a loss of $184,000 to Africa; and the financial cost to South Africa is estimated at $37 million. Moreover, Africa spends $4 billion a year on the salaries of foreign experts (p. 62). Such injustices cannot be left to thrive simply because neoliberal policies subscribe to it. Something needs to be done to avoid creating many more unnecessary violent conflicts resulting from injustices and exploitation.

Apart from Africa contributing to the industrial revolution, we need to underscore the fact that African commerce, institutions, ways of life and all other ingredients of a free and able society were felled to give room to colonialism, neocolonialism and neoliberalism for the benefit of Europe as opposed to that of Africa. To know how advanced and developed Africa was, try to imagine. Who offered any aid or handouts, loans and whatnot to precolonial Africa? Who treated Africans so as to become healthier than others and be enslaved? There were institutions and systems that ran Africa swiftly and efficiently. Here I am talking of institutions. There is evidence all over the place to suggest that Africa taught Europe metallurgy, especially iron smelting (Young and Sessine 2000; and Blakely 2006) which Africans started many years before Europe which was so ignorant so as to regard the Americas as the new world while it actually was not. Again, due to European *holier-than-thou* mentality, what Europe did not know was not known to anybody. This is why everything that is not known to Europe is taken as if it is not known to the entire world. Regarding commerce and international relations and links, historical records show that Africa did trade with Far Asia many years before Europe became aware of it. Dussubieux, Kusimba, Gogte, Kusimba, Gratuze, and Oka (2008) maintain that archaeologists share the same certainty that most of the glass beads in Sub-Saharan Africa that predate European arrival were imported from India; also see Shillington (2012; and Wood 2012). This proves assertions that Africa had already established commercial and international links with Asia before Europe did. Remember; this is many years before Europe did not know even the way to India. Refer to how Christopher Columbus made a goof calling Americas' Inuit Indians and Caribs West Indies (Malhotra, Thorpe, Hypolite, and James 2007) after failing to reach India thanks to his ignorance of the place and its people while Africans had already used monsoon winds to conquer the Indian Ocean. Apart from trading with Asia, Africa boasts of being one of the harbingers of iron technology which started many millenniums in Egypt under Nubians before the arrival of Europeans. Furthermore, Bantu speaking people who are believed to have originated from the grasslands of Cameroon are renowned for their iron technology (Illiffe 2017). This shows that no society was barren or static in any forms despite variances in development. What provokes is Europe's hegemonic tendency of wanting to discover and own almost everything while the evidence is out there that Europe was the last to join ancient civilisations such as China and Egypt, among others.

178

Now let us delve into development; be it cultural, material, moral, social or political and whatnots. As introduced above, development is a relative term that needs to be qualified in order to functionally make sense. The question we may ask is: Development in what and who determines it using what criteria and why? Is it development in development or development in underdevelopment? Where does this development take us and where does it take us from; who is included and who is excluded and why? Is it based on time, needs and inclusivity or exclusivity individuality and or commonality? Is this development universally achievable? Does this development accommodate equity and justices among others? Who gains and who loses and why? These questions, *inter alia,* are very important but provocative due to the fact that some development like that of Western Europe and the Americas was attained and necessitated by others whose development was arrested, destroyed and stagnated through exclusivity and exploitation. This is the story many Africans, especially academics need to tell and tell and retell so that the coming generations should know the real truth. It is hard; I know. However, nobody should condemn us to silence while we can still think and tell our story however incredibly difficult it may be. Sometimes, what is referred to as development can essentially turn out be a scam of keeping us hostage thanks to ever-changing goalposts as Europe has carried it out for a long time. When I consider different financial and economic policies the IMF and the WB have introduced to Africa without any viable success, I tend to believe that everybody needs to define development depending on possibility but not superimposition of defect and experimental polices that tend to max out without successes as it is in the case of economic experiments on Africa. Easterly (2009) maintains that IFI's policies are based on failed and recycled ideas and old fashioned way of thinking that have always achieved the same, failure. In other world, the IFIs, as far as Africa is concerned, have always tried to solve new problems with old solutions. Further, there is consensus that IFIs' neoliberal policies have failed to promote development (Vreeland 2006; Castro 2008; and Klees 2008), especially in Africa which is why I query and regard them to be an economic scams. Again, such recycled and failed ideas are viewed as nuggets if not magic bullets from developed world that can develop Africa while the same authoring such litany are the same who colonised Africa and still do the same. Due to the confusion and convolution of the definition of development, among other concepts, Europe has always pumped into the academia and mainstream public. Even Africans or countries subscribing to such scams are referred to as progressive, democratic, modern and whatnots while the duo is hard at learning. When it comes to learning the trio namely Africa, Europe and the IFIs do not show any signs of achieving development by doing just the same expecting different results which is madness in essence. Redressing and treating Africa justly due to being colonised and enslaved by Europe by forcing Europe to redress it is the only doable way forward. If Africa is redressed and treated justly in trade, it surely will catch up with others quickly. This is the only viable way of ushering development to Africa.

As for Africa, I may argue that it was developed in its own way based on its needs and time. For example, when colonisers arrived in Africa, they found that Africa was evergreen thanks to its knowledge of conserving environment. What happened when Europe started to consume timbers and other forestry products at large scale? Isn't Africa facing deforestation due to this massive and careless consumption that has been going ever since? How many natural organisms Europe made extinct? A good example can be drawn from Ankole, longhorn cattle, in Uganda. This elegant breed of cow is now facing extinction after the goofy Western-backed governments blindly destroyed its habitats by giving it to wealth investors who ended destroying them in order to give room for their so-called hybrid cows (Reid 2016). In the name of acquiring more productive cattle, Ankole ended up being duped so as to lose one of its symbols and economic assets. Again, if you look the dangers hybrid cows and their products pose compared to natural African cows, you can decide by yourself who was developed and who was not and how. Furthermore, look at how Africa is losing its elephants and rhinos due to the greed geared and enhanced by neoliberal policies based on careless consumerism and free market. Currently, China and other Asian countries are decimating elephants and rhinos in Africa. Aren't Asian emerging economies robbing Africa of its resources simply because the international system sanctifies this greed embedded in capitalism, consumerism, individualism and materialism? If precolonial Africa was able to conserve its resources before the coming of colonial ticks, how can one say it was underdeveloped? Who is developed; the one who decimates everything; or the one who conserves it? Who is developed and underdeveloped between the materialists and moralists *vis-à-vis* environmental protection? You can judge by yourself, particularly when it comes to environmental challenges and degradations the world is now facing; whereby Africa produces a fraction of the second in global warming, overconsuming and whatnots. Currently, some parts of the world face draught, famine, overwarming and overconsumption. The list is long. For those who come from the societies where rainmaking was a technology that Western cultural coloniality felled, think there is a solution to draught problem. Rainmaking in some African societies was a real thing but not a hoax. Mukhopadhyay (2009) testifies that:

> Traditional African rainmakers are slowly gaining recognition. The scientific world has begun embracing them as partners in unravelling the never-ending mysteries of Mother Nature. In fact, climate experts are looking up to indigenous African knowledge as a probable salvation to the devastating effects of climate change (p. 1); also see Håland (2005); Gandure, Walker and Botha (2013); and Babane and Chauke (2015).

I understand; some detractors may dispute this fact; and thereby treat it as a myth while, at the same time, subscribe to mythologies such as religious protection from evils that are based on beliefs. If it is accepted and possible that God gave *manna* to Israelites, what is wrong with accepting the fact that Africans had rainmaking technology? Isn't this development in its own right? Risiro, Mashoko, Tshuma, and Rurinda (2012) concur maintaining that "the study found that traditional methods of weather forecasting can be utilised for the purposes of short term and long term seasonal weather predictions by local communities" (p. 565). Who are using these natural methods if not the rainmakers Africa used to have? I like using the words natural or pre-modernism in order to avoid falling in

181

the trap of using the derogative term, traditional. Considering some aspects of African traditional societies, as they are derogatorily referred to, as opposed to the modern European, *vis-à-vis* development, one finds that they were more developed in some aspects than the so-called developed and modern European ones. For example, up until now, African women have never negated their infants or denied them their right to being breastfed. What is the situation in the so-called developed countries where women are denying their infants breastmilk? Thanks to their ignorance of the importance of mother's milk, economically, psychologically and physiologically, some women in the so-called developed countries, under the ignorance of modernity, do not breastfeed their babies for their peril and that of their infants. It is recently when Western countries came to know the centrality of breastfeeding to the mother and baby as opposed to Africans who naturally knew this for thousands of years so as to make it a right. Even African animals know when, why and how long breastfeeding should be carried out. Had such collective and systemic failures been detected in Africa, many noises would be heard not to mention the condemnation and references of savagery. McGuire (2011) notes that:

> Although much is known about rates of breastfeeding in the population, mothers' breastfeeding practices have not been well understood until recently. The Infant Feeding Practices Study II, 42 conducted during 2005–2007 by the U.S. Food and Drug Administration (FDA) in collaboration with CDC, was designed to fill in some of the gaps, (p. 6); also see the Office of the Surgeon General (US, and Centers for Disease Control and Prevention (2011); Afshariani (2014); and Byers (2015).

Despite being a basic, natural and simple knowledge in Africa, and in order to covertly acquire knowledge, the same failures will go to Africa to teach breastfeeding based on their ignorance and failures and go away priding themselves of civilising Africans while the fact is that they do so to covertly acquire knowledge. Geared by ignorance and selfishness, and latching on materiality and individuality devoid of morality, women who deny their infants breastmilk care more about their *beauties* and bodies but not the development and wellbeing of their innocent infants. Apart from such human catastrophe, resulting from ignorance, to infants in the developed world, consider environmental danger mining is now posing in Africa after the introduction of toxic and contaminant chemicals all geared by greed (Bugri 2008; and Keeley and Scoones 2014). Many mining companies from the so-called developed countries are contaminating African soil pointlessly (Eisler 2003; and Kitula 2006) after introducing mercury and other dangerous chemicals in mining. Later, once chips are down, they will blame this phenomenon on Africa while they are the ones who largely contributed in creating the problem[s]. Generally speaking, as indicated hereinabove, I think we need to agree on one thing that Western development is more materialistic while African development is didactic. This is why Africans did not need or colonised any people due to the fact that they were satisfied with their material wellbeing and they knew how morally wrong doing so it is.

When it comes to social development, the story of the religion, prior touched, suffices to tell it all. Since the introduction of cultural colonialism embedded in religions, Africans have lost their true moralistic culture and values. They are now the shadows of who they used to be. They acquired new identities from names, beliefs, fashions, education, languages and whatnots. Africa, if I may say so, needs to invent new uncontaminated Africans who will rebel, redefine and push it to the future. The Africa we have today is problematic, especially when I look at the engines that are supposed to propel it to the future. Young people are now risking their lives to go to Europe and America for greener pastures (Lucht 2011). Despite being the creator and harbinger of this phenomenon Europe is still living in the state of denial. This has resulted into the surge of nationalistic parties in Europe which look for thwarting it without addressing its historical underpinnings as found in slavery, colonialism and perpetual exploitation resulting from them. The academics, too, are perishing under the brain drain dressed as brain gain while it is a brain game. Leaders left so many years ago after they started receiving orders from their former colonial masters. A few Africans left with courage and sanity of addressing Africa's quandaries are discouraged by the black colonial governments that do not need them for the fear of awakening their people. So, when it comes to development, Africa needs to turn things around for the better by deconstructing everything renowned to have pulled it back.

Although many academics tend to delve into how Europe exploited Africa so as to develop; and thereby cause Africa's underdevelopment, they fall short of addressing another important facet. This is nothing but intellectual imperialism (Chambers and Balanoff 2009; Mäki 2009; and Firchow 2015) that Europe has always chaperoned in the international arena; and under which Europe has dominated Africa for many years. In this section, I will address the whole issue of definitions and meanings in order to show the advantage Europe has over Africa shall things remain colonial as they have always been. By suggesting that there must be deconstruction and overhaul of definitions and meaning, I want to contribute to the tools that can help us to grasp whatever concepts propounded. Definitions are the foundations of our understanding of what is propounded. Ironically, when it comes to social science and other sciences, Africa has been at the receiving end. Almost all intellectual and academic discourses taught in African institution of higher learning were created in Europe charged with defining everything. This puts Europe at an advantageous position to dominate in academics as it has been in other areas. For example, when we are told of development, we need to ask: Development in what and how. Who defined what, why and how? Is there any agreement/disagreement or negotiation of the terms? By answering these questions we will be able to understand development based on an informed decision. We will be able to gauge if this definition[s] accommodate our definition[s] aspirations, understanding[s], yardsticks, and above all, is compatible with what we deem to be true development. For, without answering these questions, we will find ourselves in the straightjacket that is aimed at trapping us in.

No doubt at all. Whatever meanings and definitions of development currently accommodated in academia have their origin in the West namely Europe and North America. This does not mean that other academics did not contribute to the dialogue. Their impact is very dismal compared to their colleagues and institutions from the

West. This is because Western grand narrative is dominant over others. This makes such meaning and definitions prejudiced and sometimes superimposed. Geisinger (2009) notes that "…development is built on the ideological separation of people and nature…" (p. 65). This shows how controversial many definitions can be, especially if we underscore the fact that apart from being propounded by the West, many definitions and meaning are measured by Western yardsticks simply because it is the Western grand narrative that is currently dominant in the international arena. This is why, for example, when you talk about development for an Africa, material development comes last after the development that is hinged on human and moral aspects of human existence and aspirations. If you prune Western masks from an African, there is no way one's development can solely be his or hers. One's development, underdevelopment, failures, success and triumphs are societal but not individual thanks to the collectivistic nature of Africans. Likewise, the formulas we use to measure Africa's development under the pretext of internationalism, which is essentially the West, are tyrannical. If you ask the West to use Africa's yardsticks of defining and measuring development, based on African philosophy, will never agree to it. For example, Jerven (2013) in addressing how statistical conclusions are reached at, notes that the statistical maps about ranking African countries according to GDP and economic growth is misleading due to the fact that there are some important elements that are ignored or not understood. He cites an example of Ghana whose GDP was undervalued. After revising everything, there was an increase of 60% that resulted into categorising Ghana s a lower-middle-income country from a lower-income country. Apart from statistical errors, Mhango (2017f) argues that true development must revolve around humanity but not criminality and duplicity, justice not injustice, morality not immorality; and material aspects must be the last thing to consider.

Despite being liable for felling Africa's propensity to development, Europe, instead of being brought to book, has self-appointed to define development based on its agendas and criteria; which is wrong. For, it is like an accused person to act as a prosecutor, a witness and a judge in his or her own case. In such a setting, there cannot be any justice whatsoever. This does not add up provided that the same Europe arrested Africa's natural development (Settles 1996; Fieldhouse 2012) for the purpose of developing itself. There is no way a tick can define development for a cow; and doing so be seen as doing justice for both parties. With cases and examples adduced above, suffice it to say, nobody can solely define or own development in all aspects of life. So, too, nobody is solely entitled to define development for others without asking crucial questions such as to whose interests, why, when, how, and above all, in what the said development is defined and measured. Arguably, defining development for others is one of colonial mentalities based on manipulative *holier than thou*, specifically when such definitions and measures, purposely or otherwise, exclude some aspects of some societies as it currently is under the neoliberal policies geared by greed and self-interests. More importantly, whatever development is defined to be and measured should revolve, mainly around humanity but not materiality. It should involve material as well as moral aspects of development in order to become meaningful and inclusive. Development that is devoid of inclusivity is nothing but a problem.

Therefore, it goes without saying that Africa is developed and underdeveloped in some areas the same way, as it has been proved herein above, others are. Therefore, we need to negotiate, agree and disagree about the concept of development. We have shown above how developed countries greedily and maliciously overconsume and waste food and other resources while other people on earth are dying of hunger and malnutrition. Such societies that are blind of others cannot be truly developed. Using African lenses: when a neighbour goes with an empty stomach, you do not have the right to waste food even if it is yours. Therefore, when I argue and urge that development should revolve around humanity I invoke such school of thought which views development as towards world's wellbeing based on interdependence and interconnectivity. The same applies to environment, economy, politics and all other aspects of life. Under Ubuntu which literary means "a person is a person through other persons" (Gade 2011: 303); also see Gade (2012), meaningful development should be inclusive as it revolves around humanity. However, such understanding of development based on collectivistic culture is totally different conceptualised from the individualistic culture's perspective. Mapadimeng (2009) argues that "Ubuntu culture could contribute to socio-economic development" (p. 78) if it is nicely applied based on its foundations.

In sum, development that is arrested or monopolised by one section of human society is deceptive, flaw and problematic thus needs to be deconstructed, overhauled and redefined altogether. Every society has its levels and aspects of development. And there is no human society that is devoid of development be it materialistic or moralistic one.

How Africa's Role in the Industrial Revolution

No doubt. Africa contributed a lot to Europe's economic and scientific development, especially if we consider the fact that Europe's leading role in development started with what is famously known as industrial revolution which Europe ushered in after accumulating capital African slaves created on top of the surplus Africa created after being a producer of raw material to end up becoming a chief consumer of processed goods from Europe, (Mhango 2015). While Europe gained significantly from slave trade, the same had many everlasting ramifications on Africa. Africa was depopulated by being robbed of the manpower that developed Europe and Americas instead of developing Africa. This helps to counter on anybody who implicates Africa as an abettor in slave trade. Although, we know a few Africans participated in this trade. Again, how did Africa benefit from this trade apart from being a big loser? The situation became worse after the introduction of colonialism. The worst for Africa came after two evils' effects were exacerbated by neocolonialism that is ongoing presently so as to make it difficult for Africa to get straight through. For example, slave trade did not only negatively impact on Africa externally but also internally (Nunn (2008b) cited in Nunn 2009). While Europe prospered, Africa became stagnant almost in everything after its economy and structures were destroyed. When I say that Africa contributed to the development of Europe, this is what I mean. It is this Africa's contribution essentially that helped Europe take off to where it currently is while, to the contrary, the same pushed Africa down to where it is. Soyinka cited in Ojo (2015) concurs with Mhango maintaining that Africa became underdeveloped due to "the twin evils of slavery and colonialism inflicted by the Western world" (p. 109); also see Koivula (2006); and Nunn (2008); Arowolo (2010); and Mhango (2017) who, as well, argue that the introduction of slavery and colonialism gave Europe an advantage to develop while Africa underdeveloped.

Although slavery has always seen based on human rights gross violations, it contributed immensely to the development of Europe economically, politically and socially. It is ironic that slavery, despite being a crime, has never inculpated those who benefited from it. This is due to the fact that if we look into the numbers and time slavery existed we can definitively maintain, without any kernel of doubt, that without slavery, Europe would not have embarked on industrial revolution. For, it was from slave's free labour that enabled Europe to have extra time to sit down and invent the machines that took over from slaves so as to usher in the so-called industrial revolution. Mazrui cited in Boateng (2005) maintains that:

> The labour of Africa's sons and daughters was what the West needed for its industrial takeoff. The slave ship helped to export millions of Africans to the Americas to help in the agrarian revolution in the Americas and the industrial revolution in Europe simultaneously.

Due to the capital Europe accumulated from slavery and colonialism, it was able to invest in researches and investments in machines that later replaced slave (Rodney 1972 cited in Boateng *Ibid.*). But what is undeniably true is the fact that without introducing slavery and colonialism, Europe would not have become the leader in development. Bryant (2006) maintains that as industrialisation ushered in a revolutionary transformation in material production and transport. This is the European advantage passed over into worldwide predominance that has gone on up until now. This is easy to see; if we revisit the real situation that enhanced Europe's development. Drayton (2005) maintains that:

Profits from slave trading and from sugar, coffee, cotton and tobacco are only a small part of the story. What mattered was how the pull and push from these industries transformed Western Europe's economies. English banking, insurance, shipbuilding, wool and cotton manufacture, copper and iron smelting, and the cities of Bristol, Liverpool and Glasgow multiplied in response to the direct and indirect stimulus of the slave plantations."

Further, slavery and colonialism felled the all already-established institutions in Africa so as to leave Africa empty handed to end up depending on its former colonial masters to establish alien institutions that have never worked for its interests since independence. Again, where did these institutions go? Nunn and Puga (2012) answer the question maintaining that "the slave trade had adverse effects on subsequent economic development because they weakened indigenous political structures and institutions, and promoted ethnic and political fragmentation" (p. 2) not to mention socio-political stagnation. Consider the suffering and perpetual trauma those born of slaves have endured in foreign lands they were forcibly taken and sold not to mention perpetual degradation and exploitation for many decades. This is why economic development achieved by means of colonising and enslaving others, those who pride themselves to be economically developed and dupe others to follow their trajectory, is wrong and unattainable without redressing their victims and historical consequences. A thug who burglarise my house and rob me of everything so as to become materially rich but morally poor cannot define my development. How can the thug's definition development define mine accurately while it means my underdevelopment? If such a thug defines my development, without returning my property, his definition and development will be totally biased, fickle, flaw, misleading and vicious as Europe's is. It is hypocritical and a big lie; to allow and expect criminals who colonised enslaved and robbed Africa to justly and judiciously define development for their victims, in particular at the time their crimes are still committed by extension under whatever system and doctrine such as neoliberalism, globalism, capitalism; you name it. Arguably, true and meaningful development must revolve around humanity but not criminality and duplicity, justice not injustice, morality and not immorality and material aspect of the concept which must be the last elements to be considered. Humanity and justice should come first. This is underscores the importance of history as a tool of emancipation becomes evidently imperative, especially for the victims. There is no way development can revolve around things first then around humanity. To make sense, development must revolve around humanity first then to materials. For the victims, subscribing to a ploy that excludes humanity in its definition of development is nothing but turning humans into things which case is dangerous as Freire cited in Snauwaert (2011) maintains that the oppressed have been destroyed precisely because their situation has reduced them to things. Therefore, the oppressed must reclaim their humanity first instead of being fighting tools. And in doing so, they must meet this condition as they strive to become human but not just being accepted and recognised as humans.

To add insult to injury, the same trend has been gone on for decades now save that the slaves that used to be shackled to go to Europe are now shackling themselves willingly thanks to brain drain or seeking greener pastures for those who happen to be undesirable in Europe. As for banking implicated above, many European banks are good beneficiaries of the money syphoned from Africa either by the way of robbing public coffers by corrupt and venal rulers or by way of capital flights if not kickbacks remitted there by multinational corporations to top up the money made during colonial and slavery times.

Additionally, to see how capital works and pushes Europe–and America that is not subject to his corpus, *inter alia*–to prosperity and material development, we can look at the Middle East today. After discovering oil, the excelled more than the countries such as Egypt and Iraq that were ahead of them simply because they have a small population and huge reserves of oil. Why didn't Africa excel despite having more precious resources? It is because colonial powers exploited Africa with its resources; which is a different case from the Middle East. Instead of being exploited, Middle East exploits and uses its oil. By exploiting its oil, Middle Eastern countries are becoming another economic power house to reckon with. As for

Europe, slaves and, later colonies, were like oil to the Middle East. However the difference is that Europe was exploiting slaves and colonies criminally as opposed to the Middle East that is enjoying its God-given resources. How much money did Europe make for over 200 years slavery existed in Europe and the Americas (Kolchin 2003; and Du Bois 2014) or 300 hundred (Bethell 2009)? Slaves were responsible for working without pay for longer periods of times producing coffee, sugarcane, cigarettes, cotton and other commodities that were then in the high demand. Imagine. How much money did Europe make by exploiting over 12 million Africans sold as slaves not to mention those many that were born in slavery thereafter for the whole over 200 years they were captivated? Bales (2012) Answers this question citing the American Slave Liberation Associations noting that:

> An estimate of 27 million people live in conditions that resembles slave's living standard. The United Nation Labour Agencies shows reservation about the estimation, but contends that there are more than 12 millions of people. It is believed that the lucrative business brings more than 10 billion of profits every year.

In ergonomics terms, if we valorise the figure of ten billion dollars annually, it means that the slaves in Americas produced trillions of dollars. And if this is calculated according to the modern labour markets and payment one get per hour, we are talking about trillions really. The tragic story does not end up here. If we calculate how much money slave owners would have paid had those slaves died in their hands been insured or deserved to enjoy human rights, we are talking about many trillions as well not to mention other trillions they would have paid had they been sued for gross violations of human rights. Here I am not talking about the sufferings the progenies of slaves suffered, and still suffer, up until now. Furthermore, I am not talking about money would have been paid as fines for rapes and negligence slave owners committed on Africans and many more. All such heinous crimes committed against Africans, if were committed today, they would force any country or countries behind them to go bankrupt not to mention being shunned internationally had the international community been fair and relevant for Africa.

Besides slavery, it is noteworthy to state that slaves were not shipped wherever they were shipped empty handed. They carried ivories, timber, and other resources with them which boosted the economies of recipient countries. It is not easy to get the actual facts and figures of how much Africa was robbed under this category. What is obvious is that slavery went hand in hand with other sorts of plunderage that left Africa high and dry. And in this criminality, Europe claimed a lion share of the loot provided that it was the only one continent that had many more future colonies at the time due to being a superpower of the time. Apart the resources slave carried with them; there are other areas in which Africa lost so as to develop Europe. Arowolo (2010) observes that for over two hundred years or so of colonisation, Europe destroyed Africa in various areas such as cultural heritage and values for which Africa was famous before colonialism but also precariously retrogressive as the continent was robbed of decades of opportunities- opportunities of self-development, self-government and, indeed, opportunities of self-styled technological developmental pace. With regard to the suffocation and annihilation of African governing institutions, the situation has worsened under Western democracy that is used as a carrot and stick bait to punish or reward some African countries depending on where and whom allies with. What transpired in Libya in 2010 speaks volume. Libya's long time ruler Muamar Gadhafi was toppled, caught and summarily killed simply because he was a dictator. Ironically, while that happened, there were many more dictators in Africa that were in bed with the same Europe. Arguably, the aspect of self-governance has cost Africa a lot. For, many West's stooges were installed in power to supervise the plunderage of Africa. Cameroon, Congo, the DRC, Equatorial Guinea, Gabon, Ivory Coast, Kenya and Uganda, *inter alia*, provide an ideal example. These countries were mismanaged by dictators and some with their families to end up robbing Africa as they augmented Europe for the peril of their peoples. Robbing their countries individually aside, they helped Europe to plunder resources while their people remained poor since acquiring their independence.

While Kenya was praised for its modernising steps by looking like European capitals, Tanzania was scorned for having a capital that did not look like European ones. Kenyans used to tell Tanzanians that they did not need to go to Europe to see modernity. They had to just go to Nairobi. Again, when you compare rural Tanzania and rural Kenya, Tanzania, up until now, is still far better than Kenya.

Ellis and Freeman (2004) observe that:

Kenya, despite its highest per capita income level in this group of countries, has the next highest poverty proportions, estimated as 52 per cent overall, 53 per cent rural, and 49 per cent urban. Tanzania and Uganda display fairly similar poverty profiles according to recent evidence, both with 35 per cent of their total population designated as poor, 39 per cent poverty incidence in rural areas in both cases, and between 26 per cent (Tanzania) and 10 per cent (Uganda) poverty incidence in urban areas (p. 6).

The major question we need to ask ourselves is: If Kenya has the highest capital in the region, where does the money go? The answer is simple that all such attractive investments Kenya is praised for belong to many European companies. Therefore, what is seen as having economic muscles is nothing but the profits for Europe. This is a typical replica of many African countries. This is how Africa has always developed Europe as opposed to how Europe underdeveloped Africa. Although the statistics above may seem to be archaic, the situation has stayed relatively the same in these countries. The simple explanation is that as an African country attracts many investments without having sound policies of enabling its people to access the means of production, chances that poverty in that country is likely to rev up in record numbers in the near future. This can be seen on how social services such as education and health were provided to the citizen. Ishumi (1994) cited in Sifuna (2007) says that between 1960 and 1970 primary school enrolments increased by 50 percent in Tanzania and 40 percent in Kenya (p. 691). This is the time Kenya was in the limelight for its economic miracles compared to Tanzania whose economy started to nosedive after it openly allied to the East so as to antagonise the West.

Additionally, Sifuna *(Ibid.)* notes that in Kenya, for example, enrolments increased from 5.9 in 2002 to 7.2 million in 2004 with a GER of 99 percent, while in Tanzania they grew by 25 percent from 4.4 in 2000 to 6.4 million in 2003, with a GER up to 108 percent (from 71 in 1990) (p. 696). When I talk about economic gearing, I think the picture one can get here is that Tanzania, despite being viewed as poor and unmodernised compared to its neighbouring Kenya, provided education as a capital to its people more practically than Kenya.

Apart from immense capitals Europe gained by the way of slavery, there is another venue through which it gained. This is through religion. Many missionaries that were established in Africa exploited Africans by overworking them under the pretext of working for God. On top of that, missionaries, even today, still collect a lot of produces and the pretext of harvest which all benefit their mother churches and countries in Europe. Harvests aside, Europe has always been a beneficiary of money siphoned from unwary African believers in various Christian denominations under the concept of paying tithe or one-tenth of their produces. This is theft by all definitions provided that it has no return. Dei and Osei-Bonsu (2014) maintain that becoming a Christian does not automatically usher one into material blessing which have never been the goal of Christianity. If this is the case, why should people pay tithes while the goal of Christianity is not material gains? This is controversial and the churches take different stances on it. For example, Ehioghae (2012) argues that "Pentecostal pastors urge their followers to give in order to experience material prosperity. The scriptural injunction to tithe is used as a basis for the gospel of prosperity" (p. 143). Who is telling the truth here? Demonstrably, such lies have helped Europe to fleece Africa and build such magnificent castles and churches dotting Europe while those fleeced are dying in penury. Ironically, even Islam uses the same loopholes to fleece Africa, for example, by canonising the trip for hajj to Mecca in which billions of dollars are fleeced annually (Mhango 2015) from Africa. This adds another aspect that Africa did not only develop Europe but also the Middle East, chiefly if we consider the fact that slave trade, for example, was carried out between Arabs and

Europeans. As for Europe particularly, Africa contributed immensely in all manners. Take, for example, the simple lie of turning *Jesus's blood* into wine as a part of the pattern of fleecing others. How many litres of wine did Africa import for the purpose of being used in Lord's mass every Sunday up until African countries started to produce their own wines.

Apart from wine that Africa used to import from Europe, there is another face of exploitation that made Africa contribute to Europe after its culture was felled. Take chalices and robes that are still used during the mass were also imported from Europe. They all used to be imported from Europe so as to contribute immensely to its economy. These were the ways of robbing Africa once again through the promotion of Western cultures attached to Christianity. Has this stopped? It is not easy to tell. This is why the centrality of wine in Catholicism can be regarded as a colonial strategy to fleece non-European countries on top of tithe. It is so simply because, as it is date for Arabs, wine is traditional European beverage that was once adored so as to be used to pay taxes in Europe (McGovern 2013). Wine is the part of Europe's inheritance (Johnson 2012; and Robinson and Harding 2015). What is Africa's inheritance in this equation? It is sad to note however that many academics and activists do not address this historical robbery as it is so as to force the international community to enact laws that would redress Africa and those born of slaves. Those who do not view slaves as machines that propelled Europe to prosperity it is boasting of today, tend to purposely push such stark reality under the carpet.

It is not an underestimation to argue that slavery gave Europe the capital that enabled it produce surpluses and financed other ventures (Williams 2014) that accorded it leisure time to sit down and think about do some researches (Mhango *Ibid.*). Despite such a humungous contribution, Africa has never received a credit for giving Europe a leg up for development. To make matters worse, slave traders and slave owners acquired young Africans (Jordan 2013) who would have developed Africa; had they not been shipped to the Americas.

Although there are no available figures to show how much Africa was robbed, we can hypothetically look at European countries that were stingingly poor which became ultra-rich after colonising Africa.

Such countries are Belgium, Portugal and Spain among others. There is no way we can say that there is justice in the world without forcing countries that developed after colonising Africa and trading in slaves to redress their victims. This is the area which academics need to concentrate on in order to avoid prevailing disparities and injustices in the world systems. So, too, the Great Britain, France, Germany, Portugal and Spain, *inter alia*, doubled their wealth after occupying and colonising Africa. To keep Africa at bay and fooled (Moyo 2011) and hypnotised, the same thieves are currently pretending to help Africa through fake philanthropic aid and other succors. Africa does not need philanthropists but, instead, it needs international legal mechanisms that can unequivocally address its past wrongs resulting from long time colonisation. Despite the *beauties* aid optimists may have about it, there is no way aid can pull Africa out of abject poverty while it is always has some strings attached (Glennie 2010). Optimism and sweet language have always been applied by neoliberalist thinkers to convince the world that aid can create economic growth and push in recipient countries. But when we truthfully consider over fifty years of aid Africa's dependency, Africa's situation is worsening but not improving due to the fact that such aid goes to corrupt governments.

Wherever corruption is blessed and rampant, the lives of the majority citizens become harder and harder provided that there are no mechanisms that force those in power to be accountable for whatever they do. One of the reasons why aid has never worked for Africa is corruption in the upper echelons of power that is endemic and systemic. For example, the United Nations Economic Commission for Africa (UNECA 2009) cited in Asongu (2013: 1) estimated that in 2004, the continent lost more than $148 billion to corruption while the *African Development Bank* (ADB 2006: 7) cited in Asongu (2012) estimated that 50% of tax revenue and $30 billion in aid for Africa ends up in corrupt hands. Such findings led to academics such as Knack (2001); Alesina and Weder (2002) cited in Menard and Weill (2016) to reach a conclusion that, empirically, aid enhances corruption. Easterly and Pfutze (2008) disclose that up until 2007, aid given to Africa had reached a whopping US$2.2 trillion. Again, where did all aid money go? The simple answer is that the aid money goes back to Western countries. Provided that such money is supervised by corrupt African leaders either it is stashed back to Western banks or spent on purchasing expensive toys, fashion designer suits, houses, mansions, yachts and other nonsenses while surprisingly perhaps, the donors sit aside a look as if they do not know this is a crime. Take an example of corrupt dictators such as Daniel Arap Moi (Kenya), Joseph Mobutu (DRC), Jean-Bedel Bokassa (CAR), Omar Bongo (Gabon) Sani Abacha and some of his predecessors (Nigeria) and Felix Houphouet-Boigny (Ivory Coast) who robbed their coffers billions of dollars to end up stashing them in Western banks, purchasing mansions and ranches in Western countries or financing bogus projects such as the world's largest church–the Basilica of Our Lady of Peace (Yamoussoukro, Ivory Coast) and an artificial lake that went with it. This is how Africa has kept on developing Europe. Even as I write, there are still some African rulers who are still burgling their coffers to repeat the same. Due to this broad-light theft, Africa still has many dictators who are lining the pockets of many European politicians not to mention stashing the loots there. This is why Western democracy has never made any impact or sense to Africa due to the fact that it has always been used in robbing Africa on top of creating perpetual conflicts and supplying weapons to stooges and warlords (Chan 2011). It is from such a backdrop that countries like Angola, Burundi, Rwanda and Uganda, *inter alia*, were able to invade and occupy the DRC in 2003 (Williams 2013). Ever since, the culprits have never been reprimanded or being brought to book. Why? It is simply because the major beneficiaries of this war were none other than Europe that was supplied with minerals and other resource plundered from the DRC.

Regarding as to how much some African venal rulers robbed their countries, Okeke (2015) maintains that Mobutu alone stashed at least US$5 billion away in foreign banks. Such an amount does not include Zaire's accumulated a public external debt of roughly US$14 billion Mobutu and his associates left behind after being overthrown (Mhango 2016). Further, the figure does not include the other chunks of loots that Mobutu squandered on shopping sprees, entertaining his friends and other extravagances while the common Congolese were dying of preventable and remediable diseases. Where was the international community when such crimes were committed? Where were human rights campaigners and organisations when such crimes against humanity were committed openly? This is the very international community we have today that can shamelessly bless such freakish regimes. As to how much Mobutu robbed his country for the whole over 30 years he was in power, nobody can tell exactly how much due to the secrecy involved. One would ask: why Mobutu was not toppled before committing such a sacrilege. Again, Europe becomes a culprit due to the fact that, along with the US, it provided Mobutu security to see to it that he remained in power for only one reason namely supplying them with resources the country is gifted with (Gordon 2008). Mobutu plundered the DRC as he wished. He was sure that he was untouchable as long as he was in bed with Europe and its allies. It is only when Europe found another stooge that it dumped Mobutu to end up being toppled and forced to flee the country in 1997. Despite being toppled, Mobutu, for many years, has caused a lot of miseries to his country and people simply because Europe was using him to rob the DRC the same it protected Bongo in Gabon and other suchlike thieves in power. Enweremadu (2013) puts Mobutu's loot at US$6.49. While assessing and considering how foolish, greedy and myopic venal rulers are, how much did Mobutu's foreign accomplices make away with? How much his consigliore, courtiers and bootlickers did steal and spent in European capitals? For all African thieves in power, it is obvious that what would have made Africa rich and thus, economically developed went to Europe to develop; and thereby helped to develop it. We may know how much corrupt presidents like Mobutu stole but not their courtiers, accomplices and who is who in their venal regimes.

With regard to robbing Africa and stashing in Europe, Abacha scored high by robbing Nigeria approximately US$20 billion not mention another former Nigeria strongman Ibrahim Babangida who made away with US$5 billion or Mousa Traore (Mali) US$ billion and Houphouet-Boigny (Ivory Coast) US$6 billion (Wanjala 2013). The figures above are about individual presidents. Apart from the fact that some of the money the above presidents acquired came from their national treasuries, much of the money came by the way of bribes. This means that those who offered them such bribes made away with much more money than those thieves got. Wherever there are bribes, all sorts of taxes, one or a firm is supposed to the government, are not paid not to mention underrating prices or values of the items involved. What makes the situation worse is the fact that once money is stolen from Africa either it is stashed in Western banks or it is used to establish investments in the West. Doing so denies Africans jobs. By denying Africans jobs, the same money stolen from their countries, ironically, creates them for the affluent citizens in the West.

Another example can be drawn from Angola, one of poorest country in Africa, despite sitting on huge reserves of oil is still as poor as Nigeria and other African countries with resources but they are still poor as well. The *Guardian* (25 January, 2013) discloses that when Angolan president Jose Eduardo dos Santos' billionaire daughter Isabel was married, her wedding cost an estimate of US$4 million. Her meteoric rise shocked many (Sharife and Grober 2013). However, the accurate and simple answer one can give as to her rise is nothing but being the daughter of the imperial president of Angola, Jose Eduardo dos Santos. To crown it all, the choir was flown in from Belgium; and two charter planes delivered food from France as if Angola does not produce food. Whose economy such goons were contributing to? Does it mean that Angolans or Congolese could not sing at this wedding? Does it mean that African cooks could not cook at this African wedding in African country? Apart from importing European choir, drinks and foods, the *Guardian* goes on reporting that Isabel has many shares in Portuguese firms such as Zon, a Portugal media conglomerate (28,8%), Portugal bank Banco BPI (19.5%) and Angola's Banco BIC (25%). This means; she corruptly makes (de Morais 2011) money from Angola and invest in Portugal while many Angolans live on about 2 dollars a day. What do you expect with such a stooge whose administration is defined by corruption at the helm (Croese 2012)? Can such a sitting duck ordering food from Europe develop food production in his country? This Angola incident is a drop in the ocean. Many African leaders spend much money and time for medical checkups and treatment not to mention shopping, taking their children to expensive schools, doing business and the likes in Europe. Such rulers, for many years, ruined their social services simply because they do not depend on or use them. Instead of investing in sound areas such as social services, they invest in anything that can help them to cling to power. This is why it is easy to find a well-supplied police force and armies in Africa with all modern gadgets of suppressing riot and threatening the citizens but not essential items and services such as education, health, electricity, clean water, running water etc. the living example is what transpired in Angola in 2011 where Margues de Morais (2012) notes that the authorities spent over US$20 for funding counter-offensive, the MPLA held pro-dos Santos demonstrations in several parts of the country on March 5, 2011. While such megalomania and prebendalism were ongoing, hundreds of Angolans either were going to bed with empty stomachs or dying of lack of medical services. When such criminality, extravagance and madness are committed the West is watching and keeping quiet provided that those squandering such money are in its good books. Interestingly, such venal and extravagant regimes get aid and loans from the West as pleased. Why should Europe bother while it knows such money will go back to its coffers?

Another advantage the West has over Africa is the fact that all money stashed in their banks ceases to belong to African *garbage* (Anonymous demonstrator cited in Marques de Morais 2013) when they die or being overthrown as it was in the case of Abacha and Mobutu. Up until now, no one knows what happened to the billions of dollars they stashed in various banks abroad.

Again, do Western countries bother? Why should they bother while they know; money given as loans always is paid back? Theirs has always been to provide aid and loans to corrupt rulers knowingly they will embezzle the money. This is logical provided that those offering aid are not offering it for free. They aim at gaining leverage, making profits or squeezing African countries into heavy debts so that they can get the loophole by which to tamper into their affairs for economic and political gains. Asongu (2013) discloses that aid channeled through government for its expenditure increase corruption, especially in the countries where there is no rule of law and good governance. It does not make sense for a country or countries to ruin the economies of others and pretend to care about them by providing fake aid that has haunted, hunted and hurt Africa (Moyo 2009) apart from making it poorer and poorer due to being swindled by West's stooges in power in many African countries. Those doubting such assertions must ask themselves: What types of resources such as mineral, agriproducts and the like that those countries naturally have? The only means to opulence for many European countries without resources were slavery, colonialism and now neocolonialism. While Africa is now wallowing in abject poverty, Europe is becoming richer and richer simply because its resources are benefiting Europe. As if it this is not enough for Africa, currently, Africa is facing another danger besides poverty. It is now facing the depletion of its resources so as to add more pangs and twangs to Africa's predicament. And this is not the first time Africa has faced such a phenomenon. Gißibl (2006) posits, for example, that the introduction and:

> The use of guns in elephant hunting was widespread and in the 1880s about 100,000 firearms a year were imported into East Africa. Although the figures are hardly reliable, in the early 1880s German and British sources estimated that some 65,000 elephants were shot throughout Africa annually (p. 123).

If we multiply the numbers of animals killed above by, at least, 30 countries in the East, Central, South and West Africa that had many herds of elephants, we can hypothetically grasp the size of the problem colonialism caused to Africa. Mathematically speaking, if we calculate the whole period Africa was under colonialism namely from the year 1900 (Iweriebor 2011) to 1960 in calculating how many elephants were killed, we find that Africa was ruled for roughly 70 years. This brings our sum to 4,550,000 elephants. If we consider all animals such giraffe, ostrich, leopards, hippopotamus, rhinoceroses, buffaloes, and many birds that colonisers and their accomplices killed either to control population or for their precious body parts, the numbers are staggering. And this speaks loudly about how Africa developed Europe. Negative effects of such capitalist greed, ignorance and madness did not only result in depletion of some species but also it exacerbated other problems such as diseases. Kjekshus (1977) cited in Neumann (2001) notes that "the elephant control policies made the most fertile valleys uninhabitable, promoted the advance of bush at the expense of cultivation, and thus encouraged the spread of tsetse fly" (p. 659). So, you can see how one step provoked negative chains of reactions that left Africa negatively affected and impacted. For, over 70 years, how many tones of timber, rubber, spices, gold, diamond, copper, artifacts, fish, ivories, hides, and many precious things Europe robbed Africa? How many acres of fertile land European missionaries and settlers grabbed? It came just recently that the Vatican is the biggest land owner on earth by having 177 million more acres in various countries in the world (McEnery 2011). You do not have to be an economist, mathematician or statistician to grasp the volume of wealth Europe robbed Africa.

The capital that would help Africa to move ahead is now slowly dwindling after resources have been overexploited. What crowns it all is the fact that whatever little money is paid to African countries as loyalties ends up being embezzled or invested in white elephants. For whose benefit let say highways in the capital serve while millions of citizens are living in abject poverty in rural areas which is phenomenal in many African countries?

Chapter Eight

How Europe and the Vatican Colluded in Robbing Africa

There are countries that were out-front in initiating the process of dividing, partitioning occupying and therefrom colonising Africa at what is famously known as the Brussels Meeting on 12th September, 1876. At this meeting, in attendance were Austria-Hungary, Belgium, Britain, France, Germany, Italy and Russia (Keltie 2014). Essentially, with respect to colonial and criminal liability, these are the very countries Africa has to start with in its drive for redress. Primarily, this meeting set the agenda that attracted other interested players such as Norway, Ottoman empire (now Turkey), Portugal, Spain, Sweden, the Netherland and the United States. As well, such countries are liable for the dent colonialism caused to Africa. Importantly, almost all countries that were involved in hatching the scheme of invading, occupying, colonising and exploiting Africa are relatively richer than Africa. Therefore, they have what it takes when it comes to redressing Africa. Arguably, redressing Africa will not bankrupt these very beneficiaries. However, the most prominent among the above colonial powers that massively exploited Africa directly are Spain, Portugal, Holland France and Britain whose merchants were fully involved in slave trade which "was founded on Christianity"(Cannon 2008: 127) not to forget the Vatican. These countries did not only get *free-working machines* but also they secured the market for their goods. For, in this trade, slaves were exchanged with manufactured goods such as cloths and guns among others (McMichael 2011). Further, Christianity did not only institute slavery but also genocide as Numbers 32: 1-6) cited in Mamdani (2014) notes that God commanded Moses to:

> Avenge the children of Israel of the Medianites: afterward shalt thou be gathered unto thy people. And Moses spake unto the people saying, Arm ye men from among you for the war, that they may go against Median, to execute the LORD's vengeance on Median And they warred against Median, as the LORD commanded Moses, and they slew every

male . . . And the children of Israel took captive the women of Median and their little ones; and all their cattle, and all their flocks, and all their goods, they took for a prey. And all their cities in the places wherein they dwelt, and all their encampments, they burnt with fire. And they took all the spoil, and all the prey, both of man and of beast . . . And Moses said unto them, Have you saved all the women alive? Behold, these caused the children of Israel, through the counsel of Balaam, to commit trespass against the LORD in the matter of Peor, and so the plague was among the congregation of the LORD. Now therefore kill every male among the little ones, and kill every woman that hath known man by lying with him. But all the women children that have not known man by lying with him, keep alive for yourselves [Sic].

For that reason, demanding redress for all evils and tragedies colonialism and slavery ushered in Africa must encompass the Roman Catholic Church as well either as a colonial agent or a free entity that sought and served its own and its masters' interests. Lu (2011) maintains that it is the duty of colonising powers and whoever participated in the international structure to commit harms and cause damages through their colonial injustices to redress the victims provided that a structural injustice approach should lead to inquire about the responsibilities that all participants in international structural injustice may have towards victims of colonial injustice. There is no way the abettors can be left to go scot-free whereas they actually participate in and benefited from this criminality. Others are still benefiting alongside those who created this criminal and parasitic system however it has changed forms and names. It does not make any sense, for example, to exonerate the church that has ever since enjoyed the rewards of its cultural imperialism after felling African cultures and ways of life.

Essentially, these are the harbingers of colonialism as the world came to know it. And indeed, they are the richest countries of the world just because they robbed Africa and other colonies they illegally occupied and exploited for decades under colonialism and imperialism. These are the same culprits who destroyed the natural African tapestry that existed before this criminal act. Under this drive geared by greed and inhumanity, Africans were treated like mere animals. Who invites cows when deciding to sell or slaughter them? With this criminal act, European colonial powers divided and partitioned Africa without inviting African chiefs and kings to discuss the move. This way, Africans were denied the rights to self-rule, choice, and plan based on their desires and needs. Apart from being a disregard and disrespect of the high order, the division and partition of Africa unleashed many miseries from colonialism, degradation, tortures and murders among many. Many Africans who resisted against colonisation were killed, exiled, imprisoned and degraded. Many organic nations or tribes as colonisers, abusively called them were divided carelessly and ruthlessly. This does not mean that European powers were ignorant of the rights to self-rule, self-organisation even self-partition. Who partitioned them the way they were and the way they are today? Of course, their divisions into nations were driven by their choices, desires, needs and plans all aimed at living harmoniously among themselves like any other human beings. However, due to their racism and disregards of human equality, colonial European powers did not recognise Africans as humans with any "national consciousness" (O'Leary 2007: 897) which vividly shows how racist and inhuman these powers were. Apart from lacking national consciousness, some sacrilegious racist went further degrading an African to level of an ape. Weingrod (2005) notes that there was dialog as to whether an African after being placed under the bottom of human family should be categorised as an ape or a human. While those doubting whether an African was an ape or human, currently in Adaman Island in India, the Jarawa people, who originated from Africa, are still being regarded as apes so as to be used as tourist attractions (Halder and Jaishankar 2014) the same way animals are used in the zoos (Liljeblad 2014) in their reserved Island (Sardar and Ambedkar 2011). Sadly, the assumption that Africans are apes did not occur during precolonial and colonial times. Also, it was not applied by whites only but also nonwhite as Rowe (2011) notes that an Indian cricketer Harbahajan Singh who ironically is also black by the look of his skin called another cricketer, Andrew Symonds whose parents are from the Caribbean during the test in Australia. Indians call Africans kalu or monkeys or absiii or chimps in India which is a widespread practice

(Mhango *forthcoming*). Although Singh's racist behaviour can be attributed to him personally, it is indicative of how he was brought up in the society and system that perceives an African as a less-human creature.

Singh was following in the footsteps of his masters who exported Indians to some African countries to exploit and sabotage Africans whom they have kept on discriminating up until today despite living there comfortably and becoming even richer than those they left in India. I addressed this issue of Indian discrimination against Africans from Mohandas Gandhi to Indian remnants living currently in Africa not to mention the others in India itself in the forthcoming volume on decolonization of education based on interrogating the dominant Western grand narrative. In same light, the same are called "zambo meant an African monkey, which Spaniards used to call the offspring of Afro-Mexicans and indigenous peoples; as other labels to describe mixed peoples showed contempt as well, such as "*no te entiendo*, (I do not understand you)" (Simms 2008: 235). This is the world we are living in however, it tries to hide bigotry against black people while, systematically this trend is inculcated in many societies be they racists expressly or indirectly. Parks and Head (2009) maintain that:

> The stereotype associating Blacks with apes and monkeys has been deeply ingrained in the political unconscious by the confluence of pseudo-science, popular culture, and mass media such that even after the end of the eugenics movement, advances in civil rights, and an increasingly pervasive understanding of racial equality, such associations continue to manifest in the later portion of the twentieth and early twenty-first centuries (p. 9).

American provides an ideal example of how racism lives on even after appointing itself the champions of human rights which include equality. This hypocritical stance has been maintained by almost all former colonialists. Jackson (2015) notes that the postcard of well-dressed monkeys walking downs streets which is aimed at catering for white notion of black coons still exists today. Many Obama's critics used to use the trope of the ape to ridicule him. Jackson goes on saying that this racist attack on Obama went viral so as to be picked up by one Belgian Newspaper that had a cartoon showing a police beating the ape saying that they had to find somebody else to write the next stimulus bill to mean Obama.

When I argue that the world needs to come together to address past colonial evil is essential, I consider such situations in which those who benefited; and still benefit from Africa abuse its people. One of the issues this volume has concentrated is redress from the beneficiaries of criminality that was committed against Africa. The countries that divided and partition Africa are all super rich compared to Africa they robbed. We need to assess the wealth such countries, under extractive styles of European colonialism and semi-colonialism (Bayly 2008), irresponsibly scooped from Africa. How many tons of farm produces, minerals, wildlife and whatnot they robbed not to mention the destruction of African economy. How much environmental harm did colonial powers caused on Africa? How much manpower Europe sucked from Africa that ended up producing without any payment in the Americas and Africa altogether? There is no way one can praise a leech for being fat by condemning the cow that it exploits and lives on. You can see this in European idioms such as a winner takes it all and sounds like a winner which legalise criminality and injustice internationally based on imperial culture. Furthermore, you can see this on how Europe still holds that it civilised Africa whereas, in actuality, it destroyed it. Mhango (2015) argues that there is no development or civilisation without humanity. He argues that the two must revolve around humanity and justice but not otherwise. Mhango maintains that colonialism is a crime against humanity that needs to be punished retrospectively due to the miseries it caused to millions of innocent victims in the colonies. So, treating the loots many European countries acquired through colonising others cannot be treated as a normal thing or a type of justice. Like it is in the case of the lion and the jungle, this is but jungle justice in which a lion is referred to as the king while in actual fact it is but a predator. Even calling European colonisers colonial powers is legally and morally wrong. Had Africa not been robbed, how would it have been today? We cannot keep on blaming Africa on its poverty without doing the same on those who sucked it dry. Keeping on blaming Africa is unfair legally and morally. However, it should be mentioned from the outset that some of the attendants of the meeting that set and agenda of colonising Africa did not directly colonise Africa. This does not mean they did not benefit from loots from Africa. Why did they attend if there were no benefits in this colonial scheme that saw Africa being destroyed in all ways for many years?

The major question that can guide our discourse is "why is it that the Native Americans, Africans and Australian Aborigines were not the ones who conquered Europe?" (Diamond and Ordunio 2011: 84). This question has not been well addressed, especially by Africans. Diamond and Ordunio answer this question saying that there is no single answer to this question. For example, they say that some thinkers wrongly think that Europeans were more 'intelligent' than those they conquered and occupied. Based on racism and ignorance, such an answer makes sense to colonialists and ignorant ones. I may say that Europeans were more brutal and inhumane, at the time, even partly today, than those they conquered. So, too, Europeans did not have enough resources for their sustenance compared to those they conquered and colonised. Essentially, colonial experience shows that Europeans of the time were able to occupy and rule others simply because they were able to tell lies and manipulate others not to mention other barbarities and brutalities applied at the time when colonies rebelled against them. Refer to how colonialism was spread in Africa. On Europeans' arrival, Africans, who were then used to trading with India and China, believed the Europeans were like any other traders they used to trade with. They did not have any reasons of fearing them provided that they had already lived and traded peacefully with the former who did not want to colonies or impose their ways of life on them. Although we tend to directly blame the division and partition of Africa geographically that ended up formulating feeble and many African states Africa boasts of today, the first division started spiritually in that Africans, for the first time, were divided between believers and sinners or nonbelievers, two inimical groups. This enabled Europeans to access Africans' secrets that they later used to fell both believers and nonbelievers equally by subjecting them to colonisation. With the courage of betraying their hosts, Europeans were able turn tables on them and easily colonise them; something that has gone on even to date.

As far as I am aware, arguably, when it comes to division, one can go further exploring negative tribalism that colonial European introduced to, or expanded on in Africa. What transpired in Rwanda in 1994 when negative and toxic tribalism culminated in genocide (Mhango in Mawere and Marongwe 2016) speaks volumes *vis-à-vis* how Europe poisoned the relationship in Africa. This trend has plagued Africa up until today causing lots of conflicts in many African countries. Rwandans who used to live peacefully, as one, were made to believe that they are different based on nonsensical things such as nose, the length of feet, wealth and others. Adam and Gilliomee (1979); Ranger (1985); Vail (1989); and Marks and Trapido (1987) cited in Muzondidya and Ndlovu-Gatsheni (2007) came to the conclusion that colonialism set into motion the politicisation of African ethnic identities aimed at constructing and reconstructing people's identities; hence creating artificial identities that have, ever since, perpetually destroyed and haunted Africa thanks to the suspicions it maliciously created. Ironically, whereas European colonial masters introduced negative ethnicity (Mhango (*forthcoming*); Ndege (2009); and Kamaara (2010) and the whole concept of ethnicity even though it "could rapidly appear natural and immemorial" (Ranger 2014: 5), they eradicated the same from Europe. Apart from Kosovo conflict that had all hallmarks of negative ethnicity, no ethnicity is heard of in Europe; and it has never been as a big problem in Europe as it has always been in Africa. Apart from colonialism, Kamaara (*Ibid.*) directly ties Christianity to negative ethnicity by taxing it to alleviate the poison it spread among Africans. Kamaara argues that the church must organise conferences, workshops, and seminars around the theme of Colonialism, Ethnicity, and the Church in Africa whereby civic education should be provided to the general public. Due to negative ethnicity the church and its masters created, Africa lost its cohesion and harmony. It is from this backdrop that Africans, for the first time, started looking at each other as different and inimical people. Such a tendency contributed a lot in the destruction of African harmony and unity which are very important elements in developing or curtailing

209

development for any society lacking them. While Africans were divided and played off against each other, colonial masters were united in their criminality. All this was done in order to avoid creating schisms that would lead to confrontations among them.

Whereas such forces of evil were working against Africans, Europe seized them in subduing and exploiting Africa. Many African traitors from such antagonistic groups sold their secrets to their enemies who posed as friends who later used them against both. Fundamentally, unsuspecting lambs were dancing with hyenas (Mhango 2016b) for their peril and that of their progenies. Instead of standing together and fighting off their common enemies, Africans found themselves weakened and ultimately subdued to end all suffering regardless who played what role in this perversity colonial agents initiated. The subjugation and control of Africa gave Europe an opportunity of plundering it for many years up until in the 50s when African realised their mistakes; therefore decided to unitedly take on colonialism and ultimately defeat it politically after paying a heavy price. Despite forcing colonial governors and regimes out of Africa, colonial Europe had already established a freeloading system that would work for its advantages even after pulling its direct colonial agents out of Africa. Ever since, black colonialists (Chinweizu 2010; James 2013; and Mhango 2016c) were installed to manage their countries on behalf of the colonial masters. Among other reasons, this is why, under such homemade colonialists or colonial agents, Africa was pauperised even more. And it is under such a parasitic system, new black colonialists (Fasching-Varner, Reynolds, Albert, and Martin 2014) became an extension of colonialism that begat neocolonialism and other related criminal and parasitic systems the world over. If anything, it is under such a notorious system, Africa became pregnant with venal dictators of all kinds whose role was nothing but to supervise the plunder of Africa notorious ones being Joseph Mobutu former Zaire (now the DRC), Jean-Bedel Bokassa (CAR), Hastings Kamuzu Banda (Malawi), Idi Amin (Uganda), Felix Houphouet-Boigny (Ivory Coast), Jomo Kenyatta (Kenya) and Omar Bongo (Gabon). All of these dictators, *inter alia*, misruled their countries for the advantage of Europe. To make matters worse, some had their children installed after their deaths for the purpose of keeping Africa serving its colonial masters. Those who were able to die in power and install their children are Omar Bongo (Gabon), Laurent Kabila (DRC), Gnassingbe Eyadema (Togo) whose sons, Ali Bongo, Joseph Kabila and Faure Eyadema respectively took over after their deaths in office.

The criminal division and partition of Africa had many negative ramifications economically, politically and socially. Empires were destroyed by being cobbled together with others they used to compete with. This way, competition was felled. Nations were divided among new superimposed colonial ones so as to sire animosity and division that have ever since gone on for the detriment of Africa and for the advantage of colonial powers. Again, colonial powers envisaged this knowing that united we stand and divided we fall. All this bought into colonial ploy which was purposely created aimed at destroying or weakening Africa organic states.

Although Europe has another reputation of being one of the leaders in technology, it must be underscored that Europe, apart from felling Africa's civilisation and technology, it robbed Africa virtually everything from materials to technology. Although this is the fact, Europe has always lived in the state of denialism that has sadly made the world ignore Europe's causal roots revolving around historical injustices Africa suffered from colonialism, neocolonialism and slavery as Europe invented and executed them. One of things that Europe was unable to steal is the technology that was used in build Egyptian pyramids. However, it tried to no avail after denying the fact that those pyramids were built by Africans namely the Nubians of Badarian and Naqada groups who occupied Egypt before Arab invasion (Kemp 2006; Starling and Stock 2007; Wengrow, Dee, Foster, Stevenson and Ramsey 2014; and Godde 2015). For, European thinkers once claimed that "the pyramids were Joseph's grain store houses" (Genesis 41-42 cited in Verner 2007: 2) which is a lie resulting from colonial mentality based on *holier than thou*. How if, at all, there is nothing like them in the Middle East wherein those who built the pyramids are wrongly purported to have originated? If you look at the pyramids found in Sudan, you will agree with me that the builders of the pyramids of Egypt are black people from the south. They are the Nubians. To discredit them, European liars claim that they were used like slaves or foreigners but not Africans! For the sake of argument, let us take this to be true though it is not. Did the Nubians build the pyramids without knowledge of doing so? Demonstrably, based on the remnants of the pyramids in Sudan, Nubian slaves replicated the technology by building their own pyramids. What did the Biblical Israelite slaves replicate after being used as slaves by the pharaohs of Egypt? Because of their marvel, grandeur, mysteries and sophistication, pyramids forced Europeans to find the way to be the part of such big by linking them with Joseph without knowing that true Jews are Arabs but not Europeans. Naturally, humans like to associate themselves with something bigger. This is why religions and God were invented and being used to exploit and humiliate others. However, European racists who assert that pyramids were built by Israelites are a little bit satisfied based on the complexion of colour that Arabs are a bitter lighter than Africans. This is mere and pure racism at work. All this aimed at showing that Africans are incapable of doing something monumental like the pyramids the Nubians built without necessarily using modern machinery. So, too, this most ancient technology still shows the world how advanced Africa was at a certain time of its history.

Some African historians have become bold enough to retell Africa's role in the history of the world before its civilisation and technology were destroyed after the introduction of colonialism (Kiggundu 1991; and Afro-Centre Alliance 2001 cited in Inyang 2009). Once one's civilisation, technology and all ways of life are destroyed and replaced, it becomes difficulty for such a society to get time to recapture them shall it not divorce the imposed ones. This is the very situation Africa has faced for many years. Pheko (2012) nicely touches on evidential items to show how Africa was not doomed or vacant technologically to include the construction of the city of Memphis in ancient Egypt in 3100 B.C prior to the Greeks who built Athens in 1200 B.C not to mention the Romans who built Rome in 1000 B.C. Further, Africans invented writing. It was Hieroglyphics before 3000 B.C. and Hieratic alphabet shortly after this. Pheko goes on to touch on the art of writing saying that it was developed about 600 B.C., while a Kushite script was used in 300 B.C. Other African scripts were Merotic, Coptic, Amharic, Sabean,

G'eez, Nsibidi of Nigeria and Mende of Mali. There were many others such as the Twi alphabet of the Twi people of Ghana. Arguably, Africa lost its clout technologically due to the fact that whatever it owned was owned by the whole society. Hence, it was not protected the same way Western technology was. Therefore, it made it easy for any person to access except for the technology of building pyramids in Sudan and Egypt.

How Tanzania's Stance Shows the Way Forward

Recently, Tanzania came to the international limelight after getting a deconstructionist president, Dr. John Pombe Magufuli, who is not afraid of taking on Europe and the international community *vis-à-vis* Africa's place in the world. After taking power in 2015, Magufuli started to do away with the *status quo* by doing things boldly and differently. For example, Magufuli openly told Tanzanians and the world that he is not going to beg while his country sits on immense reserves of resources. This is a new and revolutionary stance for ever-complying African presidents who take begging and dependency as God-given while they are manmade. Magufuli took the world by storm so as to shake those who used to be unshakable in their boots as far as the exploitative world order has been preying on Africa is concerned. For, Magufuli took on mega corruption involving local stooges and their foreign masters. It is an open secret that some conmen go to Africa to invest not just because they want to do so. They do so in order to sabotage Africa's development. For example, Magufuli (1 June, 2017) https://www.youtube.com/watch?v=qexXY_S9_D8 said that over 190 factories Tanzania sold to investors were felled; and for 20 years nothing have ever been produced. This means that some investors buy Africa's facilities to sabotage them so that Africa can keep on depending on industrialised countries.

According to the *Presidential Press* (29 March, 2017), Magufuli formed an eight-person team to probe copper concentrate two mining companies were exporting for smelting. In this exercise, the taskforce president former inspected only 277 containers owned by just one Acacia Mining Company. Hypothetically, this is just one month shipment which makes 63,156 containers full of concentrate without adding undeclared amounts the company used to illegally add for 19 years since this business started. If we go by the statistics the taskforce presented, this means Tanzania would have lost Tshs328.55tn whose royalties is Tshs13.142bn which, for 19 years times 12, makes a sum of $146,863,349,772; if you divide this by 4% royalties mining companies pay to the government you get $5,874,533,990. That is more than a third of the current Tanzania's foreign debt of $14.12bn as of 31 December 2014. If a single company can stick up such a mindboggling amount, how much have other many mining company already stolen for the same time? Apply the same rationale to all Sub-Saharan Countries minus Botswana and South Africa. Additionally, at the same time of the probe, Tanzania budget for the year 2016/2017 was $13,192,022,180.48 which presupposes that the royalties the government lost is equals a third of its annual budget. Also, this amount is way bigger than a five-year grants from the MCC package worth $698 million for water, roads and power projects Tanzania won back in 2008 (*Guardian* (1 April, 2016) which shows how Africa is not supposed to depend on handouts from Western countries or their organisations that use such a loophole to lord it over Africa pointlessly.

Further, the taskforce found that the shipment was underdeclared. So, too, the taskforce found that there were more amounts of minerals than those the companies declared; and thus no tax or royalties were paid. Additionally, the taskforce discovered more many types of undeclared minerals.

Magufuli's move was unprecedented and unique for Tanzania and Africa in general. It marks the beginning of the end of business as usual in which African countries were turned into El Dorado if not no man's land. Ironically, under neoliberal colonial policies, this rip off is called investment which aims at boosting the economy of the host country! Is this really investment or divestment if not daylight thuggery? By the look of things, we now have tangible and watertight evidence to show that Africa's developed not only Europe but also the rest of the world including China, India and other economic powers that have taken Africa for a ride. Again, how much would such an amount do for Tanzania if its resources were well and reasonably managed and used? How much does Africa lose annually if a single country's lost over $146bn in 19 years; and that loss caused by a single company?

It came to light that Tanzania's been involved in this fiendish-cum-lossmaking business since 1998. Simple calculus tells us that Tanzania has, ever since, lost more than it needs even for the running of the business of the government for ten years without necessarily begging or borrowing had such resources been reasonably managed for the good of the country. The situation is the same almost in all African countries. Here we are talking of minerals not to mention other lossmaking outlets such as tax evasion, capital flight, fuel theft, procurement, overcharging in many national projects and so on. If you look at this sacrilege, you will find, as Magufuli put it: Tanzania is supposed to be a donor country but not a begging one as it has always been. Again, what is amiss? The answer is simple that two things are amiss namely commons sense and patriotism, chiefly for those in power abusing it. This being the case, how can Africa do away with such madness if not *folie de grandeur* without addressing issues *pro rata* or reciprocally? Africa needs to embark on paradigm shift in which new ways of addressing its problems must be envisaged and meshed with historical reality as far as Europe's contribution in the underdevelopment of Africa is concerned. Africa needs a new crop of leaders who are not comfortable with begging and graft just like many current ones who take pride in begging and dependence while their countries sit on huge reserves of resources (Mhango 2017). Currently, African has many rulers who cannot tell their people that begging is bad, mostly for countries that become witnesses of the plunderage of their resources. This needs to change for Africa to move forward. Pelizzo and Bekenova (2016) note that many African leaders need to adopt Magufuli's type of leadership in order to get through the turbulent times many Africans are going through, mainly resulting from the lack of will to take mega graft on.

Importantly, what was unearthed in Tanzania is but a typical replica of what has been ongoing in Africa. Whereas this parasitic business has been ongoing in Africa, parasitic neoliberal thinkers make Africa believe that it is suffering from a natural resource curse (Goldberg, Wibbles and Mvukiyehe 2008; Stevens and Dietsche

2008; Tsui 2010; and Frankel 2012) while in actuality; Africa has always suffered from robbery, mismanagement, and corruption perpetrated by foreign beneficiary countries that use local agents in power. If Tanzania, which is behind other resource giants such as the Angola, Nigeria, Sudan, and the Congo with massive wealth in oil, diamonds, or other minerals (Frankel 2010) has lost such humongous amount, how much have such giants lost for over 50 years of their independence? Where has this wealth gone? The answer can be found in *How Africa Developed Europe*. This is why this volume is using the current or cutting edge data to add up to what *How Europe Underdeveloped Africa* succinctly brought to the fore.

Suffice it to say, this is how Africa developed Europe; and how Europe underdeveloped Africa. We need to have sane and truthful leaders *a la* Magufuli shall he stay the course. However, Magufuli is a creature of Tanzania's constitution, Africa still has a lot of Magufulis; say, its colonial systems do not allow them to come forth; and show us how things must be done for the betterment of Africa and Africans. Whether Magufuli's experiment will succeed or fail, it remains to be seen.

In sum, in maintaining its state of denialism, Europe, after occupying, colonising and exploiting Africa, formed parasitic controlling systems that would enable it to exploit Africa perpetually. To make matters worse, these systems were internationalised under what is now known as the international community which, in a sense, is nothing but the enacting an international-colonial regime hell-bent to exploit former colonies. Under the same systems, former colonial masters and other emerging powers have retained the role of exploiting poor countries mainly African ones. This internalisation of colonial system offers an upper hand to hegemonic powers to keep poor countries under their control economically, politically and socially as we will later see in addressing these three systemic aspects of all nations. This oxymoron is known as neoliberalism or globalism which in practices in nothing but illiberal neoliberalism or narrow and toxic globalism (Navarro 2007) under which the countries in the North benefit while those in the South lose. Essentially, this is a capitalist drive that Europe envisaged and unleashed against former colonies. Plehwe, Walpen, and Neunhöffer (2007) maintain that what makes this system toxic is the fact that it does not necessarily address systemic exploitation. Once any system is left to operate free by exploiting others, chances of such a system to gain while its victims lose are high. And this translates easily into the narrative discussed here, if anywhere, about how Africa developed Europe. We now need to delve into three facets to see how Africa developed Europe bit by bit.

How Africa Internalised and Reinforced Underdevelopment

If you compare the Americas and the way its indigenous people were felled, you can see why Africa is an exception to the general rule. When you consider how immense the resources that Africa has are, you can easily understand why colonisers did not take Africa for good just the same way they did to other places such as the Americas, and Australia wherein they enacted the genocide (Wolfe 2006; and Amadahy 2009) that killed indigenous people to give room for settlers to occupy these lands forever. Many of the settlers either were exiled criminals or paupers who had failed to make it in Europe. By exploiting Africans and enjoying their forced labour, such criminals and lazy people became so much affluent so as to start having influence back home they were either expelled from or forced by their status in the society to risk going to Africa. Based on the history of colonialism and the history of African resistances, we discover that the only part of Africa that colonisers wanted to take for good namely South Africa, can understand how resilient and resistant Africans are. Due to the beauty of Africa, its fertile land, lakes, rivers and other resources, if Africans were not resistant, Africa would not been spared from the fate the said continents above suffered. This dispels the beliefs that Africans were easily colonised whereas the case is the opposite. Furthermore, this informs us as to how Africans have soldiered on despite facing all sorts of miseries from poverty, wars, exploitation and being defined by others.

Many a time, Western countries have sought to make Africa believe that it is unendingly poor by defining it as a third world. Defining Africa as a third world is nothing but abusing and belittling it all based on robbing it of its self-confidence. To do away with such colonial definition Africa needs to have its own episteme based on its history and philosophy (Mudimbe 1988 cited in Escobar 2011) all aimed at interpreting, reinterpreting, defining and redefining terms for Africa instead of depending on misleading and hegemonic external sources and thoughts based on coloniality and externality for the purpose of exploiting it perpetually. In other words, Africa needs to delve in its internality as opposed to exteriority in seeking the answers for its problems either locally or externally enacted. If needs be, externality must compliment internality but not allowing the current regime and corpus of ideas about Africa to keep on dominating and defining Africa. Without doing so, Africa will always remain disadvantaged due to the myth the West created so as to keep on perpetually exploiting Africa through dubiously reinventing it.

For example, when the founders of African countries championed the liberation and independence thought that Africa will change from being a colonial backyard to self-reliant continent; which is possible shall Africa redefine itself and show the world how it helped in developing Europe and now other emerging powers such as Brazil, China and India that are now involved in the new scramble for Africa (Carmody 2016). Africa had some notable figures such as Julius Nyerere (Tanzania), Kwame Nkrumah (Ghana) and others who wanted to emancipate Africa as opposed to other despots (Dorman 2006) such as Felix Houphouet-Boigny (Ivory Coast), Jomo Kenyatta (Kenya) Hastings Kamuzu Banda (Malawi) and others who sabotaged and emaciated this dream of truly emancipating Africa by acting against it covertly and overtly so as to cause severely suffering from "the bureaucratic-oligarchic syndrome" (Ashman, Fine and Newman 2010: 5). When such a schism appeared, Africa started to wobble under its own leaders for the benefit of Europe. Therefore, true emancipation did not come to be due to the fact that some of the very founders quickly cascaded into becoming stooges and despots who did not only oppose the move to emancipate Africa but robbed their countries while others put them on lean as it was in the case of the abovementioned traitors to mention a few among others. Politically, the possibility of emancipating Africa seems impossible from this point. For, ever since, African countries received their independence divided and

218

stifled. The situation worsened when the Cold War kicked in so as to create a good bolthole for despots and stooges to extend their tentacles and tighten their grips on power in many African countries. It is at this time another colonial blow kicked in. this was none other than *coup d'états* sponsored either by the East of the West depending on who allied with and supported whom. The West is accused of overthrowing many Marxist and socialist governments in Africa. However, Collier (2008,2009) cited in Souaré (2014) maintains that coups in Africa were the results of the failure of democracy provided that elections were not free and fair; and therefore, the West must brace itself to accept military juntas. This means; coups can return shall the West decide for its own interests.

Historically, when the first government of the first African country to gain independence, Ghana, was toppled simply because its first president Kwame Nkrumah, was a staunch anti-capitalism crusader that cost him his presidency, the doors were open for coups that followed thereafter either motivated by power greed or backed by the West as we will show in some countries. For example, the fall of the iconic Nkrumah did not only opened the floodgates for coups that followed therefrom but also motivated coup makers that it was possible to topple the government and rule the country illegally. For, those who were cagey about coups were motivated; and found it easier to carry them out as it was evidenced in the neighbouring Togo four years before wherein the military junta led by an anti-communist Etienne Gnassingbe Eyadema seized power in bloody coup that saw the first Togolese president Sylvanus Epiphanio Olympio being brutally murdered in the wake of the coup. If anything, one of the causes of Africa's underdevelopment can be traced in the coups due to the fact that they produced brutal, corrupt and inept rulers who held Africa at ransom for many years. What do you expect when you put a drunkard or a thief at the top of a family? This is the very plight Africa faced for many years in which Europe robbed Africa left, right and center unabated. As well, much time and resources, mainly manpower such as academics and professionals were lost at this time provided that many dictators either exiled or killed them for fear that they would dislodge them from power. Uganda provides an ideal example. After taking over in 1972, former Ugandan dictator, Idi

Amin whom Britain backed and installed (Mhango 2016), exiled and killed many academics as the West turned a blind eye. Despite killing hundreds of thousands innocent Ugandans, the so-called international community turned a blind eye as long as its European allies were in Uganda robbing the country. It is no secret that the international community knew everything when Amin was killing innocent Ugandans. Yet, this was not important provided that the interests of Europe in Uganda and in the region were protected by such a maniac. As it is in the case of Africa in general, after Tanzania toppled Amin after attacking it, the same criminals who conspired with Amin, abandoned and exposed him. When the British backed and installed Amin (Roberts 2012), they thought he was just a bumbling buffoon (Mhango *Ibid.*) who would not turn tables on them or know that he was used to do Britain's dirty laundry. Once he started issuing grandiose anti-colonial statements (Leopold 2009; Taylor 2009; and Hale 2011), the British decided to abandon him to end up being toppled and forced to flee the country in 1979. This shows how the belief and concept of Africans being the beasts in the jungle still goes on in the minds of its former colonisers. To help both sides, we need to decolonise them equally due to the fact that they both suffer from racist *sanctius, quam tu* mentality and its effects.

The story of how Africa developed Europe from coups does not end up with Uganda. It goes as far as the giant source of resources, the DRC, whose first president was, as well, overthrown after Belgium and France sponsored their stooge, Mobutu, to misrule the country for over thirty years (Mhango *op.cit.*). If anything, this barbaric and criminal act resulted in indescribable sufferings for Congolese whose sin was nothing but being created and placed in the country with immense reserves of various resources. Essentially, as it has generally always been for Africa, resources became a curse for the DRC in lieu of blessings. There was no way resources would be blessings to the DRC even Africa because by installing venal dictators and goons, Europe assured itself of a freebooting opportunity. Although some European thinkers tend to make Africa believe that it is poor because of mismanagement and other ills, this is hypocritical. How would Africa grow economically amidst corruption Europe has always enhanced by protecting such venal

220

rulers? How could Africa grow economically amidst unfair trading terms with Europe and its allies? In economic terms, Africa is like the sack trapping water placed on the bucket that is Europe. This is why the 27 European Union (EU) members have the GDP of US$ 14.8 trillion compared to Africa's US$ 2.2 trillion (Cilliers 2010). There are no miracles about this exploitation and unfairness which the international community has condoned simply because it is the part of conspiracy against Africa. Apart from being economic sabotage, what has been ongoing unabatedly is nothing but economic racism blatantly and perpetually committed against Africa.

When an academic Walter Rodney (1972) scientifically showed how Europe underdeveloped Africa, over four decades down the line, Africans, mainly leaders, have refused to rebel against Europe. They still go there begging pointlessly; and without any logical reasons provided that many of them rule countries with immense resources of all types. Moreover, African rulers still measure their economies and economic performances based on European standards but not African standards. Apart from depending on Europe to assess performances in their countries, African sitting-duck-like rulers still go to Europe burning billions of dollars for checkups after destroying their economies through corruption and mismanagement. So, too, African rulers still steal public money and stash it in Europe not to mention sending their children for higher education to Europe to come back and use it to rob the *hoi polloi*. Furthermore, Africans still use almost everything European when it comes to their aspects of life. They still use European names not to mention foreign religions to seek their insurance in the *afterlife*. Some lay, poor, uneducated and disgruntled African youth still die at sea seeking to get in Europe which they regard as the country of honey and milk. While thousands of energetic youth are perishing at sea, a few corrupt and privileged Africans are becoming richer and richer on the expenses of the poor (Harriss, Hunter and Lewis 2003). Africa needs to change such dependency quickly; shall it desire to pragmatically move forward as a society and as a people. Without rebelling the same way Africa did against colonialism, it will always languish in manmade miseries; all resulting from allowing itself to be defined by its former colonial powers.

Again, in spite of being categorised as a continent made of almost all the third world countries, Africa is always rich. What essentially makes it look poor but not actually poor, is nothing but the measure and scales used to measure its wealth. And indeed, this is done purposely in order to make Africans feel and internalise lies that they are poor while they actually are not. When the so-called economist and researchers term Africa as the continent that lives under a dollar a day, they do not consider other aspects such as what the so-called poor families do. How, for example, can one term a family that gets all three meals a day poor not to mention being able to send its children to school, paying tax and, above all, live happily? I do not see how Africa can be actually poor while it still supplies the whole world with precious resources of all kinds. Mhango (2017) argues that whether Africa is underdeveloped, thus dependent or not, depends on the definition, lenses and means one uses to reach at such a conclusion. Mhango argues that when you allow another person to define you, he or she will distort or wrongly define, redefine and try to reinvent you as it is in the case of Africa which has always been defined by its enemies. Keeping on doing so is like allowing Africa to remain with albatross around its neck. Mhango's main argument is that that Africa needs to define itself by redefining the terms and definition others use to define and describe it. Is it logical and right to define the wealth of Africa in terms of dollars or whatever Western modes? If the West allows Africans to define it, surely, it will cease to be as rich and as innocent as it portrays itself. This means that Africa needs to not only define itself but also interrogate other definitions almost on everything as it rebellious move aimed at helping Africa to do away with mythical miseries and poverty. For, while it is evident that the West has considerably robbed Africa, no time in history of the world Africa has ever robbed any continent on earth. For centuries, the West has become richer and richer thanks to perpetually exploiting Africa; and nobody sees any anomaly in this as to how a continent blessed with huge reserves of precious resource could live in abject poverty while those robbing it live in stinking opulence. To make Africa's situation more perilous and precarious, "all sources of exploitation" (Fanon 1967: xviii-xix cited in Gyete 2016: 52) have remained the same; as they revolve around precious resources exploited or cheaply bought from Africa going to Europe to be processed and brought back to Africa to be sold at exorbitant prices. The pillaging of Africa has recently been exacerbated by the fact that Asia is now robbing Africa the same way the West has done for many years. The holdup of Africa is not only in terms of resources but also in fluid money. Up until 2013, according to Ajayi and Ndikumana (2014), through capital flight, saw Africa losing to Europe that had held billions of dollars whereby Britain holds US$64.3, France US$15.1, the US US$8.7, US$ 7.6 Portugal, US$4.1 Belgium and US$3.1 in Cayman island (p. 330). How much can this money do for Africa had it been reimbursed to African knowingly how they were stashed illegally? Aren't such countries accomplices in fleecing Africa? Isn't this against human rights? Ajayi and Ndikumana go on disclosing that in the year 2010 Africa lost US$423 billion (p. 24). Those who wonder how small countries with minimum resources such as Portugal and Spain, *inter alia*, became rich, can, at least, get the glimpse of the criminality that has been ongoing for decade as the international community watch helplessly and uselessly. Although claiming that the international community is an accomplice may be seen as an overstatement, the fact of the matter is that it knows and does nothing to stop such criminality due to the fact that the so-called international community is the West thanks to its dominance in world affairs. Chaikin and Sharman (2009: 42) cited in Heggstad and Fjeldstad (2010) explicitly point finger on it noting that "the major obstacles to the recovery of stolen assets are said to be the lack of capacity in developing countries to negotiate the complex legal issues, and the uninterested shown by some developed countries in assisting the repatriation process" (p. 9). Which are these developed countries apart from Western countries? Further, to show how Africa meaningfully developed Europe, Boyce and Ndikumana (2012) disclose that if we assume that flight capital were to earn the modest interest rate measured by the short-term United States Treasury Bill rate, the corresponding accumulated stock of capital flight from the 33 countries stands at $1.06 trillion in 2010 (p. 1). Is this all? Ndikumana (2014) puts the loss to US$1.3 trillion in the same period (p. 16) while Nkurunziza (2012) puts at US$ 1.8 trillion (p. 15); also see Nkurunziza (2015). As far as Africa developing Europe is concerned, here we are talking about capital flight only. If we include what Europe robbed Africa for the entire time it occupied and colonised it plus what it made under neocolonialism and neoliberalism, not to mention what it is currently fleecing from Africa, we are talking about zillions of dollars. For example, Engler (2008); and Bliss 2009; Wyler and Sheik 2008) cited in Douglas and Alie (2014) respectively note that wildlife, fisheries and wild-sourced timber are worth an estimated US$332 billion annually; of which US$10-20 billion is illegal (p. 272). Apart from Africa, which continent still has animals to sell legally and illegally? This is not easy money, particularly for the poor continent like Africa that has always been treated as a misfit. This means, such a humungous amount of money was injected into European economies without doing anything except condoning graft. While all this systemic criminality has been ongoing, despite evidence been all over the place, there still are devising other methods for Africa to become poorer and poorer whereas the same does not address the root causes which gyrate around Europe's entrenched systemic criminality! To add insult to injury, the international community has condoned such criminality, the same is dubiously pampering Africa by introducing hawkish projects such as the Millennium Development Goals (MDGs) which are unfair (Easterly (2009) simply because "they do not go far enough to address unfair social relations associated with crossing a line of minimum adequacy" (Maathai 2011: 15) based on the world order despite the fact that the United Nations thinks is the solution to Africa's problems. This is a double standard and sad. Instead of wasting time and opportunities, if indeed, the international community seriously wants to help Africa out of manmade poverty and underdevelopment, it must decolonise the concept of development. For, without disinfecting the entire current structural set up of development, Africa will always lag behind in terms of Western-defined development. Currently, the world is run by a predatory system that benefits the West as opposed to Africa and the likes. Francisco and Antrobus (2009: 164 cited in Obeng-Odoom (2013) posit that "the MDGs have been nicknamed 'most distracting gimmick'" (p. 158). Africa should stop buying into such ploys. Instead, it must agitate for its redress due to the crimes Europe and its partners committed to it under slavery, colonialism; and now neocolonialism that have maintained the *status in quo*. As a victim of the above evils, I would prefer the redress and returning of the billions stashed in Europe to the MDGs and other abracadabra. Despite this chicanery, there are some thinkers who maintain that the MDGs are the way to go (Bourguignon, Bénassy-Quéré, Dercon, Estache, Gunning, Kanbur, Klasen, Maxwell, Platteau and Spadaro 2010). However, practically, the MDGs have never improved Africa's situation as far as eliminating poverty is concerned. Further, if Africa wants to move forward so as to rival others, it must think about its own model and way of attaining development through seeking to be redressed for Europe's past criminality. Keeping on being fooled that MDGs and other Western policies will pull it out of poverty is a blatant lie. This Africa shall not do.

How Africa Takes Some Things for Granted

There are things that Africans dumbfoundedly take for granted; however, they have been ones of tools that Europe used on using Africa for its development. Nothing has cost Africa dearly as taking many things for a long time for granted while those exploiting take nothing for granted. In this chapter, I am touching on such things that Africans have never suspected as being the sinkholes that sink their money for the development of Europe. One of those things is religion. Since its introduction to Africa, religion, especially Roman Catholicism has helped Europe to keep tabs on Africa as far as spying it is concerned. So, when Europeans brought Christianity, Africans did not suspect that it would be used as a tool of spying on and brainwashing them. It is at this time, through its missionaries, Christianity played a very vital role in subjugating Africans already for colonisation. Missionaries, among other colonial agents, paved the way for colonial administrators to come and take over under full-fledged colonialism. Before and during the introduction of colonialism, religion played a very pivotal role of penetrating the continent; and thereby scooping its secrets. Nothing colonial powers used as the information that missionaries relied back home. Such information was vital for making easy the colonisation of Africa.

Apart from spying on Africans, Christianity was used as a tool of cultural destruction that condemned African cultures to ungodliness and devilishness. For example, after introducing Christianity in Africa, Europe used missionaries to easily spy on Africa under the pretext of penitential (Macalister 2012; Mhango 2015; and Stejskal 2016) which has been going unabatedly despite the systems and styles of spying being overhauled. These colonial agents paved the way for the full occupation and thereafter colonisation of Africa that saw Africa's resources and people being robbed for many years as I have indicated hereinabove. Despite overhauling this spying strategy, the dent had already been made to the disadvantage[s] of Africa. For, from it, Africa ended up being colonised and exploited for many decades. This colonial strategy was easily carried out under the pretext of *forgiving* sins. Interesting, even after uncovering such damning realities on such criminality Europe committed on Africa, neither Africa nor the international community has ever advocated or introduced the process of suing such criminals and the governments that benefited from their criminal activities in Africa or sought to stop it. The international community has nothing to lose except to prove that it practically preaches what it does and means. This is why I am saying that Europe is not supposed to be afraid of delivering restorative justice to itself and Africa. In so doing, I am not seeking to exonerate Europe, as noted above, but to help both parties to move forward peacefully and judiciously. What is sought is reconciliation based on resolving a problem and negative effects it caused to both parties. This is very important. Why are the victims of sexual abuses, rapes and the like being redressed today after their plights become known but Africa's is not redressed?

Quite so, all religions, whose agents enhanced colonialism, have the duty legally and morally to make official apology to Africa and redress it for the wrongs they either committed or abetted to. For example, the Catholic Church whose management is under the Vatican has a duty along with Europe to right the wrongs it enacted and unleashed. Gallego and Woodberry (2010) note that:

> In most former colonies, the first schools founded by missionaries (as in British colonies) or were managed by priests as

226

agents of the colonial power (as in most Belgian, Portuguese and Spanish colonies) (p. 295).

These schools were used as nurseries that produced many personnel for colonial governments. Almost all clerks, and later, first elites were the products of mission schools. It is from these schools first African stooges were picked and groomed to become presidents and who's who after colonial powers handed over fake independence to Africa. Apart from hatching elites and workers for the colonial governments, missionary schools were used as spying institutions that ended up corrupting Africans who went through them.

Essentially, Africa's first intellectual blow started with missionary schools. Magesa (2002) cited in Gifford (2008) maintains that:

> Colonialism and Christianisation were the two events that hold pride of place in the profound… misshaping of the African continent' and besides legitimating the plunder, missionaries played a key role in destroying the African soul (p. 21).

In some cases, they were the ones that encouraged a colonial power to occupy a country. Bottazzi, Goguen and Rist (2016) cite an example of Sierra Leone that was seen as unfit for European settlement. But after missionaries discovered minerals, the perception about the country changed; and thus was occupied. Had it not been for the missionaries to assure British colonial government of the suitability and viability of Sierra Leone economically, there would not have been the change of heart for British government.

Apart from hijacking Africa intellectually, missionaries grabbed many acres of land. Okuku (2006) notes that in Uganda, for example, under the 1900 agreement between the British and Baganda, colonial government destroyed precolonial system of land owning by introducing one that was known as mailo or square miles under which land was preferentially offered to kings, chiefs, church and the colonial state. Apart from showing how the church and colonial governments were one thing, the offer of land shows how Europe started corrupting African leaders something that has gone up until now. Land that kings, chiefs and church were given was not just a mere lagniappe. It symbolised more connection among these institutions that his-story tells. This corruption helped Europe in many ways. You can see this on how African traitors were used either to sell their colleagues during slavery or ruling them under what was famously known as indirect rule (Acemoglu, Chaves, Osafo-Kwaako and Robinson 2014) whereby colonisers sat back and left indigenous leaders to rule their people. This is evidence that Europeans did not bring the art of administration to Africa. Instead, they brought colonialism and duplicity. For, in trying to minimising the costs of running a colony, colonisers built in the already existing African systems. This type of rule was more corrupt and cheaper for the colonisers; and it helped Europe to collect a lot of money by the way of taxes without providing any social services that the legitimate governments used to provide. To motivate indigenous people to betray their original administrational systems, they offered them some favours and turned them into unsuspecting accomplices. The difference however is that whereas European colonisers carried whatever mission, Europe benefited as opposed to African accomplices or black colonisers whose continent lost everything either due to their greed or ignorance if not both. Colonisers did not need to necessarily import anything except a couple of administrators who would use African precolonial institutions and personnel to run the colonial governments cheaply under what was known as colonialism-on-the-cheap (Herbst 2014). Under this system, colonialists made sure that Africans were running their show as they watched and fleeced Africa. This is why the argument that Africans lacked administrational institutions and organisational capacity does not hold water at all. For example, Richens (2009) discloses that by the 'high-noon of empire'–the late 1930s –there were barely 3,000 European administrators ruling over an African population approaching 90 million (p. 5). This shows that Africans were good at administering their affairs. They were better and more frugal than current big governments that are nothing but black holes in African countries simply because they aped and are now using European systems in administering their countries.

As for the land grabbing and distribution in Uganda, while such criminality was committed, the church did not defend those whose lands were taken. How could it defend them while it was part of the crime? This has been the stance of the church in many issues it has stakes. This move was very critical for the warfare of the majority of people. For, it was used to punish kings and individuals who did not support colonialism.

Essentially, the land the church received did not lay idle. It was worked on and produced a lot for the benefit of the mother church in Europe. As if this was not enough, African converts were overworked in these lands for many hours and paid nothing or less under what was known as church's time that was different from normal time. There was no difficulties in getting labourers, especially where indigenous were rendered landless. People needed jobs in order to be able to survive and pay tax to colonial governments. This is completely different from what the church was supposed to stand for; namely to defend the poor as Jesus once ordered (Luke 14:13; Mark 10: 21; and Matthew 19: 21).

Similarly, the Roman Catholic Church used to exploit its converts in Africa by spending their money without telling them how the money was spent. It established many activities by which it made a lot of money whereas its African converts were becoming poorer and poorer by day. Berry (2012) sees no difference between church financial system and medieval fiefdoms wherein a few dioceses subjected their finances to robust auditing while parishioners had little knowledge or say in how bishops control the use of their contributions. This has gone on even today. Bishops are like demigods who cannot be questioned about how they spend the money they solicit from the believers. It shows how the church has remained as a colonial extension whose role, up until now in modern society, is negligible and objectionable so to speak. This is because, as the modernity as Europe espouses engulfed Africa, immorality became the order of the day so as to involve even the clergy themselves. Refer to the case of adultery, fornication, violation of children and sexual scandals or clerical child sex abuse (Donnelly and Inglis 2010; Hungerman 2013; and Keenan 2013) that recently swamped the Roman Catholic Church.

Over and above, to easily deceive and dupe Africans, Europeans used God as a tool under the religion after finding that moral roots were so deep in Africa; not to mention trust among Africans and whoever that interacted with them. It is sad to note that Africans were not aware of the fact that religion had already tortured and failed miserably in Europe after causing a lot of miseries such as massacres, burning people at stake, drowning and many fierce divisions among Europeans under the inquisition (Murphy 2012). Therefore, the Europeans of the time exported their problems to Africa knowingly how many society will turn against each other for the benefit of colonisers. Christianity was first introduced as a tool for dividing and spying on Africans. And indeed, it worked for the advantage of Europeans as opposed to the interest of Africa. In his book, *Things Fall Apart*, Chinua Achebe explains this phenomenon nicely not to mention other writers such as Ngugi wa Thiong'o, and Camara Laye among others.

With religion came education that, in essence, was aimed at poisoning African minds. Davidson (2014) notes that whatever missionary schools taught was "from a racist standpoint that whatever that came from Europe was good and useful; and whatever that came from Africa was reverse or not worth studying" (p. 88). This tendency still exists even in the current international arena. This is why for example; genocide was carried out in Rwanda in 1994 without the international community stepping into it as they did at the same time in Kosovo. As I am writing this volume, genocide has been going in Darfur; and, ironically, the international community has never adequately addressed it. As for the international community, nothing comes to Africa except bad governance, corruption, wars, diseases, and other miseries even if there always has been the West behind them.

Just like former European colonial masters, the Roman Catholic Church has what it takes to make an apology and redress Africa for the wrong it either; or helped to commit *vis-à-vis* Rwandan genocide. As any beneficiary of the crime, the Roman Catholic should share the loots with the victims in order to prove itself morally. It does not make sense for the church to teach morality while it sits on immoral past. Among all players, the Catholic Church under the Holy See needs to lead the way. The Catholic Church needs to emulate the person on which its preaching is based namely Jesus Christ who is "a teacher of morality, in fact, he is *the* teacher of Christian morality" (Meier 2004: 45). Therefore, if the Church keeps on denying and negating the issues of issuing a formal apology and redressing Africa, it will, in fact, be recanting the teachings of Jesus it has for many years preached. For, so doing, is no different from betraying and exploiting Jesus and his message of peace and justice for the world. Before Europe invented racism in Spain 1492 (Mhango *forthcoming*) there had been only three African popes namely St. Victor I (189-199); St. Militiades (113-132); and St. Gelacius I (492-496), *inter alia*, who "made significant contributions to the growth of Christianity and the development of the catholic faith." Oddly, despite such exemplary contributions to the faith, their people, Africans are still treated like the second-class race in Africa and in the world at large. Are Africans really the children of God the Almighty or the lesser God (Crone 2010) with lesser deities, lesser minds and lesser things (Lovejoy 2011) and lesser everything so as to be abused, betrayed and maltreated like this? This is the challenge Africa needs to overcome so as to stand up; and tell Europe to redress it for the contributions it made for the development of Europe not to mention the evils Europe committed.

Apart moral decadency and deficiency, the Catholic Church is liable for racism in that it has never elected a black pope in the so-called modern times despite the fact that one in every four Christians is found in Sub-Saharan Africa (SSA) (*Pew Research Center* 2011).

Even Europe, which says it is a Christian, is not spared from this reality. Durand cited in O'Mahony (2009) notes that:

> Pius XII certainly made the distinction between free and oppressed European peoples his own and he seemed to support the idea of a renewed Christianitas. This was a new Europe built around a free Western Europe, founded on democracy, seeking institutional forms for union and collaboration on Christian foundations (p 183).

Interestingly, despite such huge contributions by Africans, their race has never been appreciated for anything except to follow but not to lead (Abera 2017). This issue has existed for many years. Jenkins (2011) discloses that in Africa, Christians have increased from 10 million in 1900 to 36 million in 2000. How much attention does the Roman Catholic Church pay to them? Just like Europe has always ignored the role Africa has religiously played in its development, the church has never bothered to appreciate Africa's contribution to its growth in the world, primarily at the time Christianity is dwindling in Europe.

Mhango (2015) chides and invites academics to re-examine and reconsider social aspects Africans take for grants while they actually have acted as the conduits if not syphons in fleecing Africa. He asks as to how much Africa has already lost much to things such as going to Mecca for pilgrimage which occurs annually not to mention money Roman Catholic churches remit to the Vatican to end up getting immaterial assurance. He goes further looking into fashion industry, music, cinema and whatnots that foreign countries use to exploit Africa.

Chapter Nine

How Can Africa Heed Its Wake-up Call

This section is intended to act as a wakeup call for African countries to wise up; and therefrom take their destiny into their hands by becoming self-reliant as they divorce the tendency of dependency as far as real and true development is concerned. The first step for Africa to do away with being labelled as an underdeveloped continent without connecting it to the development of Europe it enhanced must start with cultivating the culture of intellectual self-defining as opposed to allowing others to define Africa. Thereafter, Africa needs to question and interrogate whatever definitions, concepts and rationales those defining it in any manner propound either about it or about world issues. Therefore, this section intends to put a finger on the crux of the matter *vis-à-vis* Africa's developing Europe.

Since attaining their political independence, over fifty years ago, African countries have pointlessly over and above believed in and lived on aid that rich countries–mostly European–have extended to them in order to make them believe that they cannot do without it. This is a strategy of keeping them at bay not to mention shifting their attention to their true path of development based on the history of exploitation of the two. Thanks to this dependency, most of the African countries have their budgets, elections and other development projects–apart from being defined by the outsiders based on their criteria and targets–always been financed and supported by donors countries.

As regards Africa's pointless dependency, to begin with, we need to interrogate if aid does really help economies to grow in economic terms (Rajan and Subramanian 2008). This will enable us to gauge if the economies of African countries have grown due to receiving aid; or what is likely to keep on happening if the manner and trend of offering aid to African countries continues as it has been unabated or without being deconstructed and interrogated. Such an approach is important, particularly in showing how the so-called development that is tied on aid may, sometimes, end up being elusive for such countries, especially when emphasis is put on material things; and thereby ignore nonmaterial ones such as culture, morality and the environment that are not included in defining development and underdevelopment. I do not think that countries renowned for polluting the earth and robbing others are truly developed compared to those that do not pollute. Addressing this development paradigm, knowing what will happen, will help African countries to start thinking out of the box about the less travelled way out of their predicaments. Polluting countries have been extending aid to Africa and other non-polluting countries so as to make them dependent on them so that they could complain or take them on. Despite this, Lensink and Morrisey (2000) invoke endogamous theory to show how aid has never brought any development to African countries positing that it negatively affects growth determinants on investment for African countries. This is obvious due to the fact that when it comes to assessing, defining and gaging, if there is growth or not, the same donors have an upper hand *vis-à-vis* the modalities of research and the results obtained thereof. The real situation can be seen on the connection between aid and corruption. Mathiason (2005) and Blanchflower (2008) cited in Mac Ginty and Williams (2009) note with concern that, in the year 2007, worldwide overseas development assistance was US$103 billion whose big chunk ended up being paid to Western consultants. Again, how much does Africa lose in such corruption spearheaded by Western firms? In trying to show the size of the problem, Ribadu (2009) answers the above question noting that the African Union (AU) reported that corruption drains the region of some $140 billion a year, which is about 25% of the continent's official GDP. This means that the aid the West offers end up being syphoned back plus more US$37 billion. Ironically, despite such firms involved in mega-corruption schemes of robbing Africa being sponsored by Western countries, they and their countries are not declared as corrupt because of the same crime they accuse Africa. It takes two to tango. Here we are talking about Western corporations. What of African venal rulers such as Joseph Mobutu (former Zaire now the Democratic Republic of Congo (DRC) Sani Abacha (Nigeria) and Omar Bongo (Gabon) among others who robbed and supervised the robbing of Africa in terms of billions if not trillions? Wrong (2005) discloses that:

> In 1999, the Economist estimated that African leaders had stowed $20bn in Swiss bank accounts. Investigations in Kenya after President Daniel arap Moi left office indicated that, at the very least, $1bn had been sent overseas by former officials. University of Massachusetts researchers have estimated that from 1970 to 1996, capital flight from 30 sub-Saharan countries totalled $187bn, outstripping those same nations' external debt.

Looking at the sheer size of the loots, it is obvious that countries whose rulers were involved in this mega theft were categorised as underdeveloped due to being pauperised by the same leaders that categorise them as underdeveloped while, at the same time, they declare Europe–that benefits from such mega corruptions–as developed. Who is holding accountable, for example, Switzerland whose economy is openly known to have advanced and grown based on looted monies from the so-called underdeveloped countries among which is Africa? Ironically, despite being the accessory to the crime, the same Switzerland still offers aid to Africa. Actually, what Europe offers to Africa as aid is but the surplus resulting from robbing it either, as indicated above, through bogus consultancy or syphoning raw materials if not capital flight not to mention underpaying its products. Despite such criminality, Switzerland is defined as a highly developed country. This is because the moral aspect that ties it to robbery is excluded in defining development.

Additionally, Hickel (2013) notes that:

> Robert Pollin, an economist at the University of Massachusetts, estimates that developing countries have lost roughly $480 billion in potential GDP as a result of structural adjustment. Yet, Western corporations have benefitted tremendously. It has forced open vast new consumer markets; it has made it easier to access cheap labour and raw materials; it has opened up avenues for capital flight and tax avoidance; it has created a lucrative market in foreign debt; and it has facilitated a massive transfer of public resources into private hands (the

World Bank alone has privatised more than $2 trillion worth of assets in developing countries).

Due to material drive and the exclusion of moral and cultural aspects in defining and rating countries in development, such figures above are not addressed. You can see how such huge amounts of money stolen from Africa are not considered in categorising or rating countries *vis-a-vis* development or underdevelopment. I cannot understand the rationale behind such ignorance and exclusionary tactics the Europe and West in general have always applied on Africa almost in everything sensible and meaningful. What is clear is the fact that Western countries are maltreating Africa in order to make Africans internalise and reinforce such anomaly so as to subscribe to the belief that they cannot live without depending on aid while they lived for many centuries before the introduction of colonials without necessarily depending on any aid.

Fundamentally, what is reported above, in the main, depends on how donor countries want things done which, in many cases; favour their verdict even if it is wrong. Willis (2011) provides an answer positing that "some theorists argued that people from the temperate parts of the world were naturally 'better' than those from the tropical zones, and so justified the domination of Europeans over the inhabitants of other places" (p. 148). Therefore, whatever theorists from the temperate parts of the world say is like *Roma locuta est, causa finite est* namely Roma has spoken, the cause if finished. Whether aid is a causal force behind growth to African economies is subject to discussion all depends on who does so. There are arguments that in defining [under-]development at an individual country level, the case is always differently positive and negative depending on how the country abides by the conditions donor countries impose on it. So, too, double standard applies to loans poor countries receive from rich countries. Sometimes, a country so loaned may be worse either in accountability, democracy and rule of law. Again, the donors/lenders will never stop extending aid or lend to such a country. Knowing that some countries are so corrupt that they cannot pay, lenders tend to be more generous by cancelling some debts. In principle, lenders like to cancel debts in order to bring down the risk of defaulting. Bjerg, Bjørnskov and Holm (2011) disclose that lower levels of debts are taken as lower risk with respect to paying the debts not to mention servicing them. This is why dictatorial regime such as the one in Uganda still enjoys donors' support despite being corrupt, dictatorial and unaccountable. However, if we consider how Uganda at the time report was issued was the darling of the West, chances that such findings were aimed at showing how donor money has performed its *miracles* to the country. Shule (2016) maintains that Uganda became the darling of the West due to the fact that it helped in toppling undesired governments that the West saw as obstacles to their interests in Africa on top of having its boots in Somalia Fisher (2012). The West does not fail their ally in anything be it legal or illegal, acceptable or unacceptable. So, sometimes, the so-called development or underdevelopment depends on the personality instead of the actuality. Oloka-Onyango (2004) lucubrates that Museveni was able to garner leverage from Western bigwigs due to maintaining close ties "from Margaret Thatcher through John Major and up to Tony Blair" (p. 36). More on why Museveni, as an example of corrupt and undemocratic African rulers, became a shining star can be found in Jans (2016) who notes that since 1992 Uganda became the darling of donors, in spite of lacking democracy and transparency, nothing would deter donors to support it at the detriment of democracy, human rights and the people of Uganda. However, Uganda's aid was only withheld once when it took a stern stance against homosexuality. Here you can see that what matters to donors, compared to the real problems African countries face and the interests of the citizens despite contributing hugely to the development of Europe, is nothing but donors' interests even whenever they harm the lives of citizens as it is in the case of Uganda and other suchlike countries. I do not know if the rights of the minority homosexuals in Uganda were more important than those of the majority Ugandans dying because of poverty resulting from corruption, unaccountable, bad and poor governance. The rights of the minority should be protected and promoted alongside the rights of the majority. Try to compare Uganda with what happened when Gaddafi decided to become a *good boy* of the West; and what transpired after he did the opposite that led to his toppling; and later demise. Put in mind; Europe in this business of safeguarding its interests in Africa has neither permanent friends nor permanent foes except permanent interests. Easterly (2009) notes that development goals are unfair to Africa due to the strings attached to aid that Africa receives.

In addressing the major question of aid, we need, *inter alia*, to explore the conditions or strings attached to aid; and the very role it plays in realising development in Africa wherever there is any or otherwise. We need to critically explore and interrogate what donors actually expect to get out the aid extended to African countries; and above all, how the aid is used by the donors and the recipients. Examining the nature, role and intentions of aid becomes important due to the fact that almost every powerful country has interests in Africa while Africa does not have any interests in these countries. Under such unequal relationship devoid of inequitable reciprocity, the outcomes are obvious that whoever complies with the conditions of aid will be deemed successful however temporarily as it was in the case of Uganda even when such aid has achieved nothing but to help the dictator to fast his grip on power. It is an open secret that aid, given for safeguarding the interests of the donors, has been the backbone of corrupt and dictatorial regimes. Bermeo (2011) notes that studies have shown that aid can entrench dictatorships so as to make transitioning to democracy less likely. As for having interests to be protected in Africa for foreign non-African countries, it goes without saying, the West is not alone. Currently, China and India are seeking leverage from Africa; all aimed at safeguarding their interests too at the detriments of Africa. To do so, the duo are extending aid in order to gain leverage by winning hearts and minds of African rulers who are the only ones that decide who should have sphere of influence on them or not. This is why I call this the second scramble for Africa after the first that ushered in colonial rule in Africa. My assumption is that if there is no equal and equitable reciprocity, chances are that the donors are likely to benefit while the recipients lose in the name of aid as it has been the case for Africa. Current example of how aid has never benefited Africa can be drawn from Tanzania, among many other African countries. After suffering for a long time in the hands of donors, Tanzania's Government recently urged its people to end donor dependence. This happened when the Millennium Challenge Corporate (MCC) cancelled aid to Tanzania. The *Reuters* (March 29, 2016) reports that "Tanzania won a five-year package of grants in 2008 worth $698 million from MCC, an independent U.S. government foreign aid agency, but the award of a second round of grants has now been shelved"[Sic].

Although I do not condone election fraud that Tanzania is accused of to have occurred in Zanzibar, essentially, what Tanzanian government thought it was aid from the Millennium challenge Corporate (MCC), seems to have been more verbal than practical, just like the project that gave birth to all this namely, the Millennium Development Goals (MDGS) which Pronk (2015) postulates that they are mere political goals resulting from a political process–that includes more or less objectivity–needs assessments and cost–benefit analysis, and thus also compromises. I can argue that the donor community wanted to use such inducements to have sort of unchecked powers to control Tanzania something that is replicated almost in all Africa countries. For the country that produces tanzanite, gold, and other precious minerals in tonnes, what is US$698 million; if it manages its resources soundly? Tanzania–that was slammed with such a denial of already promised aid–produces natural gas; and it is the home of Lake Victoria, the largest national park Serengeti and many more among resources that the country is endowed with. Yet, in categorising and defining economic development of the country, such economic bases are ignored or left out of the equation. The *Guardian* (April 1, 2016) quoted Tanzanian president John Pombe Magufuli as saying "we have to stand on our own [...] Tanzania will persevere" after the MCC denied his country the monies. If this was not out of anger, many African leaders need to think this way so that they can responsibly and creatively avoid and thwart such dependency in order to pull their countries out of wanton dependency and beggarliness; and thereby define their levels of development based on internationally agreed upon criteria. Ironically, when donor countries default on their promises no punitive measures are taken against them simply because 'blessed is the hand that giveth than the one that taketh'; one may argue. So, too, recipients have no authority to question their donors. This is the tendency that emanates from colonial legacy. Africa needs to radically and systematically change this anomaly-cum-anathema. More fundamentally, Africa, if indeed wants to become free and prosperous in benefiting from and enjoying its resources, needs to think out of aid-dependency box; and stop living on handouts while it is sitting on immense untapped resources. One would wonder why such huge reserves of minerals and resources are not included in the formula of defining and rating development. Yes, it baffles to find a country that has no resources such as Switzerland–whose economy, *inter alia*, depends on stolen money–is ranked higher in development than countries like the DRC with all huge land mass and resources.

Besides defaulting, donors apply various ruses to coerce and dupe poor countries into their traps. An ideal example is the whole project known as the Heavily Indebted Poor Countries (HIPC) that the World Bank (WB) initiated in 1996 aimed at cancelling debts for some highly indebted countries of which many are in Africa. If you look at HIPC's *modus operandi*, you find that it is more of a hoax if not a ruse hegemonic countries use to pull poor countries in more debts than a serious commitment to alleviate or fight poverty in poor countries. Debt cancellation is more of a mirage than a reality due to the fact that since its inception, nothing has changed as far as Europe's exploitation of Africa is concerned. Arnone and Presbitero (2016) note that, actually the HIPC is a soft loan strategy that the lenders apply as means of avoiding default by their debtors which would lead into losing their money. To avoid this, the lenders add more money or cancel some debts so as to keep up the game of fleecing Africa. Due to the over touted and propagandised understanding that aid is a panacea for resolving Africa's problems, there is a major question we may ask: Is there any respite that the debt cancellation has ever brought to African countries? How many countries were pulled out of poverty; thus, out of underdevelopment through aid? Moyo (2009) notes that debt cancellation is essentially the cause of more poverty due to the fact that it adds more debts– not to mention serving the debts–and creates; and thereby perpetuates vicious-debt circle for Africa. Such a situation has over and above created and enhanced corruption and visionless regimes that have ruled Africa for a long time. What do you expect when you sink millions of dollar in such a hole? The DRC under Mobutu's kleptocratic regime provides an ideal example of how debts become a burden to many African countries. Under Mobutu, the DRC would borrow as it deemed fit without looking at the other side of the coin in that the money borrowed ended up being squandered by Mobutu in his oft-shopping sprees in Europe. It does not mean that loaners did not know this naked truth. They did. Again, why would they bother while they knew the DRC will always be there? Therefore, the loans they extended to the DRC would be paid even if it was through nose. The donors knew the dangers of what they were financing. This has never been part of their business. Theirs has always been the rip off of poor countries provided that there are guarantees that such countries will pay in the future. Reno (1997) cited in Wright (2008) observes that Mobutu's regime in the former Zaire fell from 17.5% of government spending in 1972 to 2% in 1990, and agricultural spending (mostly subsidies) fell from over 40% of the budget to 11% in 1990. Meanwhile, during that time, the president's share of the budget increased from 30% to 95% (p. 974). While Zaïre was cascading into manmade poverty; hence underdevelopment, the countries that conspired with Mobutu to rob it were rated as developed. Had moral aspect been included in the elements used to rate countries in development—it is obvious—such countries would not feature high in development. What such blind rating does is like rating a thug as a richest person on earth without underscoring the fact that the wealth the said thug purports to own belongs to others. As argued above, countries such as Switzerland and other heavens for illicit money are not supposed to be rated without incorporating moral aspect in the whole process. This is the argument Africa and the so-called underdeveloped countries should rise in order to partake of the process of analysing, defining and rating development. For, once only the rich are allowed to define development, they will make sure that their definition will force others to follow them and learn from them even if it realistically not supposed to be so.

Furthermore, Africa needs to markedly stop trusting whoever comes to it with whatever from definitions and models of production or economy. For, despite the fact that the West kept on pumping aid to Africa, Africa remained relatively poor (Glennie 2010) due to the fact that aid offered does not aim at resolving the real problems African countries face as they result from Europe's colonial past. Due to the failure of aid, Africa effectively needs to come up with its own economic model and policies in order to get out of elusive and manmade underdevelopment as defined by the West. To begin with, Africa needs to now know where the confusion-cum-problem of rating Africa as underdeveloped emanates. It is upon the victims to see things in their true colours so that they can urgently and quickly do something about the problems resulting from the lack of African perspective of things. Complaining is Africa's right. Again, it is not the pretext of staying aside and looks as if Africans are not victims who have been negatively affected for over five decades. The way towards real and sustainable development lies on Africa's awakening to see to it that it takes its destiny into its own hands. And doing so is nowhere except in taking charge of defining the terms of whatever Africa is part of. That is it.

Suffice it to say, whether Africa is underdeveloped or otherwise is like a myth that needs to be revisited, deconstructed and demystified, especially for the Africans whose role in reaching such a conclusion is amiss. For the development to be meaningful; and thereby make sense, past evils–slavery, colonialism and neocolonialism caused–need to be accommodated, addressed and considered in defining development. As indicated in this discourse, nothing makes Africans feel sidelined, mainly those who do not subscribe to such a conclusion, is the fact that many criteria used to define development are wanting. So, too, those who appointed such criteria have ignored so many more important elements that would make sense had they been considered in reaching the conclusion of whether one country is developed or underdeveloped. Therefore, the demystification of the said myth is looming and crucial. Therefore, efforts must be made to see to it that the process of decolonising development is done in order to get a fitting definition resulting from a dialogue on what should be exclude and what should be included and why. Importantly, there is nobody who can do this job except African academics that need to address the matter academically and courageously so as to make a bulletproof case backed by facts as far as the true history of Africa and the history of colonialism, exploitation and slavery is concerned. To do away with being referred to as an underdeveloped continent without considering the causal factors, Africa needs to face those defining and ranking it as underdeveloped in order to have a say in the process so as to be part of it. Africa is habited by humans not animals. Africans are capable of doing and perceiving things just like anybody else. Therefore, it is a grave insult to keep on defining Africa as if Africans have no knack to participate in propounding definitions of whatever they are part of. I can say that at this point and time Africa needs to reorganise itself to see to it that it changes the way it has been doing things after the results proved that the ground is tilted; and therefore things have never worked to its favour. Suppose Africa redefines its economy modal based on its aspirations, needs and time. Such as leapfrog can be reached if Africa embarks on producing what it can locally consume before pointlessly producing for the external market. It is obvious that Africa is not as technologically developed as Europe is currently. For, it still heavily depends on agriculture for consumption and for export which takes a big chunk of Africa's agro-outputs. Given that Africa has never had any say in price setting, it needs to produce what it can have a say on and consume altogether first. Many African farmers produce cash crops to end up spending a little money they get on purchasing foods of which some are pointlessly imported.

How Cultural Imperialism Misdefined Africa

Since its first contact with Europe, Africa has lost a lot to cultural imperialism. Cultural imperialism has no watertight definition. Luis Ramiro Beltran (1978b: 184) cited in Kraidy (2017) defines cultural imperialism as "a verifiable process of social influence by which a nation imposes on other countries its set of beliefs, values, knowledge, and behavioral norms as well as its overall style of life"(p. 26). For this volume, cultural imperialism means the situation in which one culture dominates another for the purpose of exploiting and subjugating as it has been in the case of Africa whose cultures Europe demonised, sabotaged and subjugated in order to invade, occupy, colonise and thereafter exploiting Africa perpetually as it has been for many decades. As mentioned prior, Africa, for example, spends millions of dollars on European fashions. This can wrongly be taken as a trivial matter. It is not. Culture is a booming business for the West or Europe. This is why, through its media, the West has always propagated the universalisation of its cultures. You can see this on how some African artists like to perform surrounded by dirty and poor background believing that this is what Europe can buy from them. And to make sure that Africans are always confined to self-negation, Europe has always praised and even bought cultural works that depicts Africa as uncouth and undeveloped continent under the pretext of originality or traditionality. Further, you can see this in much of natural African art and music many artists believe can attract European consumers by exposing their manmade poverty or nudity with the belief of selling their culture and products to Europeans. Go to any European country. You will be showed the best of it but not the worst of it as it currently is in Africa due the ignorance and cultural imperialism that inculcated self-denial in Africans. The ideal example can be drawn from Congolese music. Currently, most of Congolese musicians are trying hard to entice Europe by degrading themselves and their people. Nowadays, many male musicians with pierced ears which is a new things in Africa not to mention wearing sagging fashions simply because they feel they are or, they want to look either European or American but not Africa like Masai, Swazi or Zulu who still use their culture to portray who they are. It does not mean that Africa did not pierce their ears. They did so by the dictate of their culture but not the so-called modernity or fashion. Further, most of Congolese modern music, in in spite of being famous globally, is full of half-naked and X-rated stuff all done in the spirit of either aping or enticing Europe. It is no longer a taboo to see naked or half-naked Congolese women on Television or youtube gyrating in order to entice viewers. Most of them have their bases in Paris but not the DRC or Congo where those who decided to stay still make money (Koné 2014; and Momo 2017) despite the fact that such acts are nothing but curses and self-degrading. Egbunike (2017) asks "if not for poverty, why would someone exhibit his/her state of nudity just for a few thousand dollars he/she is not even sure of getting" (p. 39). To show how they follow Europe's *diktat* and taste, such nude girls hide their breasts but not private parts such as buttocks and others as African culture dictates. In doing so, they are aping Western Magazines such as Playboy (Ncube n.d year) which degrades women by turning them into merchandise or objects anybody can buy, use, abuse and exploit as he deems fit simply because he is able to buy them. Congolese dancers are degraded without knowing that they are used as advertising slots for the group of high-living *bon vivant* Congolese immigrants to Europe known as mikilistes, or the high fashion group known as sapeurs (Tsambu 2015). This is not a true African culture in which nudity is a taboo. This is because in many, if not all, African cultures, everything is owned communally including the dignity of the society that depends on individual members of the society. As well, purposely showing one's nudity is prohibited in many African cultures (Coly 2010; Emefa and Selase 2014). For example, in Nigeria, nudity is punishable by law under Nigerian law that also regulates women dress code (Tamale 2014). It is not only African cultures that prohibit nudity. In China mainland, for example, nudity along with kissing are prohibited (Bettinson 2017). The situation is the same in India (Prasad 1998 cited in Anujan, Schaefer and Karan 2012). However, thanks to the influx of Western culture, nudity is a norm accepted through the backdoor of modernity in many African cultures (Ojua, Lukpata and Atama 2014). Nudity is not a curse only in African cultures. Even the Bible the white man exported to Africa, it is a curse as well. Refer to what is known as "the Curse of Ham" in which Ham gazed the nudity of Noah, his father, without covering him (Gen., 9:20–27 cited in Mathee 2016). Such an act warranted not only the curse but also the punishment as stated in Gen., (9:22-27) cited in Burridge (2008) which goes on justifying slavery arguing that Abraham is blessed by God with "male and female slaves" as a wealthy slave-owner (Gen., 24:35). So, whoever thinks that using nudity as a curse is an archaic African thing of the past must think twice before passing the judgment.

In many African cultures, woman's nudity is a weapon that can be used when they are pushed to the extremes; otherwise showing the nudity of women is regarded as curse to the understanding that women are the givers of life (Maathai 2006: 22 cited in Hunt 2014; and Tamale 2016). Nudity is a very serious weapon that some African modern rulers fear the most. When narrating how Mali's former president was cursed by woman's nudity, Stevens (2009: 596) cited in Diabate (2011) notes that "the genital curse is the ultimate sanction a woman has, and even the just threat of it, making a motion of opening her wrapper in front of a man, 'is often enough to cause the most angry and aggressive of men to back down'" (p. 59). Women nudity can be used in a form of an opportunity arising from the use of nakedness as a political tool (Sutton 2007) but as a last recourse of nonviolent and peaceful conflict resolution whenever other means have failed. This is why nude music cannot be enjoyed by all members of family together due to its horrific nature. Again, why are they doing so? It is simple that they were made to believe that anything European is better than anything. This is completely contrary to the whole essence and meaning of one's identity as represented by his or her culture. Again, since Europe introduced the so-called modernity, things have changed dramatically. However, the situation is completely different in Europe, especially in France and Germany, for example, where nudity is acceptable. For, it is regarded as a celebration of woman's beauty (Scherer 2010). Historically, nudity has never been a problem to Europe due to its symbolism and the way it is exploited, particularly under capitalism. Brusa and Barilan (2009) note that "in the Hellenic arena, athletes competed unclothed, but they were not considered nude, since the foreskin covered the tip of the penis, whose exposure was a sign of sexual arousal" (p. 475). As for the European women, whether to expose themselves or not is not an important matter. Chalmers (2013) discloses that "'modern' women are more open about nudity so that exposure is unimportant" (p. 218). This is why African cultures are consistent that nudity is a curse which is different from European's. Sometimes, nudity may mean freedom, beauty and womanhood but not manhood. This is why Jesus' public stripping acts as a symbol of salvation. However, Stahl (2008) notes that such stripping stripped Jesus of his Christian symbol of divinity so as to portray him as human while he was a god. However, "nudity in Roman art signify prowess" (p. 297). Arguably, this explains why Jesus was crucified nakedly despite being total indignity and violence in uncontaminated African lenses. Contrary, to Africans, nudity does not signify and prowess. Instead, it signifies bestiality; and this is why females are allowed to use it as a last resort and a powerful weapon in peacemaking whereby nudity forces people in power to reckon with whatever they are doing. Ebila and Tripp (2017) note that once women use nudity as the weapon to voice their angers none can surpass it. Despite such special use of nudity, when Europeans came to Africa alleged that Africans were walking naked. Some may, as per the European standards. Again, they used to cover their private parts to show how nudity was not allowed.

Thanks to moral differences noted above, using its contagious culture, Europe destroyed Africa's morality so as to become what it is today. Merriam (1982) cited in Knight (2013) notes that art has the pivotal role of building the identity of the culture such artistic work comes from. If you consider what the example of Congolese music and what it is doing, you find that Europe corrupted Africans to the extent that they have become the agents of abusing their own culture either in the name of making money or trying to look modern or altogether. They are blind. They cannot see the richness their cultures have. Importantly, Cultural imperialism does not end up with arts and music. Even European tourists who tour Africa like praising negative things under the guise of culture. Essentially, Africa is made to believe that it cannot do anything of its own. Africans, especially, the high and the mighty, still buy expensive carpets, cloths, shoes, wine and other items from Europe while they can be produced locally. An ideal example is that of the dandyism or *La Sape or elegance* (Pritchard 2017) in Congo and the DRC. Due to lack of self-confidence and self-esteem, many rich Africans buy, for example, European suits and other clothes based on the tags on them but not quality or anything simply because they fit their dandyism. Lewis (2015) defines a dandy noting that:

> More specifically, the dandy is mostly a British construct who came into being in the eighteenth and nineteenth centuries, but who simultaneously has French roots. He was classified as an individual whose self-importance, impeccable dress, and manners attract attention and afford status. A black dandy can be defined as a self-

fashioned gentleman who intentionally appropriates classical European fashion with an African disaporan aesthetic and sensibilities.

This is very sad provided that, in this context, no African can be a gentleman without being associated with European culture but not his African culture. Europe knew what it was doing when it introduced such garbage to Africa. The dividends are now seen on how many rich Africa devour European fashions as they shy away from their organic African ones.

Thanks to cultural imperialism, it reached the point at which an African dandy would spend a fortune on a pair of Italian shoes or a Suisse watch that would enable him to buy a plot of land had such person not been brainwashed to end up devouring every garbage from Europe https://www.youtube.com/watch?v=W27PnUuXR_A. It is sad that the governments made of pro-west stooges have never intervened to educate its people the dangers such self-negation poses to them as people. Who would stop such madness if at all those supposed to do so were totally immersed in this poor of cultural garbage. In the DRC, under what was known as bungled philosophy Mobutuism the president himself was in the fore front; and liked to dress in collarless "à bas le costume" (literally "down with the suit") jackets "along with flamboyant leopard skin hats that he had custom-made in Paris" (Jorgensen (2014: 22). Ironically, the leopard was not from European forests or parks. If such a president would partake of such cultural imperialism who else would promote African culture and fashions? How many Mobutus does Africa still have today? Dandyism was injected purposely in order to attract and trap elites as Mbikayi (2015) notes that "in the age of colonialism, imperialism, revolution and nation-building, black dandies started combining the political, social and cultural 'power of visibility' in places such as Vauxhall, London" (p. 17) which Ogborn (1997: 450, 453) cited in Mbikayi (*Ibid.*) describes as 'a key site in eighteenth-century cultural production' (p. 17) whose beneficiary is none other than Europe. Apart from fake elegance, there are other areas Africa is robbed for the benefit of Europe.

Lack of self-confidence does not end up only in fashions. It goes far deeper and wider so as to be felt even in our assumptions and behaviours. For example, when I was putting the finishing touch on this volume, I came to a story in Kenyan leading English Daily, the *Daily Nation* with the heading "Kenyan club where Queen Elizabeth stayed turns 120 years" (Marete 2017). After reading the story I asked myself many questions? Does Britain treasure the hotels where Kenya's first delegates for its independence stayed? Do they have the names of the ladies Kenya's first president who studies and lived in Britain slept with? Do they pay any damn about the leaders of Kenya the same way Kenya seems to put high premium on the Queen as the head of Britain? Who cares? In all those questions above, I got one answer that Kenya is a British ex-colony and Britain is the ex-master to Kenya. Further, I think this is why many African capitals still have streets with the names of their colonial masters on but not vice versa *vis-à-vis* the same in Europe capitals. Due to being a deconstructionist, I understood why the Queen's stays in Kenya many years ago was still a big and real deal. It is because of the belief that by preserving the hotel in which the queen spent a few days British tourists would go there and thereby enable Kenya to get money. I do not know if the writer and his audience know; and want to know where their leaders stayed in Britain at the times they were negotiating Kenya's independence in the Lancaster house. Interestingly, while such a country was dressing itself down in the name of money, it failed to understand that they money the same country loses to capital flight is bigger than the peanut such a club can generate simply because the queen of England spent her nights there. As per Ndikumana and Boyce (2010), Kenya lost US$735.8 in from 1970 to 2004. Africa needs to abandon such mindsets that set them apart from development strategies.

Currently, in many African capitals, it is a common sight to see youth in American *swaggers* or tubular body moving with shoulder swagger or hourglass body moving with hip sway (Johnson, Gill, Reichman and Tassinary 2007:321) or boldness (Lott 2013) but not African ones. The African who whose boldness and heroism revolved around his ability to defend his society is long gone. Instead of being proud of a spear and shield, an African has now been relegated to being bold and proud about parochially being more of an American than anything! Half-naked youth dress in American styles as the signs of Americanness, masculinity and modernity. By devouring such a culture, America makes big bucks through selling its culture to the world without any reciprocity. Further, many shoes and clothes are sold to Africa simply because they are American. Through the propagation of its pop culture, America has dominated the world economically, politically and culturally. How does one become an American? There are many things that can define America which are, *inter alia*, consumerism, machoism and, above all, hegemony. American pop culture is intentionally propagated in order to achieve socio-economic and political dominance in the world. The message the world gets from America can be summarised as:

> Symptoms of a global dystopia where identity, citizenship, and social agency are manipulated by industries of mass persuasion that shapes them into niche subcultural markets for a global and soulless capitalism (Kraidy 2017: 15).

In this sense, culture is a booming business. This is different from African perspective in which culture was the property of the society but not individuals' as it is the case in capitalism. You can see this on how swaggerers like things such as coke, American fashions, basketball that is now threatening the football and rap music. In all these, African does not have anything to gain or offer except to lose. America and Europe make billions of dollars of revenues through advertisements and propagation of their cultures. Cultural imperialism does not end up with fashion alone. It goes far deeper than one can expect. Due to cultural imperialism as it was shaped by the church and later Islam, it is only an African that does not have his or her unique identity. Look at an Arab, Chinese and Indian, for example. They behave, dress, eat, and appear typically Arabic, Chinese and Indian. Even when it comes to their entertainment, they subscribe to their cultural bases and sell the same to Africa without any reciprocity. You cannot find Arabs, Chinese or Indians watching Nollywood, Nigeria film industry that, at least, used to represent Africa before sinking into aping Western everything. Ask yourself.

How much Hollywood and Bollywood dominate in African sitting rooms? Is there any reciprocity? Go further. Look at how much money and time Africans spend on watching European leagues such as Germany Bundesliga, UK premier League, la Liga, Italian, Serie A, and Spanish among others. Who is watching African leagues in Europe or America? What transpired in Kenya after two British football teams played a match in 2013 speaks volume as to how Africa has always lost to Europe almost in everything. *Reuters* (9 December, 2013) reports that "a Kenyan soccer fan unable to cope with Manchester United's loss to northern rival Newcastle United, committed suicide over the weekend, a senior Kenyan police official said on Monday." What can we call this? Is fanaticism, ignorance or love? How many Europeans are ready to commit suicide for anything African while they were taught that Africa is the continent of beasts and savages? Ironically, African governments do not see the dangers such brainwash causes to their people simply because such buffoonery produces citizens that cannot rebel against their corrupt regimes that have always been in bed with Europe vending them. Again, such things can be trivialised. Importantly, they are very important to ponder on so as to stop Africa from contributing to the development of others while denying itself the same. Here we are talking about males. When it comes to females, they too are not left out *vis-a-vis* cultural imperialism aimed at benefiting Europe economically has always relegated and maltreated them to the status of being mere objects men can own, used and even abuse as they deem fit the same way Africa has been genderised and used and abused.

Currently, beauty is a very booming industry in Africa even though, in the main, it benefits Europe more than Africa as far as economic gains are concerned. Boxlll (2016) notes that:

> The politics of beauty and sexuality is not something that should be taken lightly. How beauty is defined, shaped and deployed in black communities, and how it is promoted and in many cases denigrated must be critically analysed if issues related to identity complexes, self-esteem problems and insecurities are to be overcome (v).

The beauty of black females is defined by white standards. For example, after Europe found that it can still exploit African females through its defined beauty by ignoring the anathema of their colour as it is perceived in European cultures, it decided to redefine it. Hobson (2013) notes that this so-called "appreciation" for black women's bodies does not necessarily challenge ideas of grotesque and deviant black woman sexuality" (p. 101) which, as we have seen hereinabove, Tamale (2011: 16) cited in Nhemachena (2016) says they are accused of being promiscuous. This is very sad if we consider the fact that Europe legalised prostitution many years ago whereas Africa has never up until now. Adair and Nezhyvenko (2017) note that, in four EU Member States, prostitution contributed 29.2 percent EU GDP and almost one fourth (23.26 percent) of total population in 2010: Austria, Germany, Greece and the Netherlands (p. 117). To the contrary, up until now, as noted above, prostitution has never been legalised in Africa where many prostitutes are found in the capital cities hunting for European tourists more than their local inamoratos. From the first contact, colonial agents, especially explorers and missionaries sowed the seed of racism. Hobson (*Ibid.*) discloses that "alarm and fabricated otherness extends itself to racialized sense of aesthetics that positioned blackness in terms of grotesquerie, whereas whiteness serves as an emblem of beauty" (p. 10) for brainwashed people who want a woman to be grotesquerie while she can adopt whiteness even artificially for self-pleasing and fooling altogether. Provided that the emblem of beauty is whiteness, any black females, and sometimes, even males yearning for lightness (Glenn 2008) will go for whatever makes her or him white hypothetically or practically. Beauty, too, means powers in the eyes of European racists as Hutton (2016) puts it that "beautiful people have the natural right to rule over ugly people. White people are beautiful while black people are ugly. Therefore, white people have the inherent right to rule over black people" (p 20) which is the take of the so-called international community when it comes to forcing those who enslaved and colonised Africa to redress Africa the same way Germany did to the Jews.

Here is where lightening chemicals made in Europe kick in. Those going for such chemicals fail to understand one or two things.

First, that those making these chemicals do not necessarily use them due to the fact that they have what is driving black people to lightening their skins. And secondly, that by self-disowning, such a people is contributing the economies of Europe unnecessarily. Thanks to losing their identity as a people, those lightening their skins do not know that the beauty they are after is fake and colonial defined as it aims at destroying their natural and true identity not to mention causing health problems such as cancers and other skin diseases resulting from using lightening chemicals (Moan, Porojnicu, Dahlback and Setlow 2008; Ladizinski, Mistry and Kundu 2011; and Dlova, Hamed, Tsoka-Gwegweni, and Grobler 2015). Further, the use of lightening chemicals causes financial problems to the victims. Shankar and Subish (2016) cite an example of south Africa where "the colonial legacy in South Asia may be one of the contributory factors for the belief that White is powerful and White is beautiful" (p. 101) which is a typical replica of the assumption of many people in many African countries where skin lightening is prevalent. Essentially, after being defined by Europe, beauty took another turn, particularly for females. Thanks to colonial legacies resulting from cultural imperialism, some people have reached the point at which they cannot define themselves. Beauty, as a socially-constructed concept, differs from one society to another based on cultural lenses. Anderson (2012) maintains that beauty is many in one due to the fact that it is a conscious, harmonious but polarised, proactive and vital human trait. Basically, there is no watertight definition of beauty, largely if we consider the adage that beauty is in the eye of the beholder. This is why it is not easy to quantify or define beauty equally universally. It is something bigger and more complicated than what we see biologically (Little 2011; Păun and Teodorescu 2014 and Wales 2014). Therefore, those who try to define and assign benchmarks for someone to qualify as a beautiful person do so at the peril of their victims who do not question the rationale of defining them. This is where objectification of a woman comes in (Cox 2012) or thingification (Ledrach 2005 cited in Mhango *forthcoming*) whereby a woman becomes an object a man can buy, own and use as pleased. I would argue that women, who know themselves more than men do, would be in a good position to define what they mean by beauty.

Again, thanks to the patriarchal dominance, men almost define everything. For, example, before being colonised, for Africans, the beauty of a woman revolved around how healthy and fit one was but not how bony and white-like she is as it currently is. Instead, they allow somebody to define them without considering the ramifications of doing so. This happened after females were objectified so as to fall prey of capitalist drive of making a buck out of whatever is possible. Once a human is turned into a thing like a car or house, it makes it easy for such a person to lose the right to self-definition. The situation becomes even worse when such *thingification* is systemic; and can be exploited economically, politically and socially as it has been the case in the world under capitalism. Mhango in Mawere (2016) maintains that whenever anybody allows somebody else to define him or her, such person will define that person as he or she wanted so as to either distort or reinvent the subject in this case.

To do away with cultural imperialism, Africa needs to enact unyielding laws that will be applied in dealing with the corruption and dehumanisation and demonisation European colonial agents sowed. China provides an ideal example. After noting that there could not be any development amidst cultural imperialism and the corruption of its cultures, banned religions from being practiced. Although this has changed, Chinese authorities do not offer more freedom to religious bodies knowing how culturally corruptive and imperialistic are.

When it comes to dealing with corruptive and cultural imperialistic elements, China pays no attention to noises about Human Rights. I do not mean to belittle the importance of human rights. However, it should be appreciated that the persons or organisations under whatever pretext that corrupt Africans by introducing foreign ideologies kill many innocent people by creating lack of cooperation and identity as I have proved in the case where Christians and Muslims kill each other simply because they were exposed to fake an new brotherhood. Why? Among other, right to culture and identity must flatteringly be enshrined in African constitutions as one of the ways of addressing the anathema resulting from cultural imperialism that helps Europe to make money out of Africa not to mention denying many Africans self-confidence.

How Europe's Redress of Africa Is a *Sine Qua Non*

In law and reality, whoever inherits the estate left by the deceased bears the responsibility and liability resulting from the said estate. Likewise, modern Europe, apart from being the creature of the colonial Europe, inherited almost everything that colonial Europe achieved and made out of colonising and exploiting Africa. Therefore, it makes sense to demand that the same Europe must redress Africa. Almost all countries and institutions that colonial Europe created are still there. Thus, Africa has somewhere to start when claiming for its redress. For, the fortunes made by the way of colonising Africa such as banks, castles, churches governments and the systems are still intact today as they go on enjoying the capital that Europe made by occupying, colonising and exploiting Africa. While Africa still enjoys the capital it got by the way of colonialism, Africa still bears what Duignan and Gann (2013) call the 'burden of empire' resulting to what Lenin cited in Duigan and Gann calls super profits, thus, the liability for the new world to redress the balance of the old is palpable. Noticeably, the so-called developed or advanced economies of the world whose wealth was gotten by the way of colonialism have legal and moral obligations to redress their victims. However, there are those who try to deny the culpability by saying *nul criminem sin lege* in that no offense can be committed without law to mean that there was no law when Europe invaded Africa. This is hogwash. No society of people can live without laws even if such laws are not necessarily the same as the ones we are using today. Legally speaking, Europe will always be liable for committing crimes against Africa and humanity for the entire era it colonised Africa. It does not make sense for the world that prides itself on being advanced and developed to push this reality under the carpet. They are precedents that inform us that whatever criminality committed to innocent people must be addressed and redressed. Why was it possible to redress Jews who suffered under Nazi Germany but it becomes impossible for Africans who suffered under slavery and colonialism? This is not the first or last time I am asking why Jews were redressed; and apology being formally issued after being subjected to holocaust under Nazi rule. Historically, Jews holocaust was the second after the Namibian Herero committed by the same German rule (Langbehn and Salama 2011). Again, ironically, nobody has ever come forcefully internationally to demand that the Herero need to be redressed. As for holocaust, it does not end up with Jews or Herero only but all Africans. Abulhawa (2013) discloses that "man has truly never known a holocaust of greater magnitude, savagery, or longevity than that perpetrated against the peoples of Africa." This is the real situation. Osahon cited in Tinsley (2011) notes that ""Africans are treated like the scum of the earth" throughout the Arab world." Aren't some of the victims Muslims, especially those from Darfur Sudan? Where is Islamic brotherhood? Again, their sin is nothing but being African and black.

Jürgen Zimmerer cited in Eckl (2008) argues that the genocide of 1904 contributed to making the Holocaust thinkable and possible. I must make it clear that asserting that Herero deserves redress does not mean negating or riding on the holocaust. For, there has been a purposeful attempts to misrepresent the plight of Herero as Janntje Böhlke-Itzen (2004) cited in Zollmann (2007) points out to the fact that Herero do base their request for reparations on a negation of this singularity of the "Jewish" Holocaust) which is misleading, *holier than thou* and utterly wrong. No humans are better than others. For racists and naysayers even admitting that Africa developed Europe is going to be difficult. This is because some still harbour under colonial carryovers that Europe civilised Africa which Mhango (2015) disputes asking "was slavery or colonialism civilisation really? Is imperialism civilisation; what sort is this?" (p. 2). Common sense dictates that the victims of all crimes committed by others on them must be addressed and dressed in order to bring the closure to this ugly world chapter.

Another precedent can be drawn from Turkey that was forced to declare the massacres of Armenians holocaust (Fisk 2015) involving over one million victims. Interestingly, it is Germany that spearheaded this action due to its first-hand experience with genocide related offences (Woods 2016). Ironically, the same Germany that hosted the Berlin Conference that brutally divided and partitioned Africa has never taken such measures towards Africa's holocaust. Again, this has been the Europe's double standard that the international community has always blessed in their conspiracy against Africa. Apart from Germany and Europe, the United Nations (UN) has never initiated any process of addressing this forgotten holocaust that took place for many years. All this has been uncompleted as if African holocaust did not occur; and if it did, was but a trivial matter under the international community. Here we are talking about 9.4 to 12 million people (Mhango *Ibid*: 136) or 24 million (Zimmerer 2007) who suffered from slavery not to mention hundreds of millions that suffered under colonialism compared to over 1 million (Hovannsian 2009; and Akçam 2012) Armenian and 6 million Jewish victims (Rodriguez 2008; and Obama 2009). From these figures two of which were committed by colonial Europe, you can see how culpable Europe will always be shall it not address them and thereby redress the victims. Grunder (1998 cited in Zimmerer 2007) wonders how holocaust committed against Africa during slavery cannot be termed as thus noting that:

> Many people died performing slave labour or were put to the sword during Christianisation. The victims' suffering was certainly just as great as in cases of intentional annihilation, and yet one cannot speak of genocide in these colonial cases, as the destruction of entire peoples was not intended. In fact, the colonial economy needed the indigenous population for exploitative purposes, (p. 108).

Ironically, despite its contribution to the development of Europe, Europe and others who benefitted from robbing Africa have always referred to it as underdeveloped, uncivilised and all sorts of names. Time for instituting a case against colonial powers in order to force them redress Africa for the ills they caused is now. This is legally possible as the *Mail & Guardian* online (Aug. 11, 2004) cited in Anderson (2005) notes that:

> A settlement agreement with the German government or eventual success in U.S. or international courts could have precedential value for

257

claims brought by other groups to redress similar wrongs committed under colonial rule" (pp. 1187-1188).

However, there is a stumbling block resulting from colonial laws. Lu (2011) notes that:

> Germany did eventually apologize for the Herero genocide on 14 August 2004, but it has consistently refused to accept liability, and hence reparative obligations, to Herero descendants, "since the international rules on the protection of combatants and civilians were not in existence at the time that war crimes were being committed in Namibia (p. 265).

In other words, such a rationale means that slavery and colonialism did not occur; and if they occurred, they were legal simply; because the so-called international law did not stipulate so. Does this real make sense? If somebody kills another person with malice aforethought, it is clear that such a person has committed murder regardless as to when he committed the crime. This is logical. Sometimes, the West contradicts itself in its efforts to get away with murder. Essentially, the West has always invested heavily on making sure that its criminal past does not lead to criminal liability. Again, how long will this criminality go on without justice being done and delivered to the victims?

Nobody can say that laws do not operate retrogressively while there is a precedent on how Jews were redressed at the time the R2P did not even exist. If those who argue that we cannot use laws retrogressively, the Jewish holocaust provides a very strong precedent. McGonegal (2009) takes redress as a way of reconciliation which turns the concept into the hopes of moving beyond violence and hostility. However, there is emphasis that no compensation can ever adequately redress wrongs. Such a take is problematic due to the fact that there is nobody that has the right to decide what the victims want to be done as the way of doing justice to them; and bring about the closure. In many African cultures, redress, whether is real or ceremonial, has unique significance. I would argue that, by Europe accepting its criminal liability; and thereby redress Africa; it will

258

assure the victims that the same criminality will never be replicated in any form and manner anywhere anymore. Those who deny or shy away from accepting liability fail to underscore the fact that Africa used to live independently before the introduction of colonialism; and just like any human society, was entitled to protection under the current R2P regime and other international laws. Desperate and poverty-stricken Africa, we evidence today living on handouts, did not exist before. This speaks to the fact that Africa was self-sufficient almost in everything. Again, how was Africa able to live independently? The answer lies in the advancement and strength of its institutions that colonialism felled and replaced with parasitic ones all aimed at robbing Africa and benefitting Europe.

Further, it defies logical to deny redressing Africans as a way of assuring them of safety and protection apart from doing justice while the same international community and the culprits are ready to protect the rights of animals. Are animals in the wild more important than Africans? Isn't this mentality of equating Africans with chimpanzees? (Weingrod 2005). Something needs to be done at the international level to see to it that all legacies that dehumanise and belittle others are adequately address so as to move forward as one human family.

Similarly, those countries whose wealth was gotten by sucking Africa dry must repay. Everything is clearly demonstrable provided that the times the colonising powers occupied their victims is clearly known. And on this, African academics and other non-African academics that support African cause must act as bellwethers in fulfilling this redemptory responsibility making sure that justice is done and be seen done. It is never easy however. Importantly, if the world wants to have sustainable growth and peace all aimed at making human lives better, whatever is needed to be put into the redress of Africa is worth doing. Besides, the type of mammon that was stolen is known. For example, mathematicians and economics can calculate the volume of wealth that colonial power robbed their colonies. Therefore, when I argue that redressing the victims is the way to go, I am not making this up. It is possible; if the international community decides to get out of the closet and face it as civilised humans and society. Without redressing Africa, Europe will always be ahead of Africa economically which is sad provided that a chunk of mankind is needlessly suffering simply because the other chunk decided to rob it. There are two important epochs that need to be considered when we talk of the redress of Africa. These are colonial and post-colonial epochs. For example, Tanganyika was ruled by two colonial powers namely the Germany and British correspondingly. From 1884 up until 1961, Tanganyika was under colonial rule whereby the Germany ruled from 1905 to 1912; and Britain from 1919 to 1961 (Kiango 2005). Under all these two epochs, the two colonial powers exploited the colony almost in everything tangible and incorporeal. For example, minerals, agricultural produces and manpower were exploited. The people of Tanganyika worked without pay for the whole time they were under colonial rules. Those who were paid for their labour received less compared to what they were legally entitled to. Apart from forced labour, colonised people were not allowed to plan and execute their plans.

Provided that the offence has already been committed, the international community needs to come together and discuss how to resolve such an impasse either based on legal or moral requirements or give and take. Importantly, reparations must be on the agenda. Although many colonial powers do not like to hear or talk about reparations, without them, injustices that colonialism enacted will still haunt the world. There is no way we can say we are equal; and we love each other without doing justice based on our history. So, too, it is not criminalising Europe or calling it names, its economy became the force to reckon with so as to become dominant based on its criminal past. Under the doctrine of vicarious liability (King Jr 2005), Europe is duty bound to redress Africa for the crimes the old Europe committed against Africa. This is logical; provided that modern Europe is the product of old Europe the same way Africa suffers from the ills old Europe caused. Notably, the West has always self-appointed to teach justice and human rights to others under what they call their Western values. However, Donnelly (2007) maintains that Asian, Western and African values "and most other sets of values—can be, and have been, understood as incompatible with human rights" (p. 290). The thing is; currently, under the banner of modernity, democracy and human rights are the world order as the

West champions them so as to make them the conditions in many aspects of its cooperation with others. If, indeed, the world wants to be true to itself, Africa, among many victims of colonialism, needs to be redressed; and its contribution to the development of Europe be appreciated. In other words, we need these values to be fulfilled to the letter *vis-à-vis* the victims of Western colonialism. As aforementioned, this is our moral obligation that can be fulfilled legally by the two sides by sitting down and deciding the *modus operandi* of addressing this anomaly to human history and wellbeing. It is sad that globalisation, neoliberalism, and modernisation do purposely avoid addressing this human scar. Instead, many neoliberalists would like Africa to believe that it can develop so as to be at par with Western countries while they do not want to redress it or changing the current international superstructure as colonialism and neocolonialism created it.

How Africa Needs Paradigm Shift Shall It Want to Catch Up

Beside reparations, Africa needs to embark on paradigm shift in order to make its case clear. Although it is upon Africa to make its case aimed at addressing the quandaries it has been in for a long time as they result from the injustices it had suffered, as well, it is the duty of Europe and the international community to contribute in the dialogue provided that the destruction of Africa was done collectively from the Berlin Conference, slavery to colonialism and neocolonialism. Therefore, it is the duty of the world to fully participate in addressing the problems Africa is facing as they were enhanced by the culprits collectively. As collective the destruction of Africa was, as well, its reconstruction needs to be collective. There is no way the world can distance itself from solving the problems Africa has today. It has a duty to other human beings not to mention the interconnectivity and interdependence. Those thinking that it is a sole duty for Africa to address its problems are wrong. Business aside, morally, we are all duty-bound to partake of each other's problems the same way we share the success of one another. The world is now globalised and interconnected. For example, when Ebola broke in West Africa, the whole world was affected due to the globalised nature of the world today. There is no way one problem in any part of the world can be solely the problem of that place, particularly when it comes to contagious diseases or poverty. Currently, Europe is grappling with the problems revolving around poverty in that many people from pauperised countries are flocking Europe in the quests for greener pastures. Although Europe is paying the price and reaping what it sowed, this phenomenon soon will be global. To do away with it the solution is, *inter alia*, to address the problem this volume has exposed and analysed.

Given that there is prodigious evidence to suggest that Africa contributed immensely to the development of Europe, for itself to forge ahead, Africa needs to reinvent itself either by creating a new political paradigm shift or go back and salvage some of its felled political systems. This will help Africa in guiding it in the process of reinventing and redefining itself based on its own aspirations, needs, plans and trajectory. This task is not easy, simple and short. It is like diving into a blue hole trying to seek its treasures despite the danger such an adventure poses. This means, Africa must brace itself for dangers and difficulties from the enemies it wants to take on internally and externally. Europe will never give up without a fight provided that its development still depends on Africa despite the fact that it has already exploited much from it. Therefore, there is a very need for Africa embarking on paradigm shift in order to recoup the time lost in developing Europe and the world. This is because the use of Western models have failed; and have reinforced exploitation and underdevelopment due to being used as means of controlling and robbing Africa. This being said, Africa needs a sound homemade system that can practically help in solving its problems, either internally or externally created, all based on its needs and aspirations. There are things such as colonialism, neocolonialism and all of their agents, forms, institutions, instruments and offshoots Africa needs to revisit and re-evaluate in order to bring in its own development based on its criteria and definitions. Thanks to colonial division, many African countries are made to believe that they can go solo and survive while rich countries in the West are embarking on unity and communalism. I may argue that Africa needs to revert back to its natural communalism in order to advance it and; thereby use it to solve its problem capitalism and other parasitic policies created and exacerbated instead of solving them. Ironically, while colonialism and capitalism divided Africa, the same are now communalising Europe under its economic communitarianism drive. Refer to the European Union (EU) formerly the European Economic Community (EEC), the Organisation for Economic Cooperation and Development (OECD), and others. It is only African natural communalism that was geared by humanity that can help Africa out of the impasse it is in. This must be the foundation for Africa to embark on paradigm shift that will divorce colonial settings. I must note here that, when I talk about communalism, it should not be misconstrued as communism which also failed to help even its founder, the former Union of Soviet Socialist Republics (USSR).

Equally disconcertingly, when it comes to communalising Africa, it leaves a lot to be desired. For, Africa has fewer communities than it is supposed to have. Prominent African communities are the Economic Community of West African States (ECOWAS), the East African Community (EAC) South African Development Community (SADC) among others. Again, when you look at what Africa has achieved, there is still a lot to be done, particularly when we consider Africa's problems resulting from its division and partition that colonial masters created. All the above communities are economic ones. Again, if we consider the fact that politics has always given an upper hand in the affairs of African countries; chances are, for Africa to benefit from such communities, there must be political confederacy. This is because all important decisions reached to establish or abolish such organisations are done or organised by political entities namely the governments of the member states. So, if Africa keeps on economic communalisation without embarking on political one, things will remain the same pointlessly. The simple logic behind this is the fact that politicians are not professionals when it comes to the management of resources and the economies of their countries. Despite this, they still have an upper hand in decision making compared to professionals.

When it comes to definition, Kimmerle (2006) defines communism as the system under and in which decision making depends on consensus based on equality and equity due to the fact that communalism ties in another African philosophy of Ubuntu or "I am because we are" (Winston, Bruce and Ryan 2008: 217) or in Xhosa *Umuntu ngumntu ngabanye abantu* (Nobavula 2011: 40) which means the same in Swahili proverb which says that *Utu* or humanity *wa Mtu ni Watu* (Gathogo 2008; Outwater 2008; Kresse 2009; Kresse 2011; and Niogu 2013) or the humanity of every human is based or connected to other humans. Nyasani (1981: 143) cited in Kimmerle *(Ibid.)* maintains that under communalism, the community or society lives like a biological body whose organs equally depend on each other; and when one part is sick, the whole body is affected. My experience in an African rural life in Tanzania tells that Ubuntu or humanity is the heart and at the heart of everything the community does. You do not live or die without the community around. This is why companies dealing with burying the dead have never made any profit in some parts of rural Africa where traditions are still observed. My experience with the Sukuma and the lake Region of Tanzania show that nobody can make it without the community; because almost everything comes from the community (Gichure 2015). Ironically, it seems; the concept of humanity for Western society is new. Disturbingly, it shows that, in spite of being occupied by humans, Europe did not have the concept of equality and humanity before interacting with Africa. Even after evidencing African humanity, Europe went on with its inhumanity based on its capitalism which is, in all senses, inhumane, (Wenzel 2008). There was no way capitalism and colonialism would accommodate humanity or apply it in dealing with other non-Europeans while it actually started practicing them by subjecting its kin under these two devilish systems. Estevez-Abe (2006) points at the human capital explanation that attributes gender segregation to women's inferior human capital. If capitalistic Europe was ready to sacrifice its own mothers, how could it bother about Africans? This shows how capitalistic Europe was. It was ready to sell its own mothers to see to it that greed succeeds something that has gone on hitherto where women are still exploited based on their gender. In the experiment Arulampalam, Booth and Bryan (2007) conducted in eleven European countries, came to the conclusion that "women are still paid less than men" (pp. 20-21). To make matters worse, colonial

Europe called this inhumanity civilisation that it has always exported to Africa based on a double standard almost in everything. The take away here is that Africa, among others, taught Europe humanity. One would take it for granted that wherever there are humans there must be humanity. Not under capitalism and colonialism. Again, how could capitalism embed humanity while it is naturally a double-faced creature (Negarestani 2013)? While capitalism as Europe invented accidentally after the renaissance that started in Florence, Italy lead by Medici family in the 15th century (Strathern 2007; Goldthwaite 2009; Kuehn 2009; Goldthwaite 2015; and Stephenson Jr 2015) blatantly neglects humanity, African Ubuntu philosophy encompasses and interweaves an individual community with the individual person to make them perform swiftly and harmoniously. I may candidly argue that Africa survived colonial onslaught because of its entrenched humanism based on equality, justice and universality. For, if we consider the miseries and sufferings colonialism unleashed to Africa, it flummoxes to note that Africans, ever since, have lived inhuman life as fostered and perpetrated under colonial and current international world order.

Additionally, Anyanwu (1989:127 cited in Higgs 2010) argues that communalism as an African philosophy "invites people to take a stand on the issue of reality as experienced by Africans" (p. 2416) based on practicality, principally, if we underscore that African communities were more utilitarian than conjectural. This shows how democracy has never been a new thing to Africa however Western countries still pride themselves on being the harbingers of democracy in Africa.

Fundamentally, communalism is about total interdependency and interconnectivity of the members of the community living and dead. Kropotkin cited in Adams (2014) adds another value of communalism by referring to it as symbolic of past struggles against imperious despots in the medieval Europe. Therefore, Africa still can use its original philosophy of communalism with Ubuntu to take on current neoliberalism entrenched in capitalism, globalism and modernism. Khoza (2005: 266) cited in Mabovula (2011) argues that communalism is "a concept that views humanity in terms of collective existence, intersubjectivity serving as the basis of supportiveness, cooperation, collaboration and solidarity" (p. 38) of the community or society. I may add that communalism also encompasses interobjectivity (Talamo and Pozzi 2011), intercompartibility (Kring Figary, Boyer, Watson, and Twiss 2014) and intesectionality of goals and purposes. Communalism can be summarised as total humanity devoid of any way any of the member of the community can be exploited by or exploit another. They are all one and interconnected; and this interconnectivity is palpable and unique. The interconnection of African communal societies was different from the current Economic globalisation that has great impact on African communalism although negatively due to the fact that Africa is opened for more exploitation not to mention the negation all the ethos and ideals of cultural relativity and cultural pluralism leading to crisis of identity Africa suffers because of the importation of foreign values (Olasunkanmi 2011). Communalism is felt and seen among the members of the community. So, too, it is, arguably, impossible to separate communalism from Ubuntu due to the fact that they equally work together harmoniously. Whatever the precolonial community did was decided based on the consent of every member of the society. Further, communalism is the force Africans used to maintain an egalitarian community the West–due to its ignorance of this foreign terrain–referred to as primordial, uncivilised, underdeveloped in order to sabotage it and superimpose its exploitative and parasitic philosophies such as colonialism, liberalism, neoliberalism and capitalism among other.

More importantly, Africa has one role left for its rejuvenation and reinvention. It needs to push the envelope to see to it that it does not repeat the same mistakes it has been repeating again. For Africa to survive, needs to deconstruct and overhaul everything based on the following fronts:

Firstly, Africa needs to agitate and make sure that it gets fair treatments in international commerce. This must be done cautiously but not just a devil's bargain knowing the system that has been benefiting and enjoying from the plunderage of Africa will never go down without a fight.

Secondly, Africa must deconstruct, recalibrate and reconstruct its structural settings. For, currently, all governmental and financial institutions are built based on Western models which put Europe ahead of Africa. For example, Africa has many imperial presidents who look like former colonial governors. Instead of leading as it used to be before the introduction of colonialism, these rulers rule and they are not accountable to those they rule. They spend their taxes unaccountably and with discretionary powers. And to cap it all, they are above the law of the land.

Thirdly, Africa needs to redefine itself by doubting and questioning how it has always been defined. For, currently, Africa is not only defined by Europe but also almost all of its vital institutions are defined by Europe. To do away with keeping on developing Europe while stagnating itself, Africa needs to stop aping Europe's structures as they were created and superimposed since colonial times. I have noted how expensive Western democracy has failed due to being superimposed and serving the interests of the West. Africa needs to address this matter by revisiting its past to see how it has been able to live peacefully and without depending on the West as it currently does. There is no way Africa can catch up with other countries without deconstructing its structures to see to it that they deliver instead of being the tools the West has always used to bully and exploit Africa.

Fourthly, Africa must make sure that it seeks justice by petitioning to the international community to hold Europe liable for Africa's miseries and underdevelopment. The *status quo* will never like this. Therefore, it is upon Africa to stand firm and see to it that justice is done by revisiting Europe's criminal past; and the way it contributed hugely to the underdevelopment of Africa, especially if we underscore the fact that the capital gains Europe made by enslaving and colonising Africa propped Europe to where it is now. Seeking justice in this regard is about holding Europe and all those who benefited from the pillaging of Africa accountable so that a new chapter can be opened for peaceful and prosperous world built on justice and equality.

Fifthly, Africa has to tweak its structures of governance such as governments and their institutions, mainly the constitutions, armies and the whole concept of democracy. For example, currently, many African militaries are used for political purposes but not security ones. They spend much money on protecting dictators but not the people. Additionally, many African armies are standby to quash any attacks from their African sisters. Such a stance is counterproductive; and therefore, Africa needs to do away with militaristic structures that must be replaced by civil ones shall it aspire to move forward. This is where the centrality of reuniting Africa, so that it can become a very strong country, emanates.

Importantly, Africa needs to change not only its structures but also laws governing everything based on its aspirations, cultures, needs and traditions. For example, before the coming of Europeans to colonise Africa, there were laws governing almost everything major one being land as the means of production. After the introduction of colonialism, capitalism kicked in so as to alter and dismantle such laws that were egalitarian by nature. There were no landless Africans then. But after colonial settlers took fertile lands in many African former colonies, African economic structure was felled; and many people were left landless. Ever since, the setting has never been tweaked; even after independence except for a few countries such as Tanzania and partly Zimbabwe. Boone (2007) notes that:

> Exploitation or expropriation of community resources by opportunistic insiders or by outsiders has caused illegitimate trampling on the rights of indigenous communities, and the erosion of traditional mechanisms that ensured the downward accountability and effectiveness of community-level authorities (p. 570).

As indicated prior, when African mechanisms of landownership were abrogated; and such a move gave an advantage to foreigners and elites who grabbed land and used it to become richer and richer while the *hoi polloi* become poorer and poorer. When it comes to politicians, some used land as the means of safely clinging unto power as it was in Kenya where its first president Jomo Kenyatta used land to reward loyalty and punish dissents (Mhango 2016). Regarding the centrality of land, there is a very special connection and relationship for Africans.

Furthermore, Africa needs to ask its former colonial masters to open their closets full of skeletons resulting from the crimes against humanity that they committed to Africa through colonialism and slavery. This is important given that the same culprits–instead of being brought to justice for whatever form of injustices under international laws–have been given another opportunity to get away with murder by setting terms of defining who is developed and who is underdeveloped. Africa needs to get its ducks in a row very; very well shall it aspire to get out of the quagmire it is wantonly in.

What makes Africa's situation impossibly untenable is the fact that the Europe, as the representative of the West, has always sought to impose its formula of development; and make Africa believe it can attain it without underscoring historical realities of Europe's development. Many thinkers lure Africa to follow the same pattern, pathway and trajectory to development while the real situation on the ground says differently. For example, some thinkers have proposed that Africa must follow the so-called Rostowan stages of development namely the traditional society, preconditions for take-off, the drive to maturity and the age of high mass-consumption (Sanusi 2010; Izuchukwu 2011; and Acs, Szerb and Autio 2016) without underscoring the fact that Europe was able to criminally accumulate the capital by colonising and robbing Africa among others. There is evidence, for example, to support assertion that South Korea that is now touted as the country that attained independence nine years before the first African country to attain independence, Ghana, grew rapidly while Ghana which is the replica of Africa is still struggling. Although it is true that South Korea is more developed than Ghana, the reason of achieving such development is different from Rostow's script of development. South Korea became developed after the US and Europe decided to support in order to show that capitalism can better perform in development than socialist or communism (McMichael 2011). This is why the twin North Korea has been left behind so as to prove that nothing can develop the world except capitalism. So, what is obvious is the fact that sometimes development is the matter or outcome of choice and priority of the West. The same can apply to the Middle East currently. Almost all so-called developed in the regions are the ones that have been in bed with the West. This is why Dubai is more developed than Iraq or Iran. It is simply they are in good books of the West. They also did not follow Rostow's development straightjacket Africa is forced to slink into. Therefore, one can say that South Korean development was enhanced by the cold war politics but not economic science.

To show how misguidedly development as a practical chicanery is, Lipietz (1987) insultingly compares the so-called underdeveloped countries to children to adults (the so-called developed countries representing adults). As argued above, how do you equate countries such as Egypt, Ethiopia, Sudan or Zimbabwe to children while they are the oldest civilisations on earth? As indicated above, the final stage of development is the age of high mass-consumption. How can Africa develop by highly consuming massively while all it consumes comes from abroad? How do you aim at massive consumption before creating home base for producing what is supposed to be massively consumed? I would argue that we need to industrialise based on our home needs before thinking about mass consumption. Even lions in the wild consume massively due to the fact that there is massive preys to consume. Telling Africa that it needs to highly consume massively without producing what it produces is as dangerous as telling the lions to massively consume goats or cows. Where will they get the cows without being in conflict with humans? Further, I think Africa has to follow its unique trajectory based on its culture and history. Whose trajectory did Europe follow? It is worth it to try. For over five decades, Africa has been experimenting capitalist trajectory to no avail. What is wrong with trying its own methods based on the salvaged remnants of African history that will shed light on how Africa was able to live for millions of years without necessarily depending on Europe?

As if it is not enough, almost all prophets of copycat development preach production as the first means to achieving development. Well, Africa has never stopped producing. However, despite producing sufficiently, it has always been robbed ever since colonialism under which produces were stolen up to neo-colonialism in which prices are fixed not to mention conditions attached to the trade regime at the time. The aim of production is to accumulate

270

capital. Again, how can Africa accumulate capital under the current exploitative international trade regime? The more Africa produce is the more it is exploited.

As argued above, there cannot be any notable development for Africa because:

a)   It misleads to argue and think that Africa should follow Western pathway and formula in attaining development. This is impossible because there is the lack of time, cultural and enhancing environment. As argued above, Europe exploited others by the way of colonialism and slavery that enabled it to achieve its current level of development. Such enhancing factors are amiss today for Africa to accumulate capital for investing in development the same way Europe did so as to come up with the industrial revolution whose major leg up was slavery.

b)   Africa will be making and repeating more serious mistakes to think that it can develop without deconstructing, restructuring and reconstituting the current international trade regime—which is exploitative and racist by all standards—there is no way Africa can attain any parity in meaningful development that will enable it to compete with Europe and other emerging powers. In addressing the anomalies found in the international trade regime today, so, too, historical injustice that Europe committed is more important. One interesting reality here is that if Europe is forced to redress Africa, it will indirectly be not only doing justice but also giving Africa a leg up as a *quid pro quo* which is *sine quo non* with true justice and the closure of the past injustices Africa suffered.

c)   Apart from the above strategies, there is no way Africa can develop without reinvesting in profitable areas such as stopping producing for the external market without addressing home needs first, especially with regard to food self-sufficiency. For example, former-colonial masters duped African countries making them believe that through producing the so-called cash crops namely crops that African countries do not consume, they would accumulate much money. Such a ruse ended up destroying Africa economically even more. For, due to the fact that African countries do not consume the so-called cash crops, consumers in the West decided how much they must pay while the producers have no say in price setting. If anything,

271

cash crops have always been a tragedy for Africa due to the fact that they have never benefited it. Instead, these colonial crops have always benefited Africa's former colonial masters. Frankema (2010b) notes that cash crops did not only facilitate the exploitation of Africans but also resulted into high disparities in income for indigenous not to mention land grabbing in some countries such as Kenya, Namibia, South Africa and Zimbabwe among others.

Mhango (2015, 2016) calls cash crops "crash crops" due to the fact that they have never ushered development in except crashing the economies of African countries. Accumulating capital is not a bad idea save that it becomes bad when you tell a continent to do the same the way the West did. There are no more countries or world to conquer, colonise and rob currently. This would make sense of the countries that robbed Africa would be forced to redress it and then talk about capital accumulation. I do not think African countries can currently accumulate as big capital as Britain or France did when they colonised Africa. Even the hype-touted countries in Asia tigers namely Hong Kong, South Korea, Singapore and Taiwan did not make it through without being given money by the same countries that looted Africa. We can, therefore, say that one of the major means of capital accumulation for countries to develop is the capital that former colonial masters robbed Africa. There is need for those countries that robbed Africa to pay reparations.

Furthermore, Africa needs to cultivate a culture of self-reliance and self-esteem to also include self-defining. Mhango (2015) underscores the importance of reunifying Africa at "the tune of how it was before 1884" when it was partitioned at the Berlin Conference of 1884-85 (p. 307). Arguably, without reuniting Africa, there is no way it can make any headways without being frustrated and sabotaged by the current colonial-created superstructure in whatever form be it the IFIs or unequal cooperation. It becomes hard to understand how Africa can get out of the impasse it is in without doing some things such as the reunification; and thereby have the same policies and strategies as a single and united country in its encounter of facing the same enemies and problems altogether. Such anathema-cum-anomaly–that Africa has always faced–interweaves external and internal causes so as to work together in making Africa what it is today whether you term it as underdeveloped or arrested developmental wise. Sometimes, it becomes hard to separated external and internal causes of Africa's 'underdevelopment' due to the fact that the two forces reinforce each other purposely or accidentally. As I have indicated hereinabove, there is no way one can talk about Europe's development without touching Africa's underdevelopment resulting from being robbed by Europe for its development. There is no feasible way one can separate the two. For, doing so is like trying to dissect ketchup in which is difficult to separate eggs from mushrooms, oysters, mussels, walnuts, or other foods that make ketchup what it is. No ketchup can be ketchup without any of the ingredients. This is the same with Europe's development as far as Africa is concerned. For ketchup to be ketchup it must accept the entirety and the roles its ingredients play in making it what it is. Therefore, the analysis or history that defines ketchup without its major ingredients does not do justice to ketchup, its ingredients and the readers. The same applies to the history of Africa or his-story as maliciously Europe concocted, doctored, miswrote and misrepresented. This is why the essence of deconstructing everything becomes eminent for the duo to do justice to each other; and thus make sense. Although in this distortion ketchup is the victim, it is upon all of us to unearth fabrications and lies behind our ketchup we all like to eat. This analogy fits well in the theme of this corpus provided that nobody can live without Africa between the duos, among others. Therefore, the former and the latter are duty bound to seek the truth so that justice can be done. So, all proposed measures can help the duo to move forward. Importantly, this corpus does not exhaust all possibilities. In sum, it adds up to the dialogue. Importantly, Africa needs to raise its voice in order to get justice resulting from Europe's criminal past. As well, the international community must abandon its stance of silence *vis-à-vis* Africa's colonial past that resulted into the development of Europe as opposed to Africa's underdevelopment. This is how Africa developed Europe. How and when? The volume has revisited every aspect, *inter alia,* countering *his-story* as it was written by Europe.

"I dream of the realization of the unity of Africa, whereby its leaders combine in their efforts to solve the problems of this continent. I dream of our vast deserts, of our forests, of all our great wildernesses" Mandela (2011).

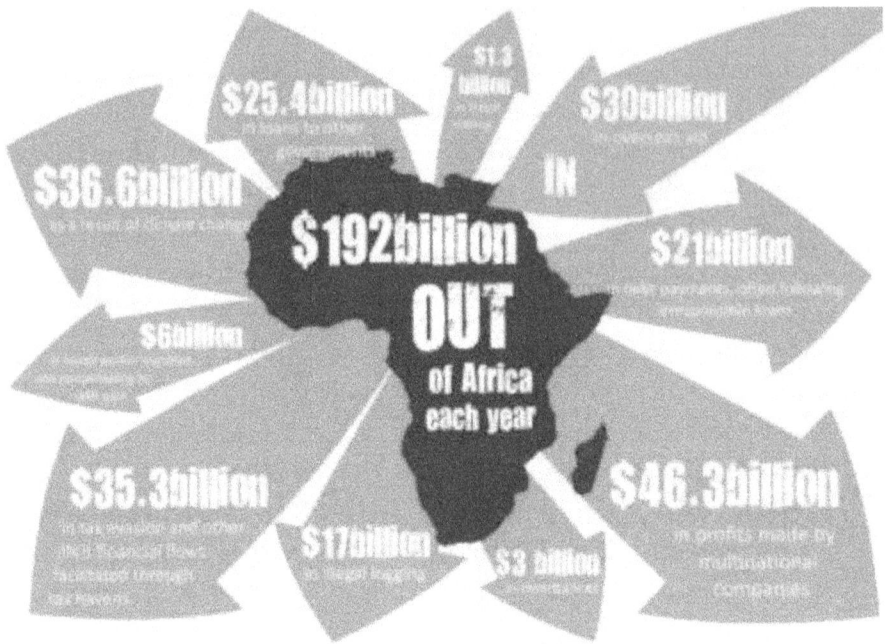

Figure 1 photo for the courtesy of thisiafrica.me

References

"Tanzania's Government Urges End to Donor Dependence as MCC Cancels Aid." 2016. *Guardian*, 1 April.

"U.S. agency freezes $473 million aid to Tanzania over Zanzibar election." 2016. *Reuters*, 29 March.

"What's so great about living in Vanuatu?" 2006. *BBC*, 13 July.

Abera, T., 2017. Ethiopianism in Today's Ethiopia. *Imperial Journal of Interdisciplinary Research*, 3(5).

Abulhawa, S., 2013. "Confronting anti-black racism in the Arab world: The Arab slave trade is a fact of history, and anti-black racism in the region is something that must be addressed." *Al Jazeera*, 7 July.

Acemoglu, D. and Robinson, J.A., 2010. Why is Africa poor? *Economic history of developing regions*, 25(1), pp.21-50.

Acemoglu, D., Chaves, I.N., Osafo-Kwaako, P. and Robinson, J.A., 2014. *Indirect rule and state weakness in Africa: Sierra Leone in comparative perspective* (No. w20092). National Bureau of Economic Research.

Acs, Z.J., Szerb, L. and Autio, E., 2016. The global entrepreneurship and development index. In *Global Entrepreneurship and Development Index 2015* (pp. 11-31). Springer International Publishing.

Adair, P. and Nezhyvenko, O., 2017. Assessing how large is the market for prostitution in the European Union.

Adams, M., 2014. Rejecting the American model: Peter Kropotkin's radical communalism. *History of Political Thought*, 35(1), pp.147-173.

Adan, A.M., 2015. Clan Politics in Somalia: Consequence of Culture or Colonial Legacy?

Adegbulu, F., 2011. Pre-Colonial West African Diplomacy: It's Nature and Impact. *Journal of International Social Research*, 4(18).

African, T.E, 2017. Kenya poll one of the most expensive in the world. *Daily Nation. Available at* http://www.nation.co.ke/news/Kenya-holds-one-of-the-most-expensive-elections/1056-4018144-10vpg41/index.html [Accessed Jul. 2017].

Afshariani, R., 2014. "Maternal Benefits of Breastfeeding." *Women's Health Bulletin 1.3*.

Aiyejina, F., 2010. Esu Elegbara: A Source of an Alter/Native Theory of African Literature and Criticism. *Lagos: CBAAC Occasional Monographs*.

Ajayi, S.I. and Ndikumana, L. eds., 2014. *Capital flight from Africa: causes, effects, and policy issues*. OUP Oxford.

Akçam, T., 2012. *The Young Turks' crime against humanity: The Armenian genocide and ethnic cleansing in the Ottoman Empire*. Princeton University Press.

Akcay, O., Dalgin, M.H. and Bhatnagar, S., 2011. Perception of color in product choice among college students: a cross-national analysis of USA, India, China and Turkey. *International Journal of Business and Social Science*, 2(21).

Alberts, M. and Mollema, N., 2013. Developing legal terminology in African languages as aid to the court interpreter: A South African perspective. *Lexikos*, 23(1), pp.29-58.

Alemazung, J.A., 2010. Post-colonial colonialism: An analysis of international factors and actors marring African socio-economic and political development. *The Journal of Pan African Studies*, 3(10), pp.62-84.

Alexander, A.C., Inglehart, R. and Welzel, C., 2012. Measuring effective democracy: A defense. *International Political Science Review*, 33(1), pp.41-62.

Allain, J. and Bales, K., 2012. Slavery and its definition.

Aluko, F. and Arowolo, D., 2010. Foreign Aid, the Third World's debt crisis and the implication for economic development: The Nigerian experience. *African Journal of Political Science and International Relations*, 4(4), p.120.

Amadahy, Z. and Lawrence, B., 2009. Indigenous Peoples and Black People in Canada: Settlers or Allies? *Breaching the colonial contract*, pp.105-136.

Amukowa, W. and Ayuya, C.V., 2013. The 21st Century Educated African Person and the Loss of Africans' Educational Identity: Towards an Afro Education Model. *Academic Journal of Interdisciplinary Studies*, 2(1), p.269.

Amutabi, M.N., 2013. *The NGO factor in Africa: the case of arrested development in Kenya*. Routledge.

Anderson, C.A., 2012. *Beauty*. First Edition Design Pub.

Anderson, R., 2005. Redressing colonial genocide under international law: the Hereros' Cause of action against Germany. *California Law Review, 93*(4), pp.1155-1189.

Aning, K. and Lecoutre, D., 2008. China's ventures in Africa: features. *African Security Review, 17*(1), pp.39-50.

Antwi-Boasiako, K.B. and Okyere, B., 2009. *Traditional institutions and public administration in democratic Africa*. Xlibris Corporation.

Anujan, D., Schaefer, D.J. and Karan, K., 2012. The changing face of Indian women in the era of global Bollywood. *Bollywood and Globalization: The Global Power of Popular Hindi Cinema, 63*, p.110.

Anyefru, E., 2011. The Refusal to Belong: Limits of the discourse on Anglophone Nationalism in Cameroon. *Journal of Third World Studies, 28*(2), p.277.

Appleby, J., Hunt, L. and Jacob, M., 2011. *Telling the truth about history*. WW Norton & Company.

Apter, D.E., 2013. *The political kingdom in Uganda: a study in bureaucratic nationalism*. Routledge.

Arnone, M. and Presbitero, A.F., 2016. *Debt relief initiatives: Policy design and outcomes*. Routledge.

Arowolo, D., 2010. The effects of western civilisation and culture on Africa. *Afro Asian Journal of Social Sciences, 1*(1), pp.1-13.

Arulampalam, W., Booth, A.L. and Bryan, M.L., 2007. Is there a glass ceiling over Europe? Exploring the gender pay gap across the wage distribution. *ILR Review, 60*(2), pp.163-186.

Asante, M.K., 2014. *The history of Africa: The quest for eternal harmony*. Routledge.

Ashforth, A., 2005. Muthi, medicine and witchcraft: regulating 'African science 'in post-apartheid South Africa? *Social Dynamics, 31*(2), pp.211-242.

Ashman, S., Fine, B. and Newman, S., 2010. The Developmental State and Post Liberation South Africa. *Testing democracy: Which way is South Africa going*, pp.23-45.

Asongu, S.A., 2012. On the effect of foreign aid on corruption.

Asongu, S.A., 2013. Fighting corruption in Africa: do existing corruption-control levels matter? *International Journal of Development Issues*, *12*(1), pp.36-52.

Austen, R.A., 2010. The moral economy of witchcraft. *Perspectives on Africa: A Reader in Culture, History and Representation*, *270*.

Babane, M.T. and Chauke, M.T., 2015. The Preservation of Xitsonga Culture through Rainmaking Ritual: An Interpretative Approach.

Bach, D., 2011. The European Union and Africa: Trade Liberalisation, Constructive Disengagement, and the Securitisation of Europe's External Frontiers. *Africa Review*, *3*(1), pp.33-46.

Bales, K., 2012. *Disposable people: New slavery in the global economy*. Univ of California Press.

Barbier, E.B., 2010. *Scarcity and frontiers: how economies have developed through natural resource exploitation*. Cambridge University Press.

Bartels, L.M., 2016. *Unequal democracy: The political economy of the new gilded age*. Princeton University Press.

Bayart, J.F. and Ellis, S., 2000. Africa in the world: a history of extraversion. *African affairs*, *99*(395), pp.217-267.

Bayly, C.A., 2007. *Indigenous and colonial origins of comparative economic development: the case of colonial India and Africa* (Vol. 4474). World Bank Publications.

Bayne, N., 2016. Challenge and Response in the New Economic Diplomacy. *The new economic diplomacy: decision-making and negotiation in international economic relations*, p.15.

Beattie, J. and Middleton, J. eds., 2013. *Spirit mediumship and society in Africa*. Routledge.

Beaujard, P., 2007. East Africa, the Comoros Islands and Madagascar before the sixteenth century: on a neglected part of the world system. *AZANIA: Journal of the British Institute in Eastern Africa*, *42*(1), pp.15-35.

Beine, M., Docquier, F. and Rapoport, H., 2008. Brain drain and human capital formation in developing countries: winners and losers. *The Economic Journal*, *118*(528), pp.631-652.

Berger, D., 2009. Taxes, institutions and local governance: evidence from a natural experiment in colonial Nigeria. *Unpublished manuscript*.

Bermeo, S.B., 2011. Foreign aid and regime change: a role for donor intent. *World Development, 39*(11), pp.2021-2031.

Berry, J., 2012. *Render unto Rome: The secret life of money in the Catholic Church.* Broadway Books.

Bethell, L., 2009. *The Abolition of the Brazilian Slave Trade: Britain, Brazil and the Slave Trade Question* (Vol. 6). Cambridge University Press.

Bettinson, G.J., 2017. Posthandover Hong Kong Cinema: Interviews with Stanley Kwan, Herman Yau, and Gordon Chan. *Cineaste, 42*(4), pp.28-31.

Bigelow, B., 2016. "Time to Abolish Columbus Day." *Huffington Post,* October 5.

Biloa, E. and Echu, G., 2008. Cameroon: official bilingualism in a multilingual state. *Language and national identity in Africa,* p.199.

Bjerg, C., Bjørnskov, C. and Holm, A., 2011. Growth, debt burdens and alleviating effects of foreign aid in least developed countries. *European Journal of Political Economy, 27*(1), pp.143-153.

Blanchard, P. and Snoep, N.J., 2011. L'invention du sauvage. *Exhibitions, Paris: Musée du quai Branly.*

Blasco, M., 2009. Cultural pragmatists? Student perspectives on learning culture at a business school. *Academy of Management Learning & Education, 8*(2), pp.174-187.

Blaut, J.M., 2012. *The colonizer's model of the world: Geographical diffusionism and Eurocentric history.* Guilford Press.

Boateng, O., 2005. How Africa Developed Europe and America. *New African,* October.

Boeschoten, A., 2013. Shakespeare's History Plays and Borgen: The Portrayal of Political Realism.

Bond, P., 2006. *Looting Africa: The economics of exploitation.* Zed books.

Boone, C., 2007. Property and constitutional order: Land tenure reform and the future of the African state. *African Affairs, 106*(425), pp.557-586.

Bottazzi, P., Goguen, A. and Rist, S., 2016. Conflicts of customary land tenure in rural Africa: is large-scale land acquisition a driver of 'institutional innovation'? *The Journal of Peasant Studies, 43*(5), pp.971-988.

Bourguignon, F., Bénassy-Quéré, A., Dercon, S., Estache, A., Gunning, J.W., Kanbur, R., Klasen, S., Maxwell, S., Platteau, J.P.

and Spadaro, A., 2010. The Millennium development goals: an assessment. *Equity and growth in a globalizing world, 17.*

BoxIll, I., 2016. Beauty &Sexuality.

Boyce, J.K. and Ndikumana, L., 2012. Capital Flight from Sub-Saharan African Countries: Updated Estimates, 1970-2010. *Political Economy Research Institute Research Report (October 2012). University of Massachusetts Amherst.*

Brett, M.G., 2008. *Decolonizing God-The Bible in the Tides of Empire.* Sheffield Phoenix Press.

Broadman, H.G., 2008. China and India go to Africa: New deals in the developing world. *Foreign affairs,* pp.95-109.

Brodie, J., 1989. The political economy of regionalism. *The new Canadian political economy, 144.*

Broedel, H.P., 2010. *The Malleus Maleficarum and the construction of witchcraft: Theology and popular belief.* Manchester University Press.

Brown, L. and Strega, S. eds., 2005. *Research as resistance: Critical, indigenous and anti-oppressive approaches.* Canadian Scholars' Press.

Brusa, M. and Barilan, Y.M., 2009. Cultural circumcision in EU public hospitals—an ethical discussion. *Bioethics, 23*(8), pp.470-482.

Bryant, J.M., 2006. The West and the rest revisited: Debating capitalist origins, European colonialism, and the advent of modernity. *The Canadian Journal of Sociology, 31*(4), pp.403-444.

Buchan, B. and Heath, M., 2006. Savagery and civilization: from Terra Nullius to the 'Tide of History'. *Ethnicities, 6*(1), pp.5-26.

Bugri, J.T., 2008. The dynamics of tenure security, agricultural production and environmental degradation in Africa: Evidence from stakeholders in north-east Ghana. *Land Use Policy, 25*(2), pp.271-285.

Burridge, R.A., 2008. Being Biblical? Slavery, sexuality, and the inclusive community. *HTS Theological Studies, 64*(1), pp.155-174.

Bush, T., 2007. Educational leadership and management: Theory, policy and practice. *South African journal of education, 27*(3), pp.391-406.

Byers, H.L., 2015. The Benefits of Breastfeeding.

Caballero, B., 2005. A nutrition paradox—underweight and obesity in developing countries. *N engl j med, 352*(15), pp.1514-1516.

Call, C.T., 2008. The fallacy of the 'Failed State'. *Third World Quarterly*, *29*(8), pp.1491-1507.

Cannon, K.G., 2008. "Christian Imperialism and the Transatlantic Slave Trade." *Journal of Feminist Studies in Religion* 24.1: 127-134.

Carmody, P.R., 2016. *The New Scramble for Africa*. Polity Press.

Carney, J.J., 2014. *Rwanda before the genocide: Catholic politics and ethnic discourse in the late colonial era*. Oxford University Press.

Castro, J.E., 2008. Neoliberal water and sanitation policies as a failed development strategy: lessons from developing countries. *Progress in Development Studies*, *8*(1), pp.63-83.

Cavalieri, M., 2013. Blackface is considered offensive for several reasons. *Quora*, 3, May (accessed in January, 2017).

Chabal, P., 2016. *Power in Africa: an essay in political interpretation*. Springer.

Chalmers, B., 2013. Cultural issues in perinatal care. *Birth*, *40*(4), pp.217-219.

Chamberlain, M.E., 2014. *The scramble for Africa*. Routledge.

Chambers, C.M. and Balanoff, H., 2009. Translating "participation" from North to South: A case against intellectual imperialism in social science research. In *Education, Participatory Action Research, and Social Change* (pp. 73-88). Palgrave Macmillan US.

Chami, F.A., 1998. A review of Swahili archaeology. *African Archaeological Review*, *15*(3), pp.199-218.

Chan, A.B., 2011. *Arming the Chinese: The Western Armaments Trade in Warlord China, 1920-28*. UBC Press.

Chemhuru, M., 2010. Democracy and the paradox of Zimbabwe: Lessons from traditional systems of governance. *The Journal of Pan African Studies*, *3*(10), pp.180-191.

Chen, Z.J., Scheffler, B.E., Dennis, E., Triplett, B.A., Zhang, T., Guo, W., Chen, X., Stelly, D.M., Rabinowicz, P.D., Town, C.D. and Arioli, T., 2007. Toward sequencing cotton (Gossypium) genomes. *Plant physiology*, *145*(4), pp.1303-1310.

Chinweizu, B., 2010. Pan-Africanism and a Black Superpower—the 21st century agenda. In *CBAAC Conference on Pan-Africanism*.

Chirikure, S., Pollard, M., Manyanga, M. and Bandama, F., 2013. A Bayesian chronology for Great Zimbabwe: re-threading the sequence of a vandalised monument. *Antiquity*, *87*(337), pp.854-872.

Chomsky, N., 1992. *Deterring democracy*. Hill and Wang.

Chomsky, N., 2015. *Year 501: The conquest continues*. Haymarket Books.

Cilliers, J., 2010. Europe and Africa-the enduring relationship.

Clarence-Smith, W.G., 2006. *Islam and the Abolition of Slavery*. Oxford University Press, USA.

Clark, M., 2006. *A short history of Australia*. Penguin UK.

Coly, A.A., 2010. A Pedagogy of the Black Female Body: Viewing Angèle Essamba's Black Female Nudes. *Third Text*, *24*(6), pp.653-664.

Corsetti, G., Guimaraes, B. and Roubini, N., 2006. International lending of last resort and moral hazard: A model of IMF's catalytic finance. *Journal of Monetary Economics*, *53*(3), pp.441-471.

Cox, F.E., 2012. 'So Much Woman': Female Objectification, Narrative Complexity, and Feminist Temporality in AMC's Mad Men. *Invisible Culture*, *17*.

Croese, S., 2012. One million houses? Chinese engagement in Angola's national reconstruction. *China and Angola: a marriage of convenience*, pp.124-138.

Crone, P., 2010. The religion of the Qur'ānic pagans: God and the lesser deities. *Arabica*, *57*(2), pp.151-200.

Crowell, B.L., 2009. Postcolonial studies and the Hebrew Bible. *Currents in Research*, *7*(2), pp.217-244.

Curran, A.S., 2011. *The anatomy of blackness: Science and slavery in an age of enlightenment*. JHU Press.

Dalaker, J. and Naifeh, M., 1997. Poverty in the United States. *US Bureau of the Census, Current Population Reports. Series P60-201. Washington, DC: US Government Printing Office.*

Dalton, H., 2016. *Merchants and Explorers: Roger Barlow, Sebastian Cabot, and Networks of Atlantic Exchange 1500-1560*. Oxford University Press.

Dave, M., 2012. How much in food do Canadians waste a year? Think billions. *Globe and Mail*, October 1.p.l. available at: https://beta.theglobeandmail.com/life/the-hot-button/how-much-in-food-do-canadians-waste-a-year-think-billions/article4580509/?ref=http://www.theglobeandmail.com & [Accessed 8 Oct. 2017].

Davidson, B., 2014. *Modern Africa: A social and political history*. Routledge.

Davis, D.B. and Zilberstein, A., 2007. Inhuman Bondage: The Rise and Fall of Slavery in the New World. *African Diaspora Archaeology Newsletter, 10*(2), p.19.

Davis, F.J., 2010. *Who is black?: One nation's definition*. Penn State Press.

Dawkins, R., 2016. *The god delusion*. Random House.

de Morais, R.M., 2011. Corruption in Angola: An impediment to democracy. *Presentation at National Endowment for Democracy, May http://www. ned. org/events/corruption-in-angola-an-impediment-to-democracy*.

De Weever, J., 2013. *Sheba's Daughters: Whitening and Demonizing the Saracen Woman in Medieval French Epic* (Vol. 2077). Routledge.

Deci, E.L. and Ryan, R.M., 2011. Self-determination theory. *Handbook of theories of social psychology, 1*, pp.416-433.

Dei, D. and Osei-Bonsu, R., 2014. The Nature, Philosophy, and Sustaining Factors of the Theology of Wealth in Africa: Theological Reflections. *Philosophy Study*, p.391.

DeLancey, M.D., Mbuh, R. and DeLancey, M.W., 2010. *Historical dictionary of the Republic of Cameroon*. Scarecrow Press.

Demirel, S. and Kılıç, Z.H., 2014. The Contribution of the Language, Culture and Vision Constructed by Qur'an and Sunnah to the World Peace. *IIUC Studies, 8*, pp.141-160.

Demirel-Pegg, T. and Moskowitz, J., 2009. US aid allocation: The nexus of human rights, democracy, and development. *Journal of Peace Research, 46*(2), pp.181-198

Deng, F., 2007. Sudan at the Crossroads. *MIT Center for International Studies Audit of the Conventional Wisdom series (March 2007)*.

Deng, F.M., 2011. *War of visions: Conflict of identities in the Sudan*. Brookings Institution Press.

Diabate, N., 2011. Genital power: Female sexuality in West African literature and film.

Diagne, S.B., 2008. Toward an intellectual history of West Africa: the meaning of Timbuktu. *The meanings of Timbuktu*, pp.19-27.

Diamond, J.M., and Ordunio. D., 2011. *Guns, germs, and steel.* Books on Tape.

Diamond, L., 2015. Facing up to the democratic recession. *Journal of Democracy, 26*(1), pp.141-155.

Dickinson, H.T. ed., 2008. *A Companion to Eighteenth-Century Britain.* John Wiley & Sons.

Diop, C.A., 1989. *The African origin of civilization: Myth or reality.* Chicago Review Press.

Dixon, J., 2013. Do Fast Foods Cause Asthma, Rhinoconjunctivitis and Eczema? Global Findings from the International Study of Asthma and Allergies in Childhood (ISAAC) Phase Three. *Journal of Emergency Medicine, 45*(3), p.482.

Dlova, N.C., Hamed, S.H., Tsoka-Gwegweni, J. and Grobler, A., 2015. Skin lightening practices: an epidemiological study of South African women of African and Indian ancestries. *British Journal of Dermatology, 173*(S2), pp.2-9.

Docquier, F. and Rapoport, H., 2012. Globalization, brain drain, and development. *Journal of Economic Literature, 50*(3), pp.681-730.

Docquier, F., Lohest, O. and Marfouk, A., 2007. Brain drain in developing countries. *The World Bank Economic Review, 21*(2), pp.193-218.

Donnelly, J., 2007. The relative universality of human rights. *Human rights quarterly, 29*(2), pp.281-306.

Donnelly, S. and Inglis, T., 2010. The media and the Catholic Church in Ireland: Reporting clerical child sex abuse. *Journal of Contemporary Religion, 25*(1), pp.1-19.

Dorman, S.R., 2006. Post-liberation politics in Africa: Examining the political legacy of struggle. *Third World Quarterly, 27*(6), pp.1085-1101.

Dotsika, E., Poutoukis, D., Tzavidopoulos, I., Maniatis, Y., Ignatiadou, D. and Raco, B., 2009. A natron source at Pikrolimni Lake in Greece? Geochemical evidence. *Journal of Geochemical Exploration, 103*(2), pp.133-143.

Douglas, L.R. and Alie, K., 2014. High-value natural resources: Linking wildlife conservation to international conflict, insecurity, and development concerns. *Biological Conservation, 171*, pp.270-277.

Drayton, R., 2005. The wealth of the west was built on Africa exploitation. *Guardian*, August, 20.

Drezner, D.W., 2007. The New New World Order. *Foreign Aff.*, *86*, p.34.

Du Bois, W.E.B., 2014. *The Suppression of the African Slave-Trade to the United States of America*. Oxford University Press.

Dube, M.W., 2017. Consuming a Colonial Cultural Bomb. *Postcoloniality, Translation, and the Bible in Africa*, p.1.

Dueppen, S.A., 2014. *Egalitarian revolution in the savanna: the origins of a West African political system*. Routledge.

Duignan, P. and Gann, L.H., 2013. *Burden of empire: an appraisal of Western colonialism in Africa south of the Sahara*. Hoover Press.

Duncan, R., 2012. *The new depression: The breakdown of the paper money economy*. John Wiley & Sons.

Dussubieux, L., Kusimba, C.M., Gogte, V., Kusimba, S.B., Gratuze, B. and Oka, R., 2008. The trading of ancient glass beads: new analytical data from South Asian and East African soda–alumina glass beads. *Archaeometry*, *50*(5), pp.797-821.

Dustmann, C., Fadlon, I. and Weiss, Y., 2011. Return migration, human capital accumulation and the brain drain. *Journal of Development Economics*, *95*(1), pp.58-67.

Easterly, W. and Levine, R., 2016. The European origins of economic development. *Journal of Economic Growth*, *21*(3), pp.225-257.

Easterly, W. and Pfutze, T., 2008. Where does the money go? Best and worst practices in foreign aid. *The Journal of Economic Perspectives*, *22*(2), p.29.

Easterly, W., 2009. How the millennium development goals are unfair to Africa. *World development*, *37*(1), pp.26-35.

Ebila, F. and Tripp, A.M., 2017. Naked transgressions: gendered symbolism in Ugandan land protests. *Politics, Groups, and Identities*, *5*(1), pp.25-45.

Echu, G., 2013. The language question in Cameroon. *Linguistik online*, *18*(1).

Eckl, A., 2008. The Herero genocide of 1904: Source-critical and methodological considerations. *Journal of Namibian Studies: History Politics Culture*, *3*, pp.31-61.

Edelman, B.G. and Luca, M., 2014. Digital discrimination: The case of Airbnb. com.

Edusah, S.E., 2011. The impact of forest reserves on livelihoods of fringe communities in Ghana. *Journal of Science and Technology (Ghana)*, *31*(1).

Egbunike, N., 2017. "Us and Them:" The Cross Cultural Communication Clash of the Big Brother Africa Reality Show. *International Journal of Communication*, *20*(1).

Eichengreen, B. and Flandreau, M., 2009. The rise and fall of the dollar (or when did the dollar replace sterling as the leading reserve currency?). *European Review of Economic History*, *13*(3), pp.377-411.

Eichengreen, B. and Temin, P., 2010. Fetters of gold and paper. *Oxford Review of Economic Policy*, *26*(3), pp.370-384.

Eisler, R., 2003. Health risks of gold miners: a synoptic review. *Environmental Geochemistry and Health*, *25*(3), pp.325-345.

Eldeen, I.M.S. and Van Staden, J., 2007. Antimycobacterial activity of some trees used in South African traditional medicine. *South African Journal of Botany*, *73*(2), pp.248-251.

Elhadi, A.M., Kalb, S., Perez-Orribo, L., Little, A.S., Spetzler, R.F. and Preul, M.C., 2012. The journey of discovering skull base anatomy in ancient Egypt and the special influence of Alexandria. *Neurosurgical focus*, *33*(2), p.E2.

Ellis, F. and Freeman, H.A., 2004. Rural livelihoods and poverty reduction strategies in four African countries. *Journal of development studies*, *40*(4), pp.1-30.

Ellis, S., 2007. Witching-times: A theme in the histories of Africa and Europe.

Emefa, A.F. and Selase, G.R., 2014. Increasing HIV Awareness through Reduced Sexual Provocations: Implications for Dipo Initiation Rite among the Krobos in Ghana. *International Journal of Innovative Research and Development*, *3*(9).

Emielu, A., 2006. Foreign culture and African music. *An encyclopeadia of Arts*, *8*(1), pp.27-34.

Enslin, P. and Horsthemke, K., 2004. Can Ubuntu provide a model for citizenship education in African democracies? *Comparative education*, *40*(4), pp.545-558.

Enweremadu, D.U., 2013. Nigeria's quest to recover looted assets: the Abacha affair. *Africa Spectrum*, pp.51-70.

Escobar, A., 2011. *Encountering development: The making and unmaking of the Third World*. Princeton University Press.

Estevez-Abe, M., 2006. Gendering the varieties of capitalism. A study of occupational segregation by sex in advanced industrial societies. *World Politics*, *59*(1), pp.142-175.

Estreicher, S.K., 2014. A Brief History of Wine in South Africa. *European Review*, *22*(3), pp.504-537.

Evans, R. ed., 2017. *Mass and Elite in the Greek and Roman Worlds: From Sparta to Late Antiquity*. Taylor & Francis.

Exenberger, A. and Hartmann, S., 2007. *The dark side of globalization. The vicious cycle of exploitation from world market integration: Lesson from the Congo* (No. 2007-31). Working Papers in Economics and Statistics.

Fage, J., 2013. *A history of Africa*. Routledge.

Falola, T., 2009. *Colonialism and violence in Nigeria*. Indiana University Press.

Fasching-Varner, K.J., Reynolds, R.E., Albert, K.A. and Martin, L.L. eds., 2014. *Trayvon Martin, race, and American justice: Writing wrong*. Springer.

Fayemi, A.K., 2009. Towards an African theory of democracy. *Institute of African Studies Research Review*, *25*(1), pp.1-21.

Feeley, A.B.B., Kahn, K., Twine, R. and Norris, S.A., 2011. Exploratory survey of informal vendor-sold fast food in rural South Africa. *South African Journal of Clinical Nutrition*, *24*(4), pp.199-201.

Feldman, N. and Martinez, R., 2006. Constitutional politics and text in the new Iraq: An experiment in Islamic democracy. *Fordham L. Rev.*, *75*, p.883.

Ferguson, J., 2006. *Global shadows: Africa in the neoliberal world order*. Duke University Press

Ferim, V., DICTATORSHIPS IN AFRICA. *ct4 | 2012, 1*, p.128.

Ferreira, M.E., 2006. Angola: conflict and development, 1961-2002. *The Economics of Peace and Security Journal*, *1*(1), pp.25-29.

Fieldhouse, D.K., 2012. *Black Africa 1945-1980: Economic decolonization and arrested development*. Routledge.

Fiorillo, J., 2010. *Great Bastards of History: True and Riveting Accounts of the Most Famous Illegitimate Children Who Went on to Achieve Greatness.* Fair Winds Press.

Firchow, P.E., 2015. *Envisioning Africa: Racism and Imperialism in Conrad's Heart of Darkness.* University Press of Kentucky.

Fischer, H., 2015. "Africa and the First World War.) *Deutch Welle*, April 16.

Fisher, J., 2012. Managing donor perceptions: Contextualizing Uganda's 2007 intervention in Somalia. *African Affairs, 111*(444), pp.404-423.

Fisk, R., 2015. "The Gallipoli centenary is a shameful attempt to hide the Armenian Holocaust." *Independent (London)* 19.

Fitzmaurice, A., 2007. The genealogy of terra nullius. *Australian Historical Studies, 38*(129), pp.1-15.

Fitzmaurice, A., 2012. Liberalism and Empire in Nineteenth-Century International Law. *The American Historical Review, 117*(1), pp.122-140.

Flint, J., 2009. *Beyond'janjaweed': Understanding the Militias of Darfur.* Geneva, Switzerland: Small Arms Survey.

Form, W.H., 2015. *Blue-collar stratification: Autoworkers in four countries.* Princeton University Press.

Frankel, J.A., 2010. *The natural resource curse: a survey* (No. w15836). National Bureau of Economic Research.

Frankema, E., 2010. Raising Revenue in the British Empire, 1870–1940: how 'extractive' were colonial taxes? *Journal of Global History, 5*(3), pp.447-477.

Frankema, E., 2010. The colonial roots of land inequality: geography, factor endowments, or institutions? *The Economic History Review, 63*(2), pp.418-451.

Friedmann, J., 1967. A general theory of polarized development.

Frynas, J.G. and Paulo, M., 2006. A new scramble for African oil? Historical, political, and business perspectives. *African Affairs, 106*(423), pp.229-251.

Furnivall, J.S., 2014. *Colonial policy and practice.* Cambridge University Press.

Gade, C.B., 2011. The historical development of the written discourses on Ubuntu. *South African Journal of Philosophy= Suid-Afrikaanse Tydskrif vir Wysbegeerte*, *30*(3), pp.303-329.

Gade, C.B., 2012. What is Ubuntu? Different interpretations among South Africans of African descent. *South African Journal of Philosophy*, *31*(3), pp.484-503.

Galbraith, J.K., 2008. *The predator state: How conservatives abandoned the free market and why liberals should too.* Simon and Schuster.

Gallego, F.A. and Woodberry, R., 2010. Christian missionaries and education in former African colonies: How competition mattered. *Journal of African Economies*, *19*(3), pp.294-329.

Gandure, S., Walker, S. and Botha, J.J., 2013. Farmers' perceptions of adaptation to climate change and water stress in a South African rural community. *Environmental Development*, *5*, pp.39-53.

Gathogo, J.M., 2008. Some expressions of African hospitality today: general. *Scriptura: International Journal of Bible, Religion and Theology in Southern Africa*, *99*(1), pp.275-287.

Geisinger, A.C., 2009. Sustainable development and the domination of nature: Spreading the seed of the western ideology of nature.

Geisler, C., 2012. New Terra Nullius Narratives and the Gentrification of Africa's" Empty Lands". *Journal of World-Systems Research*, *18*(1), pp.15-29.

Geschiere, P., 2013. *Witchcraft, intimacy, and trust: Africa in comparison.* University of Chicago Press.

Getye, Abneh, 2016. The Contribution of African Philosophy in Challenging Western Hegemony and Globalization. Diss. AAU.

Gichure, C.P., 2015. Human Nature and Identity in Muntu Anthropology and Ubuntu Worldview.

Gifford, P., 2008. Africa's Inculturation Theology: Observations of an Outsider. *Hekima Review*, *38*, pp.18-34.

Gill, B. and Reilly, J., 2007. The tenuous hold of China Inc. in Africa. *Washington Quarterly*, *30*(3), pp.37-52.

Gill, B., Huang, C.H. and Morrison, J.S., 2007. Assessing China's growing influence in Africa. *China Security*, *3*(3), pp.3-21.

Gißibl, B., 2006. German colonialism and the beginnings of international wildlife preservation in Africa. *From Heimat to Umwelt: New perspectives on German environmental history*, pp.121-144.

Giuliano, P. and Nunn, N., 2013. The transmission of democracy: from the village to the nation-state. *The American Economic Review*, *103*(3), pp.86-92.

Glenn, E.N., 2008. Yearning for lightness: Transnational circuits in the marketing and consumption of skin lighteners. *Gender & society*, *22*(3), pp.281-302.

Glennie, J., 2010. *The trouble with aid: why less could mean more for Africa.* Zed Books Ltd.

Global Christianity–A Report on the Size and Distribution of the World's Christian Population. 2011. *Pew Research Center.* Available at: http://www.pewforum.org/2011/12/19/global-christianity-exec/ [Accessed 12 Jun. 2017].

Gluckman, M., 2017. *Politics, law and ritual in tribal society.* Routledge.

Godde, K., 2009. An Examination of Nubian and Egyptian biological distances: Support for biological diffusion or in situ development? *HOMO-Journal of Comparative Human Biology*, *60*(5), pp.389-404.

Goldberg, E., Wibbels, E. and Mvukiyehe, E., 2008. Lessons from strange cases: Democracy, development, and the resource curse in the US states. *Comparative Political Studies*, *41*(4-5), pp.477-514.

Goldenberg, D.M., 2009. *The curse of Ham: Race and slavery in early Judaism, Christianity, and Islam.* Princeton University Press.

Goldthwaite, R.A., 2009. The Return of a Lost Ledger to the Selfridge Collection of Medici Manuscripts at Baker Library. *Business History Review*, *83*(1), pp.165-171.

Goldthwaite, R.A., 2015. *Private Wealth in Renaissance Florence.* Princeton University Press.

Gong, S., 2007, April. Chinese workers in Africa. In *unpublished paper presented at the conference 'Rethinking Africa's "China Factor": identifying players, strategies, and practices* (Vol. 27, p. 664).

González, R.J., 2009. Going 'tribal': Notes on pacification in the 21st century. *Anthropology Today*, *25*(2), pp.15-19.

Gordon, G.S., 2008. An African Marshall Plan: Changing US Policy to Promote the Rule of Law and Prevent Mass Atrocity in the Democratic Republic of the Congo. *Fordham Int'l LJ*, *32*, p.1361.

Gordon, R., 2016. Moving targets: hunting in contemporary Africa.

Granger, M.D. and Price, G.N., 2007. The tree of science and original sin: Do Christian religious beliefs constrain the supply of scientists? *The Journal of Socio-Economics*, *36*(1), pp.144-160.

Green, J., 2015. *Popes Coloring Book*. Courier Dover Publications.

Grisham, L., 2010. The Independence of Love: Leah and Kambili's Rise from Colonialism. *Prologue: A First-Year Writing Journal*, *2*(1), p.2.

Grocott, C. and Grady, J., 2014. 'Naked abroad': The continuing imperialism of free trade. *Capital & Class*, *38*(3), pp.541-562.

Grosfoguel, R., 2013. The structure of knowledge in westernized universities: Epistemic racism/sexism and the four genocides/epistemicides of the long 16th century. *Human architecture*, *11*(1), p.73.

Guerra, M.F., 2008. An overview on the ancient goldsmith's skill and the circulation of gold in the past: the role of x-ray based techniques. *X-Ray Spectrometry*, *37*(4), pp.317-327.

Gurib-Fakim, A., 2006. Medicinal plants: traditions of yesterday and drugs of tomorrow. *Molecular aspects of Medicine*, *27*(1), pp.1-93.

Gwinn, J.D., Judd, C.M. and Park, B., 2013. Less power= less human? Effects of power differentials on dehumanization. *Journal of Experimental Social Psychology*, *49*(3), pp.464-470.

Habashi, F., 2009. Gold in the ancient African Kingdoms. *De. Re Met*, *12*.

Hahn, N.S.C., 2007. Neoliberal imperialism and pan-African resistance. *Journal of World-Systems Research*, *13*(2), pp.142-178.

Håland, E.J., 2005. Rituals of magical rain-making in modern and ancient Greece: A comparative approach. *Cosmos: The Journal of the Traditional Cosmology Society*, *17*(2), pp.197-251.

Halder, D. and Jaishankar, K., 2014. Online Victimization of Andaman Jarawa tribal women: an analysis of the 'human safari' 'YouTube Videos (2012) and its effects. *British Journal of Criminology*, *54*(4), pp.673-688.

Hale, M.M., 2011. *On Uganda's Terms: A Journal by an American Nurse-midwife Working for Change in Uganda, East Africa during Idi Amin's Regime*. CCB Publishing.

Harrison, G., 2013. *Neoliberal Africa: The impact of global social engineering*. Zed Books Ltd.

Harriss, J., Hunter, J. and Lewis, C. eds., 2003. *The new institutional economics and third world development*. Routledge.

Hasian, M. and Wood, R., 2010. Critical museology, (post) colonial communication, and the gradual mastering of traumatic pasts at the Royal Museum for Central Africa (RMCA). *Western Journal of Communication*, *74*(2), pp.128-149.

Haugen, H.Ø., 2013. China's recruitment of African university students: policy efficacy and unintended outcomes. *Globalisation, Societies and Education*, *11*(3), pp.315-334.

Hayes, C. and Hromic, H., 2014, September. Constructing Twitter Datasets using Signals for Event Detection Evaluation. 22nd International Conference on Case-Based Reasoning.

Heggstad, K. and Fjeldstad, O.H., 2010. How banks assist capital flight from Africa: a literature review.

Heldring, L. and Robinson, J.A., 2012. *Colonialism and economic development in Africa* (No. w18566). National Bureau of Economic Research.

Helgesen, G., 2002. Imported Democracy. *Globalization and democratization in Asia: the construction of identity*, p.73.

Herbst, J., 2014. *States and power in Africa: Comparative lessons in authority and control*. Princeton University Press.

Hickel, J., 2013. The Donors' Dilemma'-Aid in Reverse: How Poor Countries Develop Rich Countries, *Global Poli*cy, December 12.

Higgs, P., 2010. Towards an indigenous African epistemology of community in education research. *Procedia-Social and Behavioral Sciences*, *2*(2), pp.2414-2421.

Hinterberger, F., Luks, F. and Schmidt-Bleek, F., 1997. Material flows vs. Natural capital': What makes an economy sustainable? *Ecological economics*, *23*(1), pp.1-14.

Hobson, J., 2013. *Venus in the dark: Blackness and beauty in popular culture*. Routledge.

Hoeffler, A., 2008. Dealing with the Consequences of Violent Conflicts in Africa.

Holley, P., 2015 "More cities celebrating 'Indigenous Peoples Day' amid effort to abolish Columbus Day." Washington Post, October 12.

Holt, S., Jebodh, R. and Gilbert, J., 2015. Minority-Related Activities in the United Nations System in 2013. *European Yearbook of Minority Issues Online, 12*(1), pp.280-314.

Holter, K., 2006. Interpreting Solomon in colonial and post-colonial Africa. *Old Testament Essays, 19*(3), pp.851-862.

Holter, K., 2008. Does a dialogue between Africa and Europe make sense. *African and European readers of the Bible in dialogue: In quest of a shared meaning,* pp.69-80.

Hopkins, A.G., 2014. *An economic history of West Africa.* Routledge.

Hovannisian, R.G. ed., 2009. *The Armenian genocide in perspective.* Transaction Publishers.

Hubbard, P., 2009. The Zimbabwe birds: interpretation and symbolism. *Honeyguide: Journal of Birdlife Zimbabwe, 55,* pp.109-116.

Hungerman, D.M., 2013. Substitution and stigma: Evidence on religious markets from the catholic sex abuse scandal. *American Economic Journal: Economic Policy, 5*(3), pp.227-253.

Hunt, K.P., 2014. "It's More Than Planting Trees, It's Planting Ideas": Ecofeminist Praxis in the Green Belt Movement. *Southern Communication Journal, 79*(3), pp.235-249.

Hutton, C., 2016. 'I Prefer The Fake Look': Aesthetically Silencing and Obscuring the Presence of the Black Body. *Ideaz, 14,* p.20.

Igboin, B.O., 2011. "Colonialism and African cultural values." *African Journal of History and Culture* 3.6: 96-103.

Iliffe, J., 2017. *Africans: the history of a continent* (Vol. 137). Cambridge University Press.

Imhonopi, D. and Urim, U.M., 2012. Nigeria's expensive democracy: A confederal option for development. *Journal of Sustainable Development in Africa, 14*(7), pp.70-80.

Inyang, B.J., 2009. The challenges of evolving and developing management indigenous theories and practices in Africa. *International Journal of Business and Management, 3*(12), p.122.

Ishengoma, J.M. and es Salaam, D., 2008. Internal Brain and Its Impact on Higher Education Institutions' Capacity Building and Human Resource Development in Sub Saharan Africa: The Case of Tanzania. *The African Brain Drain–Managing the Drain: Working with the Diaspora,* p.37.

Iweriebor, E.E., 2011. The colonization of Africa. *Africana.*

Izuchukwu, O., 2011. Analysis of the contribution of agricultural sector on the Nigerian economic development. *World review of business research*, *1*(1), pp.191-200.

Jackson, J., 2015. Structural differentiation and the poetics of violence shaping Barack Obama's presidency: a study in personhood, literacy, and the improvisation of African–American publics. *Language sciences*, *52*, pp.200-214.

Jackson, J.G., 2015. *Introduction to African civilizations*. Ravenio Books.

Jackson, R.H. and Rosberg, C.G., 1982. Why Africa's weak states persist: the empirical and the juridical in statehood. *World politics*, *35*(1), pp.1-24.

Jacobsen, S.L. and Nielsen, J.K., 2014. Sub Saharan Africa's underdevelopment, causes of it, and what the future might hold. *Master of Science in Strategy, Organisation and Leadership*.

Jaffee, D., 2014. *Brewing justice: Fair trade coffee, sustainability, and survival*. Univ of California Press.

Jaffer, G., 2012. "Tinted prejudice in China" CNN, July 24.

James, J., 2013. "Concerning Violence": Frantz Fanon's Rebel Intellectual in Search of a Black Cyborg. *South Atlantic Quarterly*, *112*(1), pp.57-70.

James, J.C., 2012. *A Freedom Bought with Blood: African American War Literature from the Civil War to World War II*. UNC Press Books.

Jans, M., 2016. *Political Conditionality in aid to Kenya and Uganda* (Bachelor's thesis).

Jarosz, L., 2009. Energy, climate change, meat, and markets: mapping the coordinates of the current world food crisis. *Geography Compass*, *3*(6), pp.2065-2083.

Jenkins, P., 2011. *The next Christendom: The coming of global Christianity*. Oxford University Press.

Jerven, M., 2013. *Poor numbers: how we are misled by African development statistics and what to do about it*. Cornell University Press.

Johnson, K.L., Gill, S., Reichman, V. and Tassinary, L.G., 2007. Swagger, sway, and sexuality: Judging sexual orientation from body motion and morphology. *Journal of personality and social psychology*, *93*(3), p.321.

Johnson, P., 2012. *History of Christianity*. Simon and Schuster.

Johnson, S.A., 2010. The Bible, Slavery, and the Problem of Authority. In *Beyond Slavery* (pp. 231-248). Palgrave Macmillan US.

Jønsson, J.B. and Bryceson, D.F., 2009. Rushing for Gold: Mobility and Small-Scale Mining in East Africa. *Development and Change*, *40*(2), pp.249-279.

Jordan, W., 1812. The Simultaneous invention of slavery and racism. *White over black: American attitudes toward the Negro, 1550*, pp.3-7.

Jordan, W.D., 2013. *White over black: American attitudes toward the Negro, 1550-1812*. UNC Press Books.

Jorgensen, K.E., 2014. Sapologie: Performing Postcolonial Identity in the Democratic Republic of Congo.

Joseph, P.E., 2010. *Dark days, bright nights: From black power to Barack Obama*. Civitas Books.

Kamaara, E., 2010. Towards Christian national identity in Africa: a historical perspective to the challenge of ethnicity to the church in Kenya. *Studies in World Christianity*, *16*(2), pp.126-144.

Kanu, I.A., African Traditional Democracy.

Kasapovic, A., 2015. Teaching Chinua Achebe's Things Fall Apart and critical literacy in the English classroom: For a democratic Swedish society.

Keegan, J., 2014. *The First World War*. Random House.

Keeley, J. and Scoones, I., 2014. *Understanding environmental policy processes: Cases from Africa*. Routledge.

Keenan, M., 2013. *Child sexual abuse and the Catholic Church: Gender, power, and organizational culture*. Oxford University Press.

Keltie, J.S., 2014. *The partition of Africa*. Cambridge University Press.

Kemp, B.J., 2006. *Ancient Egypt: anatomy of a civilization*. Psychology Press.

Kenyan fan commits suicide after Man Utd's loss to Newcastle. 2013. *MailOnline*. Available at:
http://www.dailymail.co.uk/sport/football/article-2520757/Kenyan-football-fan-commits-suicide-Manchester-United-lose-Newcastle-United-Old-Trafford.html [Accessed 7 May 2017].

Kiango, J.G., 2005. Tanzania's historical contribution to the recognition and promotion of Swahili. *Africa & Asia*, 5(1), pp.157-166.

Kihato, C.W., 2015. "Go Back and Tell Them Who the Real Men Are!" Gendering Our Understanding of Kibera's Post-election Violence. *International Journal of Conflict and Violence*, 9(1), p.13.

Killingray, D. and Plaut, M., 2012. *Fighting for Britain: African Soldiers in the Second World War*. Boydell & Brewer Ltd.

Kim, N.C. and Kusimba, C.M., 2008. Pathways to social complexity and state formation in the southern Zambezian region. *African Archaeological Review*, 25(3-4), pp.131-152.

Kimmerle, H., 2006. Ubuntu and communalism in African philosophy and art. *Prophecies and protest-Ubuntu in glocal management*, pp.79-91.

King Jr, J.H., 2005. Limiting the Vicarious Liability of Franchisors for the Torts of their Franchisees. *Wash. & Lee L. Rev.*, 62, p.417.

Kirzner, I.M., 2010. The Meaning of" Economic Goodness": Critical Comments on Klein and Briggeman. *Journal of Private Enterprise*, 25(2).

Kitching, G., 2010. *Development and Underdevelopment in historical perspective: populism, nationalism and industrialisation* (Vol. 103). Routledge.

Kitula, A.G.N., 2006. The environmental and socio-economic impacts of mining on local livelihoods in Tanzania: A case study of Geita District. *Journal of cleaner production*, 14(3), pp.405-414.

Klees, S.J., 2008. A quarter century of neoliberal thinking in education: Misleading analyses and failed policies. *Globalisation, Societies and Education*, 6(4), pp.311-348.

Knight, S., 2013. Exploring a cultural myth: What adult non-singers may reveal about the nature of singing. *The phenomenon of singing*, 2, pp.144-154.

Koduru, S., Grierson, D.S. and Afolayan, A.J., 2007. Ethnobotanical information of medicinal plants used for treatment of cancer in the Eastern Cape Province, South Africa. *Current Science*, pp.906-908.

Kohn, M. and Reddy, K., 2006. Colonialism.

Koivula, T. and Kauppinen, H., 2006. *Promoting peace and security in Africa: is the European Union up to the challenge?* Maanpuolustuskorkeakoulu.

Kolchin, P., 2003. *American Slavery: 1619-1877*. Macmillan.

Koné, Y., 2014. The Popular Movement of Coupé-Décalé. Anthropology of an Urban and Coastal Dance. *Global Journal of Anthropology Research, 1*, pp.20-24.

Kraakman, R.H., 2009. Vicarious and corporate civil liability. *Tort law and economics, 1*.

Kraidy, M., 2017. *Hybridity, or the cultural logic of globalization*. Temple University Press.

Kresse, K., 2009. Knowledge and intellectual practice in a Swahili context: 'wisdom' and the social dimensions of knowledge. *Africa, 79*(1 1), pp.148-167.

Kresse, K., 2011. "African Humanism" and a Case Study from the Swahili Coast. In *Humanistic ethics in the age of globality* (pp. 246-265). Palgrave Macmillan UK.

Kring, S.A., Figary, S.E., Boyer, G.L., Watson, S.B. and Twiss, M.R., 2014. Rapid in situ measures of phytoplankton communities using the bbe FluoroProbe: evaluation of spectral calibration, instrument intercompatibility, and performance range. *Canadian Journal of Fisheries and Aquatic Sciences, 71*(7), pp.1087-1095.

Kubiesa, J., 2014, March. Review of Michael Lundblad, the Birth of a Jungle: Animality in Progressive-Era US Literature and Culture. Oxford and New York: Oxford University Press, 2013. In *Postgraduate English: A Journal and Forum for Postgraduates in English* (No. 28).

Kuehn, T., 2009. Household and Lineage in Renaissance Florence: The Family Life of the Capponi, Ginori, and Rucellai.

Kumah-Abiwu, F., 2016. Beyond intellectual construct to policy ideas: The case of the Afrocentric paradigm. *Journal of Pan African Studies, 9*(2), pp.7-28.

Künzle, V. and Reichert, M., 2011. PHILharmonicFlows: towards a framework for object-aware process management. *Journal of Software: Evolution and Process, 23*(4), pp.205-244.

Labrecque, L.I. and Milne, G.R., 2012. Exciting red and competent blue: the importance of color in marketing. *Journal of the Academy of Marketing Science*, *40*(5), pp.711-727.

Ladizinski, B., Mistry, N. and Kundu, R.V., 2011. Widespread use of toxic skin lightening compounds: medical and psychosocial aspects. *Dermatologic Clinics*, *29*(1), pp.111-123.

Laird, S.A. ed., 2010. *Biodiversity and traditional knowledge: equitable partnerships in practice*. Routledge.

Lamb, D., 2011. *The Africans*. Vintage.

Langbehn, V. and Salama, M. eds., 2011. *German colonialism: race, the Holocaust, and postwar Germany*. Columbia University Press.

Langmia, K., 2006. The role of ICTs in the economic development of Africa: The case of South Africa. *International Journal of education and Development using ICT*, *2*(4).

Lanning, G. and Mueller, W.M., 1979. *Africa Undermined*. Penguin Books.

Larkin, B., 2013. The politics and poetics of infrastructure. *Annual Review of Anthropology*, *42*, pp.327-343.

LaViolette, A., 2008. Swahili cosmopolitanism in Africa and the Indian Ocean world, AD 600–1500. *Archaeologies*, *4*(1), pp.24-49.

LeBaron, G. and Ayers, A.J., 2013. The rise of a 'new slavery'? Understanding African unfree labour through neoliberalism. *Third World Quarterly*, *34*(5), pp.873-892.

Lentz, C., 2010. Travelling emblems of power: The Ghanaian seat of state. *Critical Interventions*, *4*(2), pp.45-64.

Leonard, A., 2011. The plight of "Big black dogs" in American animal shelters: Color-based canine discrimination.

Leonard, T.C., 2008. Richard H. Thaler, Cass R. Sunstein, Nudge: Improving decisions about health, wealth, and happiness. *Constitutional Political Economy*, *19*(4), pp.356-360.

Leopold, M., 2009. Sex, violence and history in the lives of Idi Amin: Postcolonial masculinity as masquerade. *Journal of Postcolonial Writing*, *45*(3), pp.321-330.

Leslie, M., 2017. *Media and democracy in Africa*. Routledge.

Liljeblad, J., 2014. Human Safaris: A Foucauldian Alternative to the Law's Treatment of the Indigenous Andaman Jawara. *AILR*, *18*, p.6.

Lindberg, S.I., 2006. *Democracy and elections in Africa*. JHU Press.

Lipietz, A., 1987. *Mirages and miracles*, Vol. 137, London: Verso.

Lipinski, B., Hanson, C., Lomax, J., Kitinoja, L., Waite, R. and Searchinger, T., 2013. Reducing food loss and waste. *World Resources Institute Working Paper, June*.

Liscák, V., 2014. Franciscan Missions to China and the Czech Crown Lands (from the 16th to the 18th Century). *Archiv Orientalni, 82*(3), p.529.

Little, B.A., 2011. Beauty: A Defeater of Naturalism. *Filosofie*, p.97.

Liu, X., 2010. *The Silk Road in world history*. Oxford University Press.

Lonsdale, J., 2014. Moral ethnicity and political tribalism. *Occasional Paper*, (11), pp.131-150.

Loomba, A., 2015. *Colonialism/postcolonialism*. Routledge.

Lott, E., 2013. *Love & theft: Blackface minstrelsy and the American working class*. Oxford University Press.

Louw, D.J., 2006. The African concept of Ubuntu. *Handbook of restorative justice: A global perspective*, pp.161-174.

Lovejoy, A.O., 2011. *The great chain of being: A study of the history of an idea*. Transaction Publishers.

Lovejoy, P.E., 2011. *Transformations in slavery: a history of slavery in Africa* (Vol. 117). Cambridge University Press.

Lu, C., 2011. Colonialism as structural injustice: historical responsibility and contemporary redress. *Journal of Political Philosophy, 19*(3), pp.261-281.

Lucht, H., 2011. *Darkness before daybreak: African migrants living on the margins in Southern Italy today*. Univ of California Press.

Lydon, G., 2009. On Trans-Saharan Trails. *Los Angeles*.

Maathai, W., 2011. Challenge for Africa. *Sustainability Science, 6*(1), pp.1-2.

Mabovula, N.N., 2011. The erosion of African communal values: a reappraisal of the African Ubuntu philosophy. *Inkanyiso: Journal of Humanities and Social Sciences, 3*(1), pp.38-47.

Mac Ginty, R. and Williams, A., 2016. *Conflict and development*. Routledge.

Machlup, F., 2014. The need for monetary reserves. *PSL Quarterly Review, 19*(78).

Maestri. N., 2014 "The Domestication History of Cotton (Gossypium): The Four Different Ancient Strands of Cotton Domestication." ThoughtCO June 14.

Mafe, D.A., 2013. God's Stepchildren: The "Tragedy of Being a Halfbreed" in South African Literature. In *Mixed Race Stereotypes in South African and American Literature* (pp. 25-56). Palgrave Macmillan US.

Major, R.H. ed., 2017. *India in the Fifteenth Century: Being a Collection of Narratives of Voyages to India in the Century preceding the Portuguese Discovery of the Cape of Good Hope; from Latin, Persian, Russian, and Italian Sources, now first translated into English.* Routledge.

Makahamadze, T., Grand, N. and Tavuyanago, B., 2009. The role of traditional leaders in fostering democracy, justice and human rights in Zimbabwe. *African Anthropologist, 16*(1&2), pp.33-47.

Mäki, U., 2009. Economics imperialism: Concept and constraints. *Philosophy of the social sciences, 39*(3), pp.351-380.

Malhotra, A., Thorpe, R.S., Hypolite, E. and James, A., 2007. A report on the status of the herpetofauna of the Commonwealth of Dominica, West Indies. *Applied Herpetology, 4*(2), pp.177-194.

Mamdani, M., 2009. Lessons of Zimbabwe: Mugabe in context. *Concerned African Scholars Bulletin*, (82).

Mamdani, M., 2014. *When victims become killers: Colonialism, nativism, and the genocide in Rwanda.* Princeton University Press.

Manalo, V., 2015. My Journey as a Social Work Professor. *Reflections: Narratives of Professional Helping (Click on Current or Archives; Registration Optional), 20*(4), pp.52-59.

Mandela, N., 2011. I dream of the realization of the unity of Africa, whereby its leaders combine in their efforts to solve the problems of this continent. I dream of our vast deserts, of our forests, of all our great wildernesses.

Mapadimeng, M.S., 2017. Culture Versus Religion: A Theoretical Analysis Of The Role Of Indigenous African Culture Of Ubuntu In Social Change And Economic Development In The Postapartheid South African Society. *Politics and Religion Journal, 3*(1), pp.75-98.

Maraga, D., 2017. "IEBC committed irregularities, illegalities in presidential poll." *Daily Nation*, September 1.

Marcus, A.S., 2005. "It is as it was": Feature film in the history classroom. *The Social Studies, 96*(2), pp.61-67.

Marete. G., 2017. "Kenyan club where Queen Elizabeth stayed turns 120 years." *Daily Nation*, 30 September.

Marks, R.B., 2006. *The origins of the modern world: A global and ecological narrative from the fifteenth to the twenty-first century.* Rowman & Littlefield Publishers.

Markus, H.R. and Schwartz, B., 2010. Does choice mean freedom and well-being? *Journal of Consumer Research, 37*(2), pp.344-355.

Marques de Morais, R., 2012. Alternating Demonstrations: Political Protest and the Government Response in Angola. *Fletcher F. World Aff., 36*, p.57.

Maslow, A.H., 1943. A theory of human motivation, *Psychological review 50 (4)*: 370.

Mathee, M.S., 2016. Curse motives in the "Curse of Ham" narrative: land for Yahweh's landless people? *Journal for Semitics, 25*(2), pp.726-747.

Matunhu, J., 2011. A critique of modernization and dependency theories in Africa: Critical assessment.

Mawdsley, E., 2008. Fu Manchu versus Dr Livingstone in the Dark Continent? Representing China, Africa and the West in British broadsheet newspapers. *Political Geography, 27*(5), pp.509-529.

Mawere, M. and Marongwe, N., 2016. *Violence, Politics and Conflict Management in Africa: Envisioning Transformation, Peace and Unity in the Twenty-First Century.* Langaa RPCIG.

Mawere, M. ed., 2016. *Development Perspectives from the South: Troubling the Metrics of [Under-] development in Africa.* Langaa RPCIG.

Mawere, M., 2010. On pursuit of the purpose of life: the Shona metaphysical perspective. *Journal of Pan African Studies, 3*(6), pp.269-284.

May, J. and Govender, J., 1998. Poverty and inequality in South Africa. *Indicator South Africa, 15*, pp.53-58.

Mayo, E., 2009. Can the west save Africa? *Journal of economic literature, 47*(2), pp.373-447.

Mazower, M., 2009. *Dark Continent: Europe's twentieth century.* Vintage.

Mbeki, T., 2011. What the world got wrong in Cote d'Ivoire. *Foreign Policy, 29.*

Mbikayi, M., 2015. *Fashionable addiction: the impact of digital identity through the cult of the body (an African perspective, with particular reference to the Democratic Republic of Congo)* (Doctoral dissertation, University of Cape Town).

Mbiti, J.S., 2015. *Introduction to African religion.* Waveland Press.

McAlister, M., 2012. Guess Who's Coming to Dinner: American Missionaries, Racism, and Decolonization in the Congo. *Organization of American Historians Magazine of History, 26*(4), pp.33-37.

McAllister, H.J., 2012. *Cape of storms Cabo das Tormentas: exploring natural events at the Breakwater* (Doctoral dissertation, University of Cape Town).

McAllister, P.A., 2009. Ubuntu-Beyond Belief in Southern Africa. *Sites: a journal of social anthropology and cultural studies, 6*(1), pp.48-57.

McCormick, D., 2008. China & India as Africa's new donors: The impact of aid on development. *Review of African political economy, 35*(115), pp.73-92.

McEnery, T., 2011. The World's 15 Biggest Landowners. *Business Insider,* 18 March (accessed October, 2017).

McGonegal, J., 2009. *Imagining justice: The politics of postcolonial forgiveness and reconciliation.* McGill-Queen's Press-MQUP.

McGovern, P.E., 2013. *Ancient wine: the search for the origins of viniculture.* Princeton University Press.

McGuire, S., 2011. US Dept. of Health and Human Services. The Surgeon General's Call to Action to Support Breastfeeding. US Dept. of Health and Human Services, Office of the Surgeon General. 2011. *Advances in Nutrition: An International Review Journal, 2*(6), pp.523-524.

McIntire, E., 2015. The International Tribunal for E-waste: Ending the Race towards Lethal Fallout. *Seattle J. Envtl. L., 5*, p.i.

McKoy, B., 2012. Tyler Perry and the weight of misrepresentation. *McNair Scholars Research Journal, 5*(1), p.10.

McMichael, P., 2011. *Development and Social Change: A Global Perspective: A Global Perspective.* Sage Publications.

Meager, D., 2006. Slavery in Bible Times.

Médard, J.F., 2014. Patriamonialism, Neo-Patriamonialism and the Study of the Post-colonial State in Subsaharian Africa. *Occasional Paper*, (17), pp.76-97.

Meier, J.P., 2004. *The vision of Matthew: Christ, church, and morality in the First Gospel*. Wipf and Stock Publishers.

Menard, A.R. and Weill, L., 2016. Understanding the link between aid and corruption: A causality analysis. *Economic Systems*, 40(2), pp.260-272.

Meredith, M., 2011. *The fate of Africa: A history of the continent since independence*. Hachette UK.

Mhango, N. N., 2017. *'Is It Global War on Terrorism' or Global War over Terra Africana?: The Ruse Imperial Powers Use to Occupy Africa Militarily for Economic Gains*. Hamilton Books.

Mhango, N., 2017. "Why AU needs to be decolonised." *Daily Nation*, 1 February (Accessed September 2017).

Mhango, N.N., 2015. *Africa Reunite or Perish*. Langaa RPCIG.

Mhango, N.N., 2015. *Soul on Sale*. Langaa RPCIG.

Mhango, N.N., 2016. *Africa's Best and Worst Presidents: How Neocolonialism and Imperialism Maintained Venal Rules in Africa*. Langaa RPCIG.

Mhango, N.N., 2016. *Psalm of the Oppressed*. Langaa RPCIG.

Mhango, N.N., 2017. "Wigs, robes a carryover of colonial courts." *Daily Nation*, 12 September (accessed December 2017).

Mhango, N.N., 2017. *Africa's Dependency Syndrome: Can Africa Still Turn Things around for the Better?* Langaa RPCIG.

Mhango, N.N., 2017. Chapter Four: Beyond the Genetically Modified Foods (GMFs) War: Reflections on the Effects of GMFs on Africa. *GMOs, Consumerism and the Global Politics of Biotechnology: Rethinking Food, Bodies and Identities in Africa's 21st Century*, p.95.

Michalopoulos, S. and Papaioannou, E., 2013. Pre-Colonial ethnic institutions and contemporary African development. *Econometrica*, 81(1), pp.113-152.

Michalopoulos, S. and Papaioannou, E., 2016. The long-run effects of the scramble for Africa. *The American Economic Review*, 106(7), pp.1802-1848.

Middleton, J. and Winter, E.H. eds., 2013. *Witchcraft and sorcery in East Africa*. Routledge.

Mills, G., 2012. *Why Africa is poor: and what Africans can do about it*. Penguin UK.

Minot, N., 2010. *Transmission of world food price changes to markets in Sub-Saharan Africa*. Washington:

Moan, J., Porojnicu, A.C., Dahlback, A. and Setlow, R.B., 2008. Addressing the health benefits and risks, involving vitamin D or skin cancer, of increased sun exposure. *Proceedings of the National Academy of Sciences*, *105*(2), pp.668-673.

Momo AM. Improvisational model of business registration for branding services in Congo-Brazzaville.

Monbiot, G, 2003. "Poisoned chalice." *Guardian*, August 19.

Morrison, W.L., 1985. What is the function of melanin? *Archives of dermatology*, *121*(9), pp.1160-1163.

Moseley, W.G., Carney, J. and Becker, L., 2010. Neoliberal policy, rural livelihoods, and urban food security in West Africa: A comparative study of The Gambia, Côte d'Ivoire, and Mali. *Proceedings of the National Academy of Sciences*, *107*(13), pp.5774-5779.

Mou, S.P., 2014. Of tribes, wars, and jungles: A study of US college students' perceptions of Africa and Africans.

Moyo, D., 2009. Why foreign aid is hurting Africa. *The Wall Street Journal*, *11*.

Moyo, D., 2011. *How the West was Lost: Fifty Years of Economic Folly--and the Stark Choices Ahead*. Farrar, Straus and Giroux.

Moyo, S., Yeros, P. and Jha, P., 2012. Imperialism and primitive accumulation: Notes on the new scramble for Africa. *Agrarian South: Journal of Political Economy*, *1*(2), pp.181-203.

Msiska, M.H. and Hyland, P., 2017. *Writing and Africa*. Routledge.

Msuya, J., 2007. Challenges and opportunities in the protection and preservation of indigenous knowledge in Africa. *International Review of Information Ethics*, *7*(9), pp.1-8.

Mueller, J.C., Dirks, D. and Picca, L.H., 2007. Unmasking racism: Halloween costuming and engagement of the racial other. *Qualitative Sociology*, *30*(3), pp.315-335.

Mugovhani, N.G. and Mapaya, M.G., 2014. Towards contestation of perceptions, distortions and misrepresentations of meanings, functions and performance contexts in South African indigenous cultural practices. *Mediterranean Journal of Social Sciences*, 5(27 P3), p.1201.

Mukhopadhyay, D., 2009. Cultural values, indigenous knowledge for climate change adaptations in developing countries. In *IOP Conference Series: Earth and Environmental Science* (Vol. 6, No. 57, p. 572006). IOP Publishing.

Murphy, C., 2012. *God's Jury: The Inquisition and the Making of the Modern World*. Houghton Mifflin Harcourt.

Mutua, M.W., 2007. (Book Review) Stanley: The Impossible Life of Africa's Greatest Explorer by Tim Jeal.

Muula, A.S., 2005. Is there any solution to the" brain drain" of health professionals and knowledge from Africa? *Croatian medical journal*, 46(1).

Muzondidya, J. and Ndlovu-Gatsheni, S., 2007. 'Echoing Silences\': Ethnicity in post-colonial Zimbabwe, 1980-2007. *African Journal on Conflict Resolution*, 7(2), pp.275-297.

Myers, D.N., 2003. *Resisting history: Historicism and its discontents in German-Jewish thought* (p. 217). Princeton: Princeton University Press.

Naicker, S., Plange-Rhule, J., Tutt, R.C. and Eastwood, J.B., 2009. Shortage of healthcare workers in developing countries--Africa. *Ethnicity & disease*, 19(1), p.60.

Nantambu, K., 2013. "Time for an African pope." *Daily Express*, Trinidad, February 27.

Nash, M.R., 2005. The importance of being earnest when crafting definitions: Science and scientism are not the same thing. *International Journal of Clinical and Experimental Hypnosis*, 53(3), pp.265-280.

Navarro, V., 2007. *Neoliberalism, globalization and inequalities: consequences for health and quality of life*. Baywood Publishing Company Inc.

Ncube, N.M., Creating the Cinderella syndrome.

Ndege, P.O., 2009. Colonialism and its Legacies in Kenya. *Moi University (July-August, 2009)*, p.3.

305

Ndikumana, L. and Boyce, J.K., 2010. Measurement of Capital Flight: Methodology and Results for Sub-Saharan African Countries. *African Development Review*, *22*(4), pp.471-481.

Ndikumana, L., 2014. Capital flight: measurement and drivers.

Negarestani, R., 2011. Drafting the inhuman: Conjectures on capitalism and organic necrocracy. *The Speculative Turn*, pp.182-201.

Neumann, R.P., 2001. Africa's 'last wilderness': Reordering space for political and economic control in colonial Tanzania. *Africa*, *71*(4), pp.641-665.

Newman, J.L., 2004. *Imperial Footprints: Henry Morton Stanley's African Journeys*. Potomac Books, Inc.

News, D.T., 2017. Makonda hands over design for Bakwata headquarters, mosque. 2016. *Allafrica*. Available at http://allafrica.com/stories/201608160276.html [Accessed 3 Jan. 2017].

Nhemachena, A., Mlambo, N. and Kaundjua, M., 2016. The Notion of the "Field" and the Practices of Researching and Writing Africa: Towards Decolonial Praxis. *Journal of Pan African Studies*, *9*(7), pp.15-37.

Niang, A.C. and Osiek, C. eds., 2011. *Text, Image, and Christians in the Graeco-Roman World: A Festschrift in Honor of David Lee Balch* (Vol. 176). Wipf and Stock Publishers.

Niemi, J., Ramsay, I. and Whitford, W.C. eds., 2009. *Consumer credit, debt and bankruptcy: Comparative and international perspectives*. Bloomsbury Publishing.

Niogu, K., 2013. Youth as Leaders: Transforming Society by Building Bridges. *Youth and peaceful elections in Kenya*, (1), p.3.

Nixon, S., 2009. Excavating Essouk-Tadmakka (Mali): new archaeological investigations of early Islamic trans-Saharan trade. *Azania: Archaeological Research in Africa*, *44*(2), pp.217-255.

Nkurunziza, J.D., 2012. Illicit financial flows: a constraint on poverty reduction in Africa. *ACAS Bulletin*, *87*, pp.15-21.

Nkurunziza, J.D., 2015. Capital flight and poverty reduction in Africa. *Capital Flight from Africa: Causes, Effects and Policy Issues*, pp.81-110.

Nørgaard, A.S., 2008. Political science: Witchcraft or craftsmanship? Standards for good research. *World Political Science*, 4(1).

Nunn, N. and Puga, D., 2012. Ruggedness: The blessing of bad geography in Africa. *Review of Economics and Statistics*, 94(1), pp.20-36.

Nunn, N. and Wantchekon, L., 2011. The slave trade and the origins of mistrust in Africa. *The American Economic Review*, 101(7), pp.3221-3252.

Nunn, N., 2007. Historical legacies: A model linking Africa's past to its current underdevelopment. *Journal of development economics*, 83(1), pp.157-175.

Nunn, N., 2008. The long-term effects of Africa's slave trades. *The Quarterly Journal of Economics*, 123(1), pp.139-176.

Nunn, N., 2009. The importance of history for economic development. *Annu. Rev. Econ.*, 1(1), pp.65-92.

O'Fahey, R.S., 2006. Conflict in Darfur: historical and contemporary perspectives. *Environmental Degradation as a Cause of Conflict in Darfur. Adís Abeba, University for Peace, Africa Programme*, pp.23-32.

O'Leary, B., 2007. Analysing partition: Definition, classification and explanation. *Political Geography*, 26(8), pp.886-908.

O'Mahony, A., 2009. The Vatican and Europe: Political Theology and Ecclesiology in Papal Statements from Pius XII to Benedict XVI. *International Journal for the Study of the Christian Church*, 9(3), pp.177-194.

Obama, B., 2009. "A new beginning." *ZSE Zeitschrift für Staats-und Europawissenschaften| Journal for Comparative Government and European Policy* 7.2: 173-186.

Obeng-Odoom, F., 2013. Africa's failed economic development trajectory: a critique. *African Review of Economics and Finance*, 4(2), pp.151-175.

Ofodile, U.E., 2008. Trade, Empires, and Subjects-China-Africa Trade: A New Fair Trade Arrangement, or the Third Scramble for Africa. *Vand. J. Transnat'l L.*, 41, p.505.

Ojo, E.O., 2015. The Atlantic Slave Trade And Colonialism: Reasons for Africa's Underdevelopment? *European Scientific Journal, ESJ*, 11(17).

Ojua, T.A., Lukpata, F.E. and Atama, C., 2014. Exploring the Neglect of African Family Value Systems and its Effects on Sustainable Development. *American Journal of Human Ecology*, *3*(3), pp.43-50.

Okeke, R.C., 2015. The Purpose of Political Power: An African Dimensional Contemplation. *African Journal of Governance and Development*, *4*(1), pp.59-74.

Okigbo, R.N. and Mmeka, E.C., 2006. An appraisal of phytomedicine in Africa. *KMITL Sci Tech J*, *6*(2), pp.83-94.

Okuku, J.A., 2006. The Land Act (1998) and land tenure reform in Uganda. *Africa development*, *31*(1), pp.1-26.

Olasunkanmi, A., 2011. Economic globalization and its effect on community in Africa. *J Sociology Soc Anth*, *2*(1), pp.61-64.

Oloka-Onyango, J., 2004. "New-Breed" Leadership, Conflict, and Reconstruction in the Great Lakes Region of Africa: A Sociopolitical Biography of Uganda's Yoweri Kaguta Museveni. *Africa Today*, *50*(3), pp.29-52.

Oussedik, F., 2012. The Rites of Baba Merzug. *Saharan Frontiers: Space and Mobility in Northwest Africa*, p.93.

Oyelere, R.U., 2007. Brain drain, waste or gain? What we know about the Kenyan case. *Journal of Global Initiatives*, *2*(2), pp.113-129.

Park, Y.J., 2009. *Chinese migration in Africa* (p. 6). Johannesburg: South African Institute of International Affairs.

Parks, G.S. and Heard, D.C., 2009. 'Assassinate the Nigger Apes' [1]: Obama, Implicit Imagery, and the Dire Consequences of Racist Jokes.

Parolin, G.P., 2010. *Citizenship in the Arab world: Kin, religion and nation-state* (p. 192). Amsterdam University Press.

Patnaik, P., 2005, August. The economics of the new phase of imperialism. In *International Conference: Acts of Resistance from the South against Globalisation*.

Păun, M.G. and Teodorescu, M., 2014. Hermeneutics can make beauty and ugly as neutral (as neutrosophic). *Social Sciences and Education Research Review*, *2*, pp.252-61.

Peek, L., 2005. Becoming Muslim: The development of a religious identity. *Sociology of religion*, *66*(3), pp.215-242.

Pelican, M., 2009. Complexities of indigeneity and autochthony: An African example. *American Ethnologist, 36*(1), pp.52-65.

Pelizzo, R. and Bekenova, K., 2016. African Politics and Policy.№. 18.

Persson, T. and Tabellini, G., 2006. *Democracy and development: The devil in the details* (No. w11993). National Bureau of Economic Research.

Pheko, M., 2012. Effects of colonialism on Africa's past and present. *Address at AZAPO commemoration of African Liberation Day, Pimville Community Hall, Soweto, 26.*

Phillips, A., 1977. "The concept of 'development'." *Review of African Political Economy 4.8*: 7-20.

Pitkänen, P., 2014. Ancient Israel and settler colonialism. *Settler Colonial Studies, 4*(1), pp.64-81.

Pittman, T.S. and Zeigler, K.R., 2007. Basic human needs. *Social psychology: Handbook of basic principles, 2*, pp.473-489.

Plaut, M., 2009. "The Africans who fought in WWII." BBC, November 9.

Plehwe, D., Walpen, B.J. and Neunhöffer, G. eds., 2007. *Neoliberal hegemony: A global critique.* Routledge.

Porter, M. E., 2000. Location, competition, and economic development: Local clusters in a global economy, *Economic development quarterly 14 (1)*: 15-34.

Porter, M.E., 2008. *Competitive advantage: Creating and sustaining superior performance.* Simon and Schuster.

Pronk, J., 2015. From post 1945 to post 2015. *Journal of Global Ethics, 11*(3), pp.366-380.

Quayson, A., 2015. Disentangling the laws: On Juan Obarrio's the spirit of the laws in Mozambique. *HAU: Journal of Ethnographic Theory, 5*(3), pp.257-261.

Raftopoulos, B. and Mlambo, A. eds., 2008. *Becoming Zimbabwe. A History from the Pre-colonial Period to 2008: A History from the Pre-colonial Period to 2008.* African Books Collective.

Rakotoarisoa, M., Iafrate, M. and Paschali, M., 2011. *Why has Africa become a net food importer.* FAO.

Raschke, V. and Cheema, B., 2008. Colonisation, the New World Order, and the eradication of traditional food habits in East

Africa: historical perspective on the nutrition transition. *Public health nutrition, 11*(7), pp.662-674.

Raskin, J., 2012. *Mythology of imperialism*. Aakar Books.

Ratzinger, J.C., 2013. *Meaning of Christian Brotherhood*. Ignatius Press.

Raymond Choo, K.K., 2008. Politically exposed persons (PEPs): risks and mitigation. *Journal of Money Laundering Control, 11*(4), pp.371-387.

Reid, A., 2016. Constructing history in Uganda. *The Journal of African History, 57*(2), pp.195-207.

Reid, R.J., 2012. *Warfare in African history* (Vol. 6). Cambridge University Press.

Release, P., 2012. Africa Can Feed Itself, Earn Billions, and Avoid Food Crises by Unblocking Regional Food Trade. *World Bank*. Available at: http://www.worldbank.org/en/news/press-release/2012/10/24/africa-can-feed-itself-earn-billions-avoid-food-crises-unblocking-regional-food-trade [Accessed 21 Sept. 2017].

Release, P., 2017." *Presidential Press*, Dar es Salaam, March 29.

Ribadu, N., 2009. Capital loss and corruption: the example of Nigeria. *US House Committee on Financial Services*.

Riccio, T., 2012. Ethiopia and Its Double. *TheatreForum*, (41), p.46.

Richens, P., 2009. The Economic Legacies of the" Thin White Line": Indirect Rule and the Comparative Development of Sub-Saharan Africa. *African Economic History, 37*, pp.33-102.

Riello, G. and Parthasarathi, P. eds., 2011. *The spinning world: a global history of cotton textiles, 1200-1850*. Oxford University Press.

Riello, G., 2013. *Cotton: the fabric that made the modern world*. Cambridge University Press.

Risiro, J., Mashoko, D., Tshuma, T. and Rurinda, E., 2012. Weather forecasting and indigenous knowledge systems in Chimanimani District of Manicaland, Zimbabwe. *Journal of Emerging Trends in Educational Research and Policy Studies, 3*(4), p.561.

Roberts, G., 2012. The British Government and Uganda under Idi Amin, November 1972 to April 1979. *BA diss., University of Cambridge*.

Robinson, J. and Harding, J. eds., 2015. *The Oxford companion to wine*. American Chemical Society.

Rodney, W., 1972. How Europe underdeveloped Africa. *Beyond borders: Thinking critically about global issues*, pp.107-125.

Rodrigez, S.V. and killed six million Jews, W., 2008, January. All European life died in Auschwitz. In *Extended version of the original. www. criticalfumble. net/forum/showthread. php* (Vol. 34267).

Roediger, D.R., 2010. *Black on white: Black writers on what it means to be white.* Knopf Group E-Books.

Rogoff, B., 2003. *The cultural nature of human development.* Oxford University Press.

Rosas, G., 2006. Bagehot or bailout? An analysis of government responses to banking crises. *American Journal of Political Science, 50*(1), pp.175-191.

Rotberg, R.I. ed., 2009. *China into Africa: Trade, aid, and influence.* Brookings Institution Press.

Rowe, D., 2011. The televised sport 'monkey trial': 'race' and the politics of post-colonial cricket. *Sport in Society, 14*(6), pp.792-804.

Rožňák, P., 2016. Security, threats and hazards in their current general and specific forms: a new theory of security. *Acta Scientifica Academiae Ostroviensis. Sectio A, Nauk Humanistyczne, Społeczne i Techniczne,* (7 (1)/2016), pp.277-290.

Samson, C., 2008. The rule of Terra Nullius and the impotence of international human rights for indigenous peoples. *Essex Human Rights Review, 5*(1).

Samuelson, B.L. and Freedman, S.W., 2010. Language policy, multilingual education, and power in Rwanda. *Language Policy, 9*(3), pp.191-215.

Sanginga, N. and Woomer, P.L. eds., 2009. *Integrated soil fertility management in Africa: principles, practices, and developmental process.* CIAT.

Sanusi, L.S., 2010. Growth prospects for the Nigerian economy. *Convocation Lecture Delivered at the Igbinedion University Eighth Convocation Ceremony, November, 26.*

Sardar, R. and Ambedkar, B., 2012. A Study on Economic, Social and Cultural Rights of Dalits in India. *Asia Pacific Journal of Management & Entrepreneurship Research, 1*(1), p.188.

Sautman, B. and Yan, H., 2006. East Mountain Tiger, West Mountain Tiger: China, the West, and" colonialism" in Africa. *Maryland Series in Contemporary Asian Studies, 2006*(3), p.1.

Schaefer, H.M., 2011. Why fruits go to the dark side. *Acta Oecologica, 37*(6), pp.604-610.

Schaefer, H.M., Levey, D.J., Schaefer, V. and Avery, M.L., 2006. The role of chromatic and achromatic signals for fruit detection by birds. *Behavioral Ecology, 17*(5), pp.784-789.

Scherer, B.N., 2010. *Globalization, culture, and communication: Proposal for cultural studies integration within higher education graphic design curriculum.* Iowa State University.

Seidlhofer, B., 2009. Common ground and different realities: World Englishes and English as a lingua franca. *World Englishes, 28*(2), pp.236-245.

Settles, J.D., 1996. The impact of colonialism on African economic development.

Severino, J.M. and Ray, O., 2011. *Africa's moment.* Cambridge: Polity Press.

Shankar, P.R. and Subish, P., 2016. Fair skin in South Asia: an obsession? *Journal of Pakistan Association of Dermatology, 17*(2), pp.100-104.

Sharife, K. and Grobler, J., 2013. Kimberley's illicit process. *World Policy Journal, 30*(4), pp.65-77.

Sharkey, H.J., 2008. Arab identity and ideology in Sudan: The politics of language, ethnicity, and race. *African Affairs, 107*(426), pp.21-43.

Shillington, K., 2012. *History of Africa.* Palgrave Macmillan.

Shinn, D.H. and Eisenman, J., 2012. *China and Africa: A century of engagement.* University of Pennsylvania Press.

Shklar, J.N., 2010. *Freedom and independence: a study of the political ideas of Hegel's Phenomenology of mind.* Cambridge University Press.

Shohat, E. and Stam, R., 2014. *Unthinking Eurocentrism: Multiculturalism and the media.* Routledge.

Shomanah, M.W.D. and Dube, M., 2012. *Postcolonial feminist interpretation of the Bible.* Chalice Press.

Shortland, A.J., 2004. Evaporites of the Wadi Natrun: seasonal and annual variation and its implication for ancient exploitation. *Archaeometry*, *46*(4), pp.497-516.

Shule, L., 2016. Uganda: A Mix of Strategies for Soft Power Goals. In *Diplomatic Strategies of Nations in the Global South* (pp. 239-262). Palgrave Macmillan US.

Sifuna, D.N., 2007. The challenge of increasing access and improving quality: An analysis of universal primary education interventions in Kenya and Tanzania since the 1970s. *International Review of Education*, *53*(5-6), pp.687-699.

Simms, E.Y., 2008. Miscegenation and Racism: Afro-Mexicans in Colonial New Spain. *Journal of Pan African Studies*, *2*(3).

Siraj-Blatchford, J., 2009. Education for sustainable development in early childhood. *International Journal of Early Childhood*, *41*(2), p.9.

Slaughter, A.M., 2009. *A new world order*. Princeton University Press.

Smith, D., 2013. Isabel dos Santos dubbed 'princess', named Africa's first female billionaire. *Guardian*. Available at https://www.theguardian.com/world/2013/jan/25/isobel-dos-santos-africas-first-female-billionaire [Accessed at 12Jun. 2017].

Smith, D.L., 2011. *Less than human: Why we demean, enslave, and exterminate others*. St. Martin's Press.

Snauwaert, D., 2011. Social justice and the philosophical foundations of critical peace education: Exploring Nussbaum, Sen, and Freire. *Journal of Peace Education*, *8*(3), pp.315-331.

Snead, J., 2016. *White screens/Black images: Hollywood from the dark side*. Routledge.

Soffer, R.N., 1969. New Elitism: Social Psychology in Prewar England. *Journal of British Studies*, *8*(2), pp.111-140.

Solum, L.B., 2006. Natural justice. *Am. J. Juris.*, *51*, p.65.

Souaré, I.K., 2014. The African Union as a norm entrepreneur on military coups d'état in Africa (1952–2012): an empirical assessment. *The Journal of Modern African Studies*, *52*(1), pp.69-94.

Spadola, E., 2013. *The calls of Islam: Sufis, Islamists, and mass mediation in urban Morocco*. Indiana University Press.

Squires, G.D. ed., 2004. *Why the poor pay more: How to stop predatory lending*. Greenwood Publishing Group.

313

Stadler, N., Iconic Spaces as Border Makers: The Tomb of Rachel and Our Lady on the Wall.

Stahl, N., 2008. "Uri Zvi before the Cross": The Figure of Jesus in the Poetry of Uri Zvi Greenberg. *Religion & Literature*, *40*(3), pp.49-80.

Starling, A.P. and Stock, J.T., 2007. Dental indicators of health and stress in early Egyptian and Nubian agriculturalists: a difficult transition and gradual recovery. *American Journal of Physical Anthropology*, *134*(4), pp.520-528.

Staszak, J.F., 2009. Other/otherness.

Stejskal, J., 2016. Go spy out the land: intelligence preparations for World War I in South West Africa. *Scientia Militaria: South African Journal of Military Studies*, *44*(1), pp.35-46.

Stephenson Jr, H.D., 2015. Unlucky in Affairs of Business-Turning Points in the life of Lorenzo de Medici.

Stevens, P. and Dietsche, E., 2008. Resource curse: An analysis of causes, experiences and possible ways forward. *Energy Policy*, *36*(1), pp.56-65.

Steyn, N.P., Labadarios, D. and Nel, J.H., 2011. Factors which influence the consumption of street foods and fast foods in South Africa-a national survey. *Nutrition Journal*, *10*(1), p.104.

Stiglitz, J.E., 2010. *Freefall: America, free markets, and the sinking of the world economy*. WW Norton & Company.

Stournaras, K.E., Lo, E., Böhning-Gaese, K., Cazetta, E., Matthias Dehling, D., Schleuning, M., Stoddard, M.C., Donoghue, M.J., Prum, R.O. and Martin Schaefer, H., 2013. How colorful are fruits? Limited color diversity in fleshy fruits on local and global scales. *New Phytologist*, *198*(2), pp.617-629.

Strathern, P., 2007. *The Medici: godfathers of the Renaissance*. Random House.

Strauss, D. A., 1999 "What is Constitutional Theory?" California Law Review (1999): 581-592.

Summers, C., 2014. Local Critiques of Global Development: Patriotism in Late Colonial Buganda. *The International Journal of African Historical Studies*, *47*(1), p.21.

Sutton, B., 2007. Naked protest: Memories of bodies and resistance at the world social forum. *Journal of International Women's Studies*, *8*(3), pp.139-148.

Tabuti, J.R.S., Dhillion, S.S. and Lye, K.A., 2003. Traditional medicine in Bulamogi County, Uganda: its practitioners, users and viability. *Journal of Ethnopharmacology*, *85*(1), pp.119-129.

Talamo, A. and Pozzi, S., 2011. The tension between dialogicality and interobjectivity in cooperative activities. *Culture & Psychology*, *17*(3), pp.302-318.

Tamale, S., 2014. Exploring the contours of African sexualities: Religion, law and power. *African Human Rights Law Journal*, *14*(1), pp.150-177.

Tamale, S., 2016. Nudity, Protest and the Law in Uganda.

Taylor, P.C., 2009. The Last King of Scotland or the Last N----r on Earth? The Ethics of Race on Film. *Contemporary Aesthetics*, (2).

Thompson, B., 2011. "Allah and the A'bda: Islam and Slavery in the Americas. الإسلام وعبودية في الأمريكي."

Thompson, P., 2017. *The voice of the past: Oral history*. Oxford university press.

Thurlow, C. and Jaworski, A., 2006. The alchemy of the upwardly mobile: symbolic capital and the stylization of elites in frequent-flyer programmes. *Discourse & Society*, *17*(1), pp.99-135.

Tickner, A.B., 2013. Core, periphery and (neo) imperialist International Relations. *European Journal of International Relations*, *19*(3), pp.627-646.

Tignor, R.L., 2015. *Colonial Transformation of Kenya: The Kamba, Kikuyu, and Maasai from 1900-1939*. Princeton University Press.

Tinsley, R., 2011. "The Great Taboo: Arab Racism." *Huffington Post*, November 9.

Toledano, E.R., 2007. *As if silent and absent: Bonds of enslavement in the Islamic Middle East*. Yale University Press.

Toplak, C., 2011. Hybridization Of Democracy In Central And Eastern Europe: Between" Imported" Democratic Model and Inherent Political Culture. *Journal of Comparative Politics*, *4*(1), p.76.

Tsambu, L., 2015. Transnationalism and transculturalism as seen in Congolese music videograms. *Journal of African Media Studies*, *7*(1), pp.51-67.

Tsui, K.K., 2010. Resource curse, political entry, and deadweight costs. *Economics & Politics, 22*(3), pp.471-497.

Tuck, M.W. and Rowe, J.A., 2005. Phoenix from the Ashes: Rediscovery of the Lost Lukiiko Archives. *History in Africa, 32*, pp.403-414.

Tucker, S.C., 2013. *The European powers in the First World War: an encyclopedia.* Routledge.

Tung, R.L., 2008. The cross-cultural research imperative: The need to balance cross-national and intra-national diversity. *Journal of International Business Studies, 39*(1), pp.41-46.

UKIP leader dumps lover over racist royal slur, 2018. *France24*, 12 January (accessed January 2018).

US Department of Health and Human Services, 2011. The Surgeon General's call to action to support breastfeeding.

Uwizeyimana, D.E., 2012. Democracy and pretend democracies in Africa: Myths of African democracies. *Law Democracy & Dev., 16*, p.139.

Van Biezen, I. and Kopecký, P., 2007. The state and the parties: public funding, public regulation and rent-seeking in contemporary democracies. *Party politics, 13*(2), pp.235-254.

Vanlauwe, B. and Giller, K.E., 2006. Popular myths around soil fertility management in sub-Saharan Africa. *Agriculture, ecosystems & environment, 116*(1), pp.34-46.

Vaughn, R.A., 2011. *Talking Trash: Oral Histories of Food In/Security from the Margins of a Dumpster* (Doctoral dissertation, University of Kansas).

Veenhoven, R., 2008. Healthy happiness: Effects of happiness on physical health and the consequences for preventive health care. *Journal of happiness studies, 9*(3), pp.449-469.

Veracini, L., 2010. *Settler colonialism: A theoretical overview.* Springer.

Verner, M., 2007. *The Pyramids: The Mystery, Culture, and Science of Egypt's Great Monuments.* Grove/Atlantic, Inc.

Vernet, T., 2009. Slave trade and slavery on the Swahili coast (1500-1750).

Victoor, A., 2011. *An Other Woman's Rape: Abjection and Objection in Representations of War Rape Victims in the DRC* (Doctoral dissertation).

Vidyarthi, M.A.H., 1995. The philosophy of colours in the Holy Quran. *The Light & Islamic Review*, *71*(4-6), pp.6-10.

von Holdt, K., 2010. The South African post-apartheid bureaucracy: inner workings, contradictory rationales and the developmental state. *Constructing a Democratic Developmental State in South Africa. Potentials and Challenges*, pp.241-260.

Voss, C., Eyol, E. and Berger, M.R., 2006. Identification of potent anticancer activity in Ximenia Americana aqueous extracts used by African traditional medicine. *Toxicology and applied pharmacology*, *211*(3), pp.177-187.

Vreeland, J.R., 2006. IMF program compliance: Aggregate index versus policy specific research strategies. *The Review of International Organizations*, *1*(4), pp.359-378.

wa Thiong'o, N. and wa Thiong'o, N., 2015. *The river between* (Vol. 4). Penguin.

Wales, K., 2014. *A dictionary of stylistics*. Routledge.

Wanangwe, J., 2016. Democracy and development in Africa.

Wang, J.Y., 2007. What drives China's growing role in Africa?

Wanjala, S.C., 2013. Fighting Corruption in Africa: Mission Impossible?

Ware, V., 2015. *Beyond the pale: White women, racism, and history*. Verso Books.

Wasserman, H. ed., 2010. *Popular media, democracy and development in Africa*. Routledge.

Weese, J.R., 2016. Witchcraft in Africa.

Weingast, B.R., 1995. The economic role of political institutions: Market-preserving federalism and economic development. *Journal of Law, Economics, & Organization*, pp.1-31.

Weingrod, A., 2005. *Homelands and Diasporas: holy lands and other places*. Stanford University Press.

Weinstein, J.B., 2008. The Role of Judges in a Government of, by and for the People: Notes for the Fifty-Eighth Cardozo Lecture. *Cardozo L. Rev.*, *30*, p.1.

Wengrow, D., Dee, M., Foster, S., Stevenson, A. and Ramsey, C.B., 2014. Cultural convergence in the Neolithic of the Nile Valley: a prehistoric perspective on Egypt's place in Africa. *Antiquity*, *88*(339), pp.95-111.

Wenzel, J., 2008. The Problem of Metaphor: Tropic Logic in Cattle-Killing Prophecies and their Afterlives. *African Studies, 67*(2), pp.143-158.

Whatley, W. and Gillezeau, R., 2011. The impact of the transatlantic slave trade on ethnic stratification in Africa. *The American Economic Review, 101*(3), pp.571-576.

White, E.F., 2010. *Dark Continent of our bodies: Black feminism & politics of respectability.* Temple University Press.

Whitford, D.M., 2009. *The curse of Ham in the early modern era: the Bible and the justifications for slavery.* Ashgate Publishing, Ltd.

Williams, C., 2013. Explaining the Great Ear in Africa: How Conflict in the Congo Became a Continental Crisis. *Fletcher F. World Aff., 37*, p.81.

Williams, E., 2014. *Capitalism and slavery.* UNC Press Books.

Willis, K., 2011. *Theories and practices of development.* Taylor & Francis.

Wilson, A., 2012. Saharan trade in the Roman period: short-, medium-and long-distance trade networks. *Azania: Archaeological Research in Africa, 47*(4), pp.409-449.

Winston, B.E. and Ryan, B., 2008. Servant leadership as a humane orientation: Using the GLOBE study construct of humane orientation to show that servant leadership is more global than western. *International Journal of Leadership Studies, 3*(2), pp.212-222.

Wiredu, K. ed., 2008. *A companion to African philosophy.* John Wiley & Sons.

Wolfe, P., 2006. Settler Colonialism and the Elimination of the Native. *Journal of Genocide Research, 8*(4), pp.387-409.

Womack, Y., 2013. *Afrofuturism: The world of Black sci-fi and fantasy culture.* Chicago Review Press.

Wood, M., 2012. *Interconnections: Glass beads and trade in southern and eastern Africa and the Indian Ocean-7th to 16th centuries AD* (Doctoral dissertation, Department of Archaeology and Ancient History).

Woods, M., 2016. "Turkey needs to admit the Armenian Genocide before it joins the EU." *Christian Today*, 18.

Wright, J., 2008. To invest or insure? How authoritarian time horizons impact foreign aid effectiveness. *Comparative Political Studies, 41*(7), pp.971-1000.

Wrong, M., 2005. When the Money goes west. *New Statesman March*, *14*, p.2005.

Wüst, A., 2010, April. Vatican. In *Elections in Europe* (pp. 2035-2046). Nomos Verlagsgesellschaft mbH & Co. KG.

Youde, J., 2010. China's health diplomacy in Africa. *China: An International Journal*, *8*(01), pp.151-163.

Young, R.V. and Sessine, S., 2000. *World of chemistry*. Farmington Hills: Gale Group.

Zambakari, C., 2011. South Sudan in the post-CPA era: Prospects and challenges. *Pambazuka News*, *542*.

Zehr, H., 2015. *The little book of restorative justice: revised and updated*. Skyhorse Publishing, Inc.

Zeleza, P.T., 2006. The inventions of African identities and languages: The discursive and developmental implications.

Zimmerer, J., 2007. Colonialism and the holocaust–Towards an archeology of genocide. *Revisiting the heart of darkness–Explorations into genocide and other forms of mass violence*, p.95.

Zollmann, J., 2007. Polemics and other arguments-a German debate reviewed. *Journal of Namibian Studies: History Politics Culture*, *1*, pp.109-130.

Županov, I.G., 2006. Goan Brahmans in the land of promise: Missionaries, spies and gentiles in the 17th-18th century Sri Lanka. *Portugal-Sri Lanka*, *500*, pp.171-210.